GETTING OUT
ALIVE

13 Deadly Scenarios and How Others Survived

Scott B. Williams

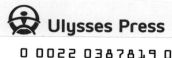
 Ulysses Press

Published in the United States by
Ulysses Press
P.O. Box 3440
Berkeley, CA 94703
www.ulyssespress.com

ISBN 978-1-56975-873-1
Library of Congress Control Number 2010937118

Acquisitions Editor: Keith Riegert
Managing Editor: Claire Chun
Editor: Bill Cassel
Proofreader: Lauren Harrison
Production: Judith Metzener, Abigail Reser
Cover design: what!design @ whatweb.com
Cover images: clouds © sebastian-julian/istockphoto.com; plane © Blue
    Fox Creative/istockpoto.com
Interior photos: See page 279

Printed in Canada by Transcontinental Printing

10 9 8 7 6 5 4 3 2 1

Distributed by Publishers Group West

NOTE TO READERS: This book has been written and published strictly for
informational purposes, and in no way should be used as a substitute for
actual instruction with qualified professionals. The author and publisher
are providing you with information in this work so that you can have the
knowledge and can choose, at your own risk, to act on that knowledge.
The author and publisher also urge all readers to be aware of their health
status, to consult local fish and game laws, and to consult health care
and outdoor professionals before engaging in any potentially hazardous
activity. Any use of the information in this book is made on the reader's
good judgment. The author and publisher assume no liability for personal
injury, property damage, consequential damage or loss, however caused,
from using the information in this book.

For my sister, Jennifer—never one to run from a storm.

TABLE OF CONTENTS

INTRODUCTION

Do you have what it takes to make it through an extreme survival situation? Do you have survival knowledge, skills, and experience? Do you have self-confidence, perseverance, and most importantly, an indomitable spirit coupled with the burning desire to live that will enable you to overcome severe adversity? If so, there is a good likelihood that you are a survivor. But you may never know for sure until you are put to the test in a real-life scenario.

We've all seen the evening news stories, television documentaries, and movies, and read the books and newspaper or magazine articles about survivors who somehow overcame seemingly impossible odds and lived to tell about it. People end up in extreme survival situations for all sorts of reasons, ranging from those who deliberately seek out adventure to ordinary people going about their everyday lives who happen to find themselves in the wrong place at the wrong time. In many cases, one or two simple mistakes or accidents can quickly throw you into a life-or-death struggle. Sometimes the situation happens through no fault of your own and there's nothing you could have done differently other than stay at home and play it safe, but even at home there are no guarantees that trouble won't come knocking at your door.

Some of the scenarios in this book, like getting lost in a jungle or marooned on an uninhabited island, may seem far-fetched in today's shrinking world where there are no more great unknowns and communication signals can be bounced anywhere via satellites. A glance through the pages of adventure magazines like *Outside, National Geographic Adventure, Backpacker,* or *Cruising World* might lead you to believe that in even the most remote locales on earth you're bound to run into a group after group of well-to-do adventure travelers, eco-tourists, and others crowding the last rain forests, uninhabited islands, and unclimbed peaks of the globe. I believed this, too, until I started exploring such places on my own. The truth is, while such travelers do manage to reach many of the most unlikely places, they are there only a tiny percentage of the time. There are still vast stretches of trackless forests where you can vanish without a trace, as well as roadless deserts and windswept island beaches where you can meet your end with no one to know, leaving your bones to bleach in the sun, undiscovered for decades or more.

The oceans of the world are still an irresistible lure to adventurers, sportsmen, and those who earn their living there on vessels of every size and description. The sea has always claimed a small percentage of those who venture over the horizon into its emptiness; small boats and ships alike are sometimes swallowed up without a trace, and this is not likely to ever change. And natural disasters such as hurricanes, blizzards, and forest fires can bring the fury of nature to even the most civilized and tamed places, so that even those who avoid adventure at all costs can find themselves in a struggle for their lives that quickly strips away the comfort of technology that usually wraps them in an illusion of safety.

This very technology that shields us from nature can be the cause of some survival scenarios, as it puts us in unnatural places like a speeding jet airliner on a collision course with the ground or 40 stories high in a man-made building that has caught on fire. Technology allows us to explore places previously off-limits to humans, like the undersea world and the highest mountain peaks, but in such an environment the equipment is the only thing keeping us alive. And in other situations, the technology that keeps us safe from threats can be used the wrong way, enabling one mentally disturbed person to wield the power of life or death over many more people than he could affect without it.

As a lifelong adventurer myself, I've sought out experiences and wild places in enough ways that I could have feasibly ended up in any of the scenarios described in this book. I've hiked, paddled, or sailed in environments as varied as rain forests, deserts, remote islands, the Alaska bush, and the open ocean. Living in south Mississippi and parts of Florida most of my life, I've been dodging hurricanes since Camille came straight over my family's house when I was five. And like most anyone reading this book, I've flown countless times on a variety of aircraft, placing my trust in aviation technology, and have been in tall buildings and crowded shopping malls where anything could happen at any time. I picked the 13 deadly scenarios detailed in this book because I've often thought about how easily I could end up in such a situation, and because each is an extreme example of how bad things can get in a hurry, changing a normal day or even an already adventurous outing into a fight for life itself.

The subject of survival is more popular than ever these days as we are bombarded by nearly instantaneous news reports from all over the world about disasters, accidents, and terror attacks. People are fascinated by survival how-to books and television shows, as well as accounts of those who have had close calls and lived to tell about it. Much of this fascination is undoubtedly fueled by our natural fears and the fact that none of us will survive life in the end. We have a need to know how other people have fared when faced with the things that frighten us the most, and what they did that caused them to either survive or fail the test and die. Recent books on the psychology of survival, such as Ben Sherwood's *The Survivors Club* and Laurence Gonzales's *Deep Survival,* have explored this fascination in depth. Both of these books also analyze the role of attitude and willpower in determining the outcome of extreme survival situations, and both authors conclude that the mental aspect of survival is far more important than learned skills, experience, or available tools. This explains many cases of quite improbable people living through experiences that have killed their stronger and more knowledgeable counterparts. In other words, the most important survival tool at your disposal is right between your ears.

But despite the fact that survival is mostly about attitude, inner strength, faith, and no small amount of luck, people interested in the subject are still fascinated with collecting the latest survival gadgets and learning the physical skills, like navigating, fire and shelter building, and foraging for wild foods. They want to imagine that they would stand a better chance because they are more prepared than the average person, and because they have studied a variety of survival scenarios in hopes they will know what to do if the time ever comes.

It is because of this hunger for survival knowledge that I am presenting these 13 deadly survival situations, along with a plausible course of action that you might take to get yourself out of each of them. I'm writing these from *your* point of view—how *you* might have ended up in each of these tight spots and what *you* might do to survive them. As you read through each scenario, you might smugly think, "I would never be stupid enough to do that!" Attempt to drive over a mountain pass in a snowstorm? "No way!" Get lost in the Amazon jungle? "I wouldn't go there in the first place!" Trapped under a rock in the mountains? "I know better than to go hiking alone!" A close call with a forest fire? "I would leave the area at the first sign of smoke!" Looking in from the outside and critiquing the actions of those who have lived or died in real-life situations, we can make such comments about any such scenario. But no matter how careful you are to avoid danger and how much you know about staying safe, there are always circumstances and factors that you can't plan for or that change faster than you can react.

Keep in mind that each story is fiction, and that how it unfolds does not necessarily represent the best course of action for surviving the given predicament, nor is it necessarily my recommendation. It's important to realize that any given scenario like this can have tremendous variations, but all of these are things that could happen and all of them *have* happened to others who successfully survived them. Along with each scenario, I will present real-life accounts of those who have been through such an ordeal, and how we can all learn from what they did to survive it. Even those who have made it out often did so after making bad decisions or stupid mistakes, so emulating them is not always the best course of action. Mostly, this is presented for your entertainment, and to make you think about possibilities you may not have given much thought to before.

As you read through each situation from the safety and comfort of your favorite chair or wherever you prefer to read, try to imagine how you would feel if you were really there. How would you do things differently than the imaginary you in the scenario? Would you be able to take action at all, or would you be frozen by fear? How would you know if you were making the right choices? Would you trust your intuition? Or would you panic and make mistakes that would make things worse? Do you think you could remain calm and apply lessons you've learned from your past experiences and accounts you've read of others who have been there? What would *you* do when faced with one of these 13 deadly scenarios? *Could you survive?*

CHAPTER ONE
CUTTING YOUR LOSSES

The coyotes are waiting patiently just outside of rock-throwing range as you lay awkwardly on your back. You can pick out their shapes among the boulders in the dim light of the new moon as they pace back and forth, curious about your predicament, waiting for you either to die or at least get too weak to put up a fight. They have all the time in the world, but for you time is running out. Even without the threat of hungry scavengers ready to take advantage of an unexpected opportunity, you will soon die of thirst in this lonely place where no one will likely find you. Daylight will be coming soon, and if you want to live, it's time to act. If you want to free yourself and have any chance of seeing civilization again, you're going to have to cut off your right leg at the knee. How could anyone end up in such a horrible predicament?

Day 1: Start of the Day Hike

It starts with a simple day hike on a benign mountain trail. You're getting tired as you carefully step from boulder to boulder, picking your way across a sloping rock field to get to a shimmering blue lake you spotted from high above on the ridgeline trail. The jumbled rocks of random sizes and shapes are difficult to traverse, forcing you to hop, crawl, and scramble to make your way through them. You are within 20 yards of the lake's edge when a stone rolls out from under you as you put your weight on it.

Fighting to keep your balance with the weight of the day-pack on your shoulders, you compensate with an extended  step, but cannot reach far enough to avoid a narrow crevice between the rock that rolled and the one it was resting against, which is also loose. You desperately try to keep from falling backward as your foot goes out from under you, the momentum stopping only when your shin slams into something hard with excruciating pain. You land on one side as you feel yourself pulled forward by your foot and lower leg as the boulders around you shift and slide. The pain in

REAL LIFE | *A Horrible Way to Die*

Consider what happened to Mike Turner, a 48-year-old Presbyterian minister and experienced backpacker who was trapped in just this way while hiking alone with his dog across such a boulder field in Wyoming's Fitzpatrick Wilderness in 1998. On a multi-day solo hiking trip, Turner was equipped with the right clothing and gear, and also had a sturdy camera tripod that he tried to use to pry the rocks away from his legs. In the beginning he was able to stay alive by wrapping himself in extra clothing and his tent, and by cooking meals from his backpack and melting snow with his single-burner stove. But he was stuck in a tough place, at an elevation of 11,500 feet.

Knowing that he had deviated well off his planned route, Turner didn't expect any rescuers to find him. Using

your shin is temporarily forgotten as you feel a crushing weight settle on your ankle and foot. You've bruised your elbow and hip in the fall as well, and you lie there for a minute, waiting for the pain to subside before trying to get back to your feet. When you try to pull your right foot out of the crack, you discover that it won't budge. The heavy stone that has settled on your foot has it pinned down to another rock beneath it, leaving no possibility of wiggling or twisting it free. You are trapped! Alone, out of sight and yelling distance of the hiking trail you wandered away from, you realize you have gotten yourself into serious trouble.

It only takes a little imagination to see how you could have ended up in such a jam. Suppose you have just recently relocated to a small city in the Colorado Rockies. You moved there for the outdoor recreation opportunities that draw so many to these mountains, and consequently, spend most of your days off exploring the excellent hiking trails in a nearby national forest.

a notebook he carefully protected in a Ziploc bag, he wrote personal notes to his family and kept a journal of his last days. He mentioned in the journal that Andy, his dog, spent a long time lying nearby. The dog later was found by other backpackers. Trapped on August 2, Mike Turner died of exposure and dehydration on or about August 11, and his body was found on August 31.

It's hard to imagine a much worse way to go, trapped and exposed, slowly dying of thirst in a place where there's little hope of someone coming along. Turner's case shows just how easily and unexpectedly even a knowledgeable hiker can end up in such a predicament. It reiterates the wisdom of being conscious and aware of every step you take when traveling off the beaten path in the wilderness.

On one such typical day, a Sunday morning, you set out alone on a high ridge trail that takes you above the timberline, where you have breathtaking views of the wilderness valleys below. A jewel-like alpine lake shining in the sun a mile or so below you proves an irresistible lure, and you leave the established path to hike cross-country to it.

It looks easy enough to reach, and you're tired of doing all your hiking on crowded trails anyway. Most of the route is across open meadows and through sparse stands of coniferous forest, but the most difficult section involves scrambling across a large boulder field on the last downhill stretch. Such boulder fields are common in mountain areas. Usually, they are stable and can be safely traversed, but the random nature of such natural rock piles means there is no way of knowing for sure if every stone has come to rest in a solid position. Sometimes, all it takes is a small amount of weight, like a human stepping on the right part of a rock, to tip the scales and cause even a large boulder to shift or roll. It's not hard to see how a person could get trapped in such a situation, and it has undoubtedly hap-

Know the Environment and the Dangers It Presents

Some dangers in wilderness travel are much more apparent than others. While you may not have considered the possibility that an experienced hiker like Mike Turner could get trapped and die while simply crossing a boulder field, you probably would know enough not to camp under a dead, leaning tree. The ways you can end up trapped while traveling through the wild are almost endless, and messing around with big heavy objects like rocks and trees is certainly a good way to increase your risks. Undoubtedly throughout human history an untold number of hapless solo travel-

pened to many lone wilderness travelers in the course of human history. There are a few documented recent cases, as well.

Day One: Sunday, Noon

A half hour has passed since the fateful misstep that resulted in your right foot getting trapped between two immoveable boulders. You're in a lot of pain, both from the pinned foot and from your bruised elbow and hip, but you've managed to position your body in a somewhat tolerable position among the hard rocks, considering your lack of mobility. Your right shin is still bleeding from a deep gash caused when it slammed into the sharp edge of a rock after your foot slipped, but it's not an arterial wound and you've almost managed to get it stopped by now. But no amount of wiggling, pulling, or squirming has enabled you to budge your trapped foot, and the stone that has rolled on top of it would be too heavy for you to lift even if you were uninjured and in a standing position with favorable leverage.

By now, you've reassessed what's in the small daypack you were carrying for your hike. It's not much, as you didn't want to

ers have been pinned by a fallen limb or tree trunk. This can happen anytime, as a dead tree or limb can fall without warning or during storms where wind or the weight of rain or snow precipitates the fall. You can also get trapped while cutting trees or branches, or while crossing piles of jumbled logs or other deadfall that can roll or shift under your weight just like rocks can.

Every environment presents its own unique dangers. Some are much more frightening than others, and it is the less obviously frightening threat that may end up being the most dangerous.

be overburdened and expected to be back to your car by late afternoon. There are two one-quart Nalgene water bottles; one is full, but the other, from which you had been drinking during the morning hike, is more than two-thirds empty. You've already eaten one of the two granola bars you packed for snacks, as well as part of the small Ziploc bag of almonds and raisins you brought. For your lunch, which you should be stopping to

REAL LIFE | *Stuck in the Mud*

Everyone has seen jungle movies where a person is swallowed up in a pool of sucking quicksand. But in reality, deep quicksand is rare and anyone caught in it can usually escape by getting in a horizontal position and swimming or crawling on the surface, depending on the exact consistency of it, which can vary.

In parts of Alaska, however, there is another kind of mud found in some of the tidal inlets along the coast that can trap an unsuspecting person as surely as cement, with no escape before the incoming rush of seawater returns and the victim drowns under a dozen or more feet of water. In 1988, 18-year-old Adeana Dickison died such a horrible death while her husband and several Alaska State Troopers attempting to rescue her failed to free her from the mud.

New to Alaska, the newlywed couple ventured out onto the mudflats of Turnagain Arm, near Anchorage, on a Honda four-wheeler, towing a trailer with gold-dredging gear. The four-wheeler got stuck, and while they were attempting to push it out, Adeana's right leg got mired in the mud. What the young couple did not know was that this treacherous tidal mud in Alaska is a fine silt that settles when the tide goes out, with a deceptively hard surface that can give under a person's weight and then build up pressure as you

consume about now somewhere along the trail in a spot with a view, you packed a dozen or so whole wheat crackers and some slices of Swiss cheese, as well as a single apple. All together, the calorie contents of your pack would be just enough to keep your energy level up to full capacity on a day hike in the mountains. Now everything has changed, and you don't dare eat all the lunch items in a single meal, as you have no idea how long

sink into it so that there is no way to pull free. The silt sets like concrete and no amount of pulling will free a leg or foot from it.

Adeana's husband dug in the silt and pulled on her leg for three hours without making any progress, finally telling her he was going for help. When he returned with tourists he flagged down on a nearby highway, even several men pulling on a rope tied around Adeana's torso could not free her. The tide was coming back in, covering the mud with 38°F water by the time State Troopers and firefighters arrived. But before they could set up the pumping equipment needed to displace the mud, the water was covering Adeana's head. She drowned as a State Trooper held her under her armpits and desperately attempted to pull her free. This Alaska tidal mud is a perfect example of a danger  unique to a specific environment that an outsider would likely be unaware of. Advance reading and research is vital to understanding the risks when venturing into new territory.

you will have to make them last. The small amount of water you have, though, is your real concern. The lake you were trying to reach sparkles in the sunlight as the wind ripples its surface so close you could throw a stone into it. But as close as that clear, cold water is, all around you there is nothing but dry, dusty boulders, and you're already thirsty from the scramble to get this far.

Aside from these meager amounts of food and water, you had also stuffed a lightweight Gore-Tex jacket into the daypack, along with a packable, wide-brimmed hat and a couple of bandanas. There's a compass that you've rarely used, a map of the national forest showing the trail you were following, a Leatherman multi-tool with an assortment of blades, pliers, can openers, and screwdrivers, and a disposable butane lighter for starting fires. In the small front pocket of the pack is another Ziploc bag containing your car keys, wallet, and Blackberry phone. You know before checking that the cell phone is useless in these mountains, far from towers, but you look anyway and verify that there is no signal and no way to call for rescue.

Weigh the Risks of Solo Travel

Traveling alone always increases the level of risk in any adventure, but more often than not my own big trips, whether sea kayaking, backpacking, canoeing, or sailing, have been solo. For one thing, it's simply hard to coordinate adventure trips with others, particularly the big adventures that require lots of time, money, or both, as well as a strong desire to go in the first place. I have always been keenly aware of the dangers of solo travel and try to remember to be cognizant of my surroundings with every step. Still, if you travel alone, you may someday find yourself in some awful predicament like the scenario described in this chapter.

You have no other means of calling or signaling for help—no emergency whistle, no flares, not even a signal mirror. Looking around among the rocks within reach, you quickly determine that there is not enough wood or other combustible material with which to build a signal fire—only a few leaves and twigs that wouldn't last more than a minute or two. All you can do is yell for help, and that you do, several times, knowing full well that you are much too far from the nearest trail for your voice to carry, even if a hiker happened to be passing by. And the chances of anyone else wandering through the area off-trail are even slimmer. You know you have to save your voice, and decide to call out at intervals of every half hour or so to increase the odds of being heard. For now, you will eat a small portion of the cheese and crackers, drink some water, and try to relax a bit.

Day One: Sunday, 3:00 PM

The sun is beating down unmercifully on the rocks around you, and the only shade you have is from your hat, bandana, and

While camping in heavily forested areas miles from the nearest road, I have several times been caught in storms that sent trees crashing down around me with terrific force. Each time as I crouched in dread in my tent, wondering if one would fall on me, I thought it would be better if it would just kill me outright rather than leave me pinned to the ground under its weight to die an agonizing slow death. Undoubtedly throughout human history, many hunters and other wilderness wanderers have perished this way. With no one with you to help you, the possible ways you can end up in such a situation are as endless as your imagination.

jacket. You cover your head and face, and drape the jacket over your bare legs to keep from getting sunburned. You've made your obligatory calls for help on the hour and half hour since eating lunch. Your shouts are answered only by silence—the silence of a vast mountain wilderness where a single human voice is pathetically insignificant. You're hot and thirsty, but don't dare take more than a couple of sips from the full water bottle. The first bottle is now empty. The gravity of your predicament is sinking in more and more as the sun arcs its way across the sky to the west. You no longer doubt that you will be spending the night here. Your trapped foot is throbbing with pain. You are incredibly uncomfortable with the limited positions in which you can move on the hard rocks. Despite the futility of the exercise, you struggle and pull with all your might to try to free yourself.

REAL LIFE | Between a Rock and Hard a Place

On Saturday, April 26, 2003, Aron Ralston, an avid rock climber and outdoorsman from Aspen, Colorado, started out for a day's adventure of riding his mountain bike and climbing near Canyonlands National Park in Utah. After parking his truck, he rode the bike 15 miles to the remote Blue John Canyon, where he would canyoneer back down to where he left the truck. While he was moving down a slot barely three feet wide, a boulder that he put his weight on shifted and pinned his hand to the rock of the canyon wall. That was the beginning of an epic ordeal that Ralston survived and later wrote about in his book *Between a Rock and a Hard Place*. Ralston's story is also told in the movie *127 Hours*, which depicts his gruesome choice in graphic detail.

Using all his rock climbing knowledge, he tried setting anchors and rigging rope tackle in an attempt to move

If only there were a large stick or something within reach that you could use as a pry bar.... But there isn't.

You give up for now and put your head down on the stones in despair. An article you read in an outdoor magazine a few years ago resurfaces in your memory. It was about a hiker, or rock climber, venturing alone into a desert canyon, climbing down a narrow slot where a boulder dislodged and somehow caught his hand, pinning him to the cliff wall. You remember reading in horror how he was faced with no choice but to cut off his arm at the elbow after being hopelessly trapped for several days. You think about the multi-tool in your pack. Is it your only hope of freedom? Could you bring yourself to do what the young climber had to do? You push the thought from your mind, telling yourself that it won't come to that. Someone will find you.

the 800-pound boulder, but couldn't even budge it. Trapped within such a hidden, inaccessible place, Ralston had little hope of rescue unless other hard-core climbers happened to come down the same route. He ran out of water by Tuesday, and was nearly freezing to death each night as temperatures dipped into the thirties.

Finally accepting the fact that there was only one way out of this situation alive, on the fifth day Ralston used a small pocketknife that he carried in a pocket of his shorts to amputate his arm at the elbow. After cutting himself free, he still had to rappel approximately 75 feet to the canyon floor, smearing the rock walls with his blood all the way down. He then walked over four miles down the canyon and had nearly reached his truck on his own when he ran into some tourists and was airlifted to a hospital in Moab by helicopter.

Day One: Sunday, 7:00 PM

The air temperature is dropping rapidly now that the sun has fallen behind the tall peaks to the west. Full darkness is still a couple hours away on this summer evening, but without the sun's warming rays, the heat of the day rapidly dissipates in the thin air at this high elevation. Along the nearby lakeshore, you see plenty of dry branches lying among the rocks that would supply you with a warm fire to last through the night—if only you could reach them. But like the water in the lake, the wood is as hopelessly out of reach as your car parked at the trailhead six miles away. All you can do is wrap yourself in the Gore-Tex jacket and huddle with your small pack, hat, and two bandanas draped over your legs to help hold in the warmth.

Day One: Sunday, 11:00 PM

You're too cold to sleep as you shiver under your inadequate protection from the elements on the cold rocks. The coldest part of the night is yet to come, in the early morning hours before dawn, yet it seems as if it has been dark for 12 hours as you lay there awake, checking your watch often and praying for daylight and the warmth of the morning sun. Somewhere in the distance you hear the eerie laughing howl of a coyote, and within minutes the sound is joined by the weird chorus of many more singing in unison. You feel the hair on the back of your neck stand up and a chill that is not from the cold runs down your spine.

For the first time it occurs to you that this mountain wilderness holds many more dangers than simply dying of thirst. You know coyotes don't normally attack humans, but what about helpless or dying humans who are unable to run or fight back? You also think of bears. While there are no grizzlies in this part of the Rockies, there are certainly plenty of black bears, and you've even seen a couple crossing the road since you moved to the area. Then there are mountain lions. A few recent, well-publicized attacks have made the news here in Colorado and in other western states. You feel incredibly vulnerable as you lie there in the dark, your mind running wild with imagination and your senses hyperalert to every little sound coming from beyond your limited range of vision.

Day Two: Monday, 10:00 AM

You've had couple of hours of sleep since daylight finally broke and the warmth of the sun's rays pushed back the cold that nearly did you in during the long night. Now that welcome warmth is turning into heat as the sun climbs higher and you squint in the brightness to look around.

The landscape is as empty as it's been since you got here. Nothing moves but a half-dozen circling vultures, wheeling high overhead in a patient holding pattern. You curse them at the top  of your lungs, as if they really care. Like the coyotes, they have all the time in the world, and if you stay where you are much longer, their patience will be rewarded. You snap out of your anger and save your voice for a couple of half-hearted calls for help. You've pretty much given up on the idea that anyone else will wander this far off the trail, especially on a weekday when there are fewer hikers out to begin with.

You take out the precious Nalgene bottle holding all the water you have left—just half a quart now. The shimmering lake taunts you with inviting clear water, so close but so far away. You imagine what it would be like to crawl into it face-first, drinking your fill, and wash away the dust and the dried blood on your scraped-up shin. But instead, all you can do is take a sip, savoring one delicious swallow as you carefully screw the cap tightly back on the bottle and put it in your pack, out of the sun. You're hungry, but with so little water, you are afraid to eat for fear of making your thirst worse.

Day Two: Monday, 3:00 PM

You've made it through the heat of the day only to dread the coming night and the cold it will bring as the sun hangs lower over the ranges to the west. There are more vultures now. Some are still circling overhead, but others have perched on an over-hanging rock wall near the lake, watching you with beady black eyes and jostling with each other for the best position. A couple of coyotes have appeared as well, perhaps some of the same ones you heard the night before. You see them pace down to the lake to drink and make eye contact as they watch you from 100 yards away.

You know what you have to do, but you're not ready to do it yet. You open the blades of the Leatherman tool and study them, feeling the sharpness against your thumb as you wonder which will hurt less, the serrated meat and rope cutter or the razor-sharp plain-edged blade. Both are only 3½ inches long. This would be much  easier if you had a big blade—something like a machete or a cleaver, or even a hatchet. Then you could close your eyes and do the deed with one mighty whack, quickly getting it over with. Instead, with either of these small blades, you will have to work at it, and you wonder if you can accomplish the task before you pass out with shock from what you are doing to yourself.

Day Two: Monday, 8:00 PM

The cold of the night has returned and four more coyotes have joined the two that have been watching you since midafternoon. They are getting bolder now with numbers and the dark of night. You can see them well enough in the faint moonlight as they pace back and forth and test the air with their noses from 50 yards away. Somehow you have to let them know that you're not helpless. Fortunately, you are surrounded by a selection of small stones among the larger boulders. You hurl a couple of baseball-sized missiles at the hungry wild dogs, missing the nearest one, but coming close enough to make them melt out of sight for now. Lucky for you they are only coyotes, as wolves or bears would not be so timid. Needless to say, you won't be getting much sleep tonight.

Day Three: Tuesday, 6:00 AM

At last dawn is breaking and you have survived the night without getting eaten alive or freezing to death. The coyotes are still nearby, and you know they won't go away until they get what they want or you free yourself and leave. It's too late to wait any longer. Your water is gone except for a final mouthful you've saved for the last. You are determined to wait only until the sun comes up, so at least you'll have its warmth if you go into shock from the pain.

You study the Leatherman tool in your right hand, having decided to use the plain blade to cut through your skin and muscle, and the serrated one to sever any stubborn ligaments or cartilage you encounter. Cutting the leg at the knee is the only way, as you cannot even contemplate how difficult it would be to hack or saw through the fibula and tibia below the joint.

Day Three: Tuesday, 7:00 AM

The first rays of morning sun have reached the boulder field. More vultures than you saw yesterday have appeared overhead, and others have landed on the perch where they sat and watched you previously. You've formulated a plan, and you begin by cutting the padding away from the nylon webbing that reinforces the straps of your backpack. Tied together, the pieces of webbing from each strap will form a strong loop long enough

REAL LIFE | *Do-It-Yourself Amputation*

You've got to be desperate to reach the point of cutting off a limb to free yourself. While there have been some remarkable stories of survivors escaping an agonizing, slow death by amputating their own limbs, others have died anyway, like a young man named Deveney, who was working as a stockman in the Australian outback in 1912. When he went missing, a search turned up his body a few days later, with one arm missing at the shoulder. Deveney had died from loss of blood, but his missing arm was a mystery until someone spotted it wedged in a hollow branch several meters above the ground in a tree. There was a cockatoo's nest in the hollow branch, and the searchers theorized Deveney had reached up to get the fledglings from the back of his horse, which for some reason moved out from under

 him, causing him to fall and get his arm wedged. Deep scars in the tree trunk bore evidence of his agony as he tried to use his spurs to climb up into the tree to get the weight off his arm. But it was wedged so tightly that the searchers had a hard time removing the arm even without his body weight on it. Despite his struggles, Deveney was unable to free the arm, and like Aron Ralston (page 22), he had no choice but to use a small knife in his free hand to cut it away at the shoulder, causing him to fall to the ground. He only made it a few meters before he bled to death.

to cinch tight around your leg just above the knee. You know you will bleed to death without it.

With no more hesitation, you secure the webbing in place and pull hard to draw up the slipknot you've formed, tying off

Since he couldn't cut at the elbow like Ralson, Deveney was unable to apply a proper tourniquet, if he even knew about the concept. Shutting off the flow of blood is obviously essential if you are going to cut off an entire limb, which will entail severing large arteries in the process.

Much more recently, a bulldozer operator named Donald Wyman, who was cutting timber in the western Pennsylvania woods to build his house, was trapped by a huge oak tree that crushed his leg and pinned him hard to the ground. Wyman tried digging with his hands to get his leg out from under the tree, but it was no use, as he soon ran into rock beneath the soil. He was out of shouting range and afraid he would bleed to death from his injuries. He amputated his leg at the knee with a dull three-inch pocketknife that he sharpened as best he could on a rock. He used the starter cord from his chainsaw to make a tourniquet and then crawled 135 feet to his bulldozer, which he then drove another 1500 feet to his pickup. The truck had a manual transmission, so Wyman had to use a metal file to reach the clutch with his hand when he shifted, but he managed to drive a mile and half to the nearest farm. A rescue crew found his severed and crushed leg, but by the time they were able to free it from under the tree and get it to the hospital, there was too much tissue damage for reattachment. Wyman was just glad to be alive. He said he had a choice and that he had too much to live for, so he did the only thing he could to survive.

the tail with several half-hitches to keep it from coming loose. You down the final swig of water in your Nalgene bottle, telling yourself it's tequila and that you will feel no pain. Going slow will only make it worse. You grip the knife handle tightly and place the edge against your flesh. In the next second, you bear down and slice, then work your way around the circumference of your knee, cutting as deep as you can until you encounter resistance. You ignore the blood as you reverse your grip on the Leatherman to bring the serrated blade into play. Just a few sawing strokes and you feel a sudden emptiness. You are free! You steel yourself against the pain and hobble and crawl to the lake's edge, where you wash away as much blood as you can and drink your fill of life-giving water. Scanning the nearby shoreline, you spot a six-foot-long piece of driftwood you can use as a crutch and walking stick. Once you are on your one remaining foot, standing tall again with the help of the stick, you feel confident the coyotes and vultures will keep their distance. Undoubtedly, they will fight over the part of you that you're leaving behind, but you still have your life. The hardest part is over, and you know you can reach down inside yourself to find the strength to make it to the trail.

TOP TEN TIPS FOR AVOIDING AND SURVIVING BEING TRAPPED IN THE WILDERNESS

1. Don't go alone. The number-one way you can avoid ending up having to make a terribly desperate choice is to have a companion with you. In most such cases, your partner will be able to free you or go get help. Remember that the more remote the area, the greater the risk of solo travel.

2. Carry a reliable communication device. If you must go alone, by necessity or choice, carry a means of calling for help. Cell phones won't help you in most remote areas because of signal problems. To be assured of getting the call out, you need a portable satellite phone or a messaging device/emergency beacon, such as the SPOT Personal Tracker.

3. Carry signal devices. A satellite communication device is great for calling outside help, but you also need a way of signaling other people such as hikers or hunters who may be in the immediate area and can help you sooner. Carry a loud emergency whistle and a signal mirror and consider hand-held flares or smoke flares such as those sold for marine use. If you have a firearm, a sequence of three evenly spaced shots is a distress signal.

4. Inform someone of your plans. Informing a reliable person where you are going, what route you are taking, and when you expect to be back can make all the difference in whether you die alone or someone comes looking for you.

5. Watch your step. When alone in the wild, you must shift into a higher level of awareness of everything around you and every step you take or move you make. Walking in the wild is not a stroll down a city sidewalk. Be especially careful when crossing rock slides and talus, boulder fields, and crevices, or when fording streams.

6. Take extra care when climbing. It's easy to get trapped by your own body weight when climbing up or down on rocks or in trees. Be wary of crevices and tree limb forks that are wide at the top and narrow at the bottom, as they can trap you if you slip and fall in

31

such a way that your weight wedges you hard into them. Jumbled logs and other deadfall can also shift under your weight and roll onto a foot or ankle.

7. **Never jump.** Avoid jumping in the outdoors if at all possible. Leaping across streams, off of rocks, or from rock to rock is a good way to break a leg or foot, or cause a large rock to roll under your weight, possibly trapping you. Move slowly and deliberately instead.

8. **Know the environment.** Do your research and learn in advance about any special dangers unique to the area, such as the tidal Alaskan mudflats mentioned earlier in this chapter. Stay alert to storms that can cause trees to fall, and avoid camping under dead tress or limbs that could fall at any time and trap you.

9. **Learn from the mistakes of others.** It pays to read true accounts like the ones summarized in this chapter just learn the possibilities of what can happen when you're alone. A lot of things that seem utterly bizarre or impossible have actually happened to some unfortunate person.

10. **Carry a sharp knife.** Those who have been so hopelessly trapped that they ran out of other options were able to save themselves only because they were in possession of a knife that they could reach and put to use. Always carry a knife when alone in the wild, and keep it as sharp as possible and in a location where you can reach it with one hand.

CHAPTER TWO

ABANDONED IN THE AMAZON BASIN

You are startled awake as the first heavy drops of rain splash against your face at the beginning of another torrential downpour. It takes a few seconds for you to realize why you are getting wet—the tarp that you had been sleeping under is *gone*. Only the veil-like mosquito net draped on a frame around your face and your lightweight sleeping bag remain. You unzip your bag, throw the flap aside, and sit up quickly as the forest floor around you turns into a muddy pool of brown water in the flooding rain. Not only is the tarp missing, but your guides are nowhere to be seen. Your backpack is gone, along with the waterproof Pelican cases that held your expensive camera gear. You are alone and without supplies, a two-day trek from the nearest village, in the trackless jungle-covered mountains along the border between Brazil and Guyana. If you are going to survive this ordeal, you are going to have to walk out of the largest rain forest on earth alone.

The Trip of a Lifetime

You spend your days in an office working a job you enjoy; but your real life's passion is wildlife photography. You've dreamed of a photo expedition to the Amazon for years and have finally managed to get both the time off and the funds to make it happen. You don't want the typical "canned" adventure to some eco-tourist lodge at the edge of the jungle. You do your research and decide on one of the most remote regions in all of equatorial South America—the headwaters of the Essequibo River. Flowing out of the Kamoa Mountains along Brazil's northern border with Guyana, the Essequibo cuts a 600-mile path of

The Jungle Is Your Worst Enemy

During World War II and Vietnam, soldiers from temperate regions found themselves thrust into a landscape where nature was as formidable a foe as the human enemy they had been sent to fight.

To those not experienced in, equipped for, or adapted to the rigors of the rain forest ecosystem, it can be one of the planet's most hostile places to travel through. An impenetrable labyrinth of vegetation, hothouse humidity, and heavy rainfall create an environment that can swallow a human with the same ease as the parched desert or treacherous sea. With visibility limited to just a few yards or even a few feet in front of you, and an enclosing canopy overhead, conventional navigation methods are useless. Even in mountainous forests, there are few landmarks and it is very difficult to get a directional fix using the sun or stars. In addition to the navigation difficulties caused by the thick vegetation, many jungle areas include rugged terrain with mountains, gorges, powerful rivers, and expansive swamps.

The endless growing season that is so conducive to a fantastic diversity of plant life is also ideal for deadly bacteria, viruses, and parasites. The slightest scratch can become a life-threatening infection, unfiltered water often causes debilitating dysentery, and the swarms of mosquitoes carry deadly illnesses like malaria, dengue fever, and yellow fever.

treacherous rapids and breathtaking waterfalls as it flows toward the Atlantic.

You talk your weekend-camping buddy into coming along with you on this adventurous self-planned trip. This involves chartering a bush plane from the coast of Guyana to take you nearly 400 miles to a jungle airstrip at a remote village on the

In addition to pesky mosquitoes, insects, arachnids, and other invertebrates thrive in incomparable abundance in this environment of constant heat and decay. Stinging wasps, bees, bullet ants, scorpions, centipedes, biting spiders, ticks, flies, and leeches are everywhere.

Larger creatures that instill even more fear in jungle travelers camouflage easily in the dense foliage, leaf-littered forest floor, and murky waters. Many of the world's most venomous snakes are found here, from the large and aggressive bushmaster—a snake so deadly that almost no one survives its bite—and common fer-de-lance to the poisonous coral snake and palm viper. In the rivers, huge anaconda snakes compete with the vicious Black caiman, a relative of the American alligator, for any unsuspecting creature that nears the water. Smaller dangers include schools of carnivorous piranhas and the tiny candiru or "toothpick" fish that is said to be attracted to urine. There have been numerous cases of candiru swimming into the urethra of people bathing in rivers, resulting in excruciating pain when the fish cannot be pulled out because of its barblike fins.

The most fearsome of all jungle predators—big cats like the Amazon's jaguar and puma—pose the smallest threat of any predator, simply because they have been hunted to such small numbers. Nevertheless, in an untamed, untouched tropical forest, every potential threat is very real.

Essequibo at the confluence of the Kassikaityu River. From there, you will hire a motorized dugout canoe to take you another 100 miles or so up the Kassikaityu to an isolated village at the limit of canoe navigation. From this village, you and your buddy intend to hire guides to trek overland to the upper Kamoa River, a route promising to take you through pristine rain forest rarely visited by outsiders. In your research you read about a scientific expedition that recently penetrated into some of the valleys in this area, discovering several new species of lizards, frogs, and tropical birds.

Forging on Alone

Trouble starts as soon as the bush plane takes off after you disembark at the village. The owner of the only outboard motor-powered dugout on this part of the river sees an opportunity and asks an exorbitant price to take you and your friend up the Kassikaityu River. You have no choice but to pay it if you want to go. Then, once you reach the more remote Indian settlement upstream, you arrange to hire four local villagers to guide you on foot through the mountains. Only one of them can speak a few words of broken English. They, too, want an outrageous price, but you fork over the cash in local currency, and plans are made to set out the next day.

After one night in the village, your friend falls violently ill and refuses to attempt the trek. Not wanting you to miss out on the trip of a lifetime, he insists you go on without him. With only a week before the bush plane picks you up, now is the time to decide. With the jungle calling, it's not a hard decision to make.

Day One: Entering the Forest

After one last night in the village, you set out with your guides on an arduous trek through trackless jungle. The one who speaks English assures you they know the way to the Kamoa

River, but there is no trail and for most of the route one of them is in front, cutting a path with a machete. A day of pushing up steep, muddy slopes in a slow, steady rain takes you into a rugged, heavily forested mountain range far from the river valley. The guides have been asking lots of questions through the interpreter about the heavy equipment they have been helping to carry. They have questions about your camera bodies and lenses, your backpack, your multi-fuel camp stove, even your LED headlamp. They want to know what each item costs, and you are embarrassed to say, knowing that any one of your pro-level lenses is worth a fortune down here. The questions make you uncomfortable, but seeing the competence and jungle-craft of the guides at work assures you that you are in good hands.

Day Two: Into the Jungle-Carpeted Mountains

A second day of even more difficult trekking takes you farther into the mountains. Deep gorges and many stream crossings make the going that much harder. The guides say that you are just another half day from the Kamoa River and that evening you make camp near a small jungle stream. You are exhausted from trying to keep up with these wiry native guides who, despite being weighed down with heavy gear, move through this terrain at a pace that makes you feel like you're running a marathon. Your feet are badly blistered from your wet hiking boots, which have stayed soaked since entering the jungle from crossing countless streams and wading through mud puddles. Nothing you've read about jungle travel could have prepared you for how difficult it really is; but the thought of penetrating this untouched rain forest is enough to make the hardships worthwhile.

Day Three: Abandoned

It only takes a few minutes for the gravity of your predicament to sink in as you realize the truth: Your guides have taken everything of value that you had—at least, everything they could get without waking you up when they left in the middle of the night. You're alone beside a small stream that probably doesn't even have a name. You know it leads down out of the mountains to a river, but which river? Are you really even in the drainage of the Kamoa River, as the guides said, or were they lying about that, too? Regardless of where you are, you realize it could have been worse. At least you're still alive. They could have just as easily

REAL LIFE | *The Teenager Who Walked out of the Amazon*

One of the most improbable jungle survival ordeals ever recorded began on Christmas Eve, 1971, when 17-year-old Juliane Koepcke and her mother boarded a flight from Lima, Peru, to Pucallpa, a city on a tributary of the Amazon where Juliane's father was in charge of a research station. Halfway into the flight, the plane entered a violent storm and a bolt of lightning tore the right wing clean off the fuselage. Juliane suddenly found herself ejected from the shattered plane and free-falling more than two vertical miles toward the forest canopy, still strapped into her seat. Somehow, the girl survived the impact with just a broken collarbone, minor cuts, and a concussion. Alone among the wreckage and unable to find her mother, she realized rescue searchers wouldn't likely spot the downed plane through the thick canopy. If she wanted to survive, she would have to walk out of the forest. Her father had taught her the most important lesson of jungle survival: Streams lead to rivers and rivers lead, eventually, to people.

Though her plan was straightforward, Juliane's trek was plagued with harrowing difficulties. In many cases such jungle streams do lead to larger rivers, but they can just

cut your throat to make sure you couldn't report them to the authorities. But they are probably very confident you'll never find your way back to civilization. And you know yourself that you're no expert tracker and that the winding route back and telltale footprints have long since vanished in the heavy rain.

You take stock of what you have left. Everything is soaked, and the rain shows no sign of letting up. You have a thin sleeping bag, mosquito net, and the T-shirt and underwear you were

as well end in an impassable swamp. Juliane had none of the equipment that most people would consider essential for jungle travel. The only food she had was some candy she found at the crash site. A bad cut in her arm and other smaller wounds quickly attracted flies and became infested with maggots. Despite her intense fear of piranhas and reptiles, she was forced to wade streams and rivers when there was no other route, leaving her covered with leeches after every crossing. She didn't concern herself with normal survival worries like building fires, making shelters, or looking for food; afraid of poisonous plants, she ate none of the strange fruits and berries in the forest. All Juliane wanted to do was get out. It was up to her to do so, and that's what motivated her to keep moving.

She walked for 10 days, following one tributary after another until she came upon a hunting hut on the banks of a river. After enduring one of the most horrific situations imaginable, Juliane had finally caught a break and the next day three Indian hunters found her. They fed her mashed-up fruit and poured gasoline in her wounds to kill the worms before taking her by canoe to a nearby settlement, where she was attended to by a doctor and eventually reunited with her father.

sleeping in. Thankfully, you rolled up your long canvas hiking pants and long-sleeved shirt the night before to use as a make-shift pillow, or they would have taken those. Your bush hat is gone, but there are a couple of bandanas in the pockets of your pants. There is also a single protein bar, a half-empty package of beef jerky, a disposable butane lighter, and a small Swiss Army knife. You have your boots and the wet pair of socks you were wearing yesterday only because they were under the mosquito net with you and not outside where the thieving guides could easily take them. Your Mini Maglite is down inside one of the boots where you left it the night before, but the batteries are dead and the spares were in your backpack. You grope around your soggy sleeping bag in the thick jungle mud, looking for something else—anything—but that's it, the complete inventory of everything man-made you have in this vast expanse of green rain-soaked death-trap.

Day Three: Getting Out Alone

The rain begins to slack off some as your mind grapples with the enormity of the difficulties and dangers you will face trying to get out of this jungle alone. You are keenly aware of these because of the thorough research you did in advance while planning the trip. You've been fascinated by jungle adventure most of your life. You've read the narratives of both the early explorers and contemporary adventurers who have found themselves in similar predicaments. You know you can't let your fears take control now or you will be doomed from the start.

In this remote, inaccessible region, nobody is going to rescue you, and stumbling upon another party of travelers is extremely unlikely. It's up to you to walk out on your own. You know that in jungles, the route to civilization is usually downstream. Big, navigable rivers usually mean villages will be found somewhere along their banks. Your only recourse is to follow the stream you've been left beside. The concept is simple, but you know it will likely be the most difficult trek of your life.

From your few days in the forest, you are keenly aware that this break in the rain won't last long. You have nothing to gain by waiting, so you wriggle into your soggy clothes and eat a small piece of the beef jerky. It's time to move out.

Day Three: Morning

This high in the mountains, streams are so small they are almost narrow enough to step across. It will be a long distance before this trickle of water becomes a river large enough to support villages, and immediately you begin running into problems. The stream banks are choked with thickets of spiny bamboo, which has tough stems armored with inch-long spikes that will rip both your clothing and skin if you attempt to push your way through. You can't attempt it without a machete, so the only way you can follow the stream is to wade down the middle, where you trip and stumble over boulders and sunken logs and sometimes sink up to your knees in the muddy bottom. Snakes are  at the forefront of your thoughts as time and again you have no choice but to duck and crawl under low-hanging vines thick with camouflaging foliage. At least you can easily quench your thirst by catching rain with the many broad streamside leaves, using them to funnel it into your mouth.

Day Three: Noon

You stop to rest during another brief break in the rain, sitting on a streamside rock. Your clothes will never dry in this environment, but you take off your boots anyway to pour the water out of them and get rid of annoying rocks that have worked their way into your insoles. Your feet have been constantly wet since you first left the village with the guides and a fungal infection has set in, causing the top layers of skin to begin peeling. It's too painful to remove your socks, so you leave them on. Blood-filled leeches have attached themselves to your calves above the top of your boots. You pry them off and throw them in back in the stream. There would be a lot more of them if not for the boots and long pants.

Insects are everywhere: an endless line of large ants carrying pieces of leaves many times their size; tiny butterflies and bees swarming around your face and neck, attracted by the sweat; and biting flies that nearly drive you wild as you slap at them to try and keep them away. You are under constant assault by things that bite, and twice you have put your hand on a tree

Jungle Survival Skills That Will Save Your Life

In the tropical forest, the safest drinking water is rainwater collected from water-catching, broad-leaved plants like bromeliads. You can also get safe water from vines, but it is difficult to cut them with a small knife.

Plant foods are varied and abundant in the jungle, but many fruits and nuts are completely inaccessible, dangling more than 200 feet up in the canopy overhead. You may be able to find some fresh nuts and fruits that have fallen on the ground before animals or insects get to them, but for the most part you will have to make do with plants that

covered with fire ants before you realized your mistake. While you haven't seen a snake yet, you're sure you've been within arm's reach of them.

Progress has been painfully slow, but at least you are moving. You have no idea what your elevation is, but the stream is dropping, and you've had to detour around several small waterfalls, climbing down steep slopes where your only option was to trust your weight to roots and vines as you worked your way down. Such travel is exhausting, and you've worked up quite an appetite. You allow yourself a quarter of the only protein bar you have and one small piece of the beef jerky; you know you're going to have to find food from the jungle if you want to maintain your strength to travel.

Day Three: Evening

With your hunger intensifying, you find yourself scanning the ground and vegetation around you for anything you might potentially eat as you continue following the course of the stream downhill. The waterway is getting wider as you go, and now there are areas of exposed muddy banks and tiny sandbars in

grow on the forest floor. These include bamboo shoots, fern fiddleheads, and palm hearts.

Animal foods are abundant in the jungle as well. But if you are without hunting weapons, larger mammals and birds are out of the question. As long as you are near a stream, there will be small fish, frogs, turtles, and crawfish that can be caught with a little persistence. Of course the easiest source of calories is under your feet in the form of grubs, snails, and insects crawling over the leaves and through the rotting layer of vegetation on the forest floor.

some of the bends. In one such sandbar, you notice animal tracks leading to the water from a raised mound with digging marks around it. You recognize it as a nest, probably of a turtle, iguana, or some other reptile. It doesn't matter at this point. You dig in the mound with your hands and are rewarded with more than a dozen small eggs with soft, leathery skins.

Knowing that all such eggs are edible, you wash them off in the stream and begin to wish you still had your multi-fuel stove and Teflon-coated camp skillet. As it is, there's nothing you can do but eat them raw. Everything around you is so wet; building  a fire seems like a hopeless proposition. You open the blade of your Swiss Army knife and puncture the skin of one of the eggs, squeezing a bit of the near-liquid yolk into the palm of your hand for a tentative taste test. It's not bad at all, and your ravenous appetite kicks in, leading you to quickly drain a half dozen of the small eggs into your mouth. With your hunger somewhat satisfied, your biggest worry now is the rapidly approaching jungle night.

Day Three: Your First Night Alone

The darkness on the ground under the dense canopy overhead is so complete that you cannot see your hand when you hold it six inches in front of your face. You decided to stay on the tiny sandbar where you found the reptile eggs, as it is the one place you can lie down where the ground is clear of rotting vegetation and all the bugs and other crawling things within it. Even so, it is terrifying to think that a deadly snake could crawl onto you in the night. At least you have the small mosquito net, which will keep things off your face. You're having a hard time falling asleep for long, as every time you doze off you are awakened by some scream, howl, bark, or other call of the myriad unseen creatures that inhabit the forest around you. You recognize some of the sounds, such as the booming roar of howler monkeys, but many are unlike anything you've ever heard. Your imagination runs wild thinking of what could be out there in the jungle night, but even so, your long struggle through the day has exhausted your body to the point that you end up getting some sleep anyway.

Day Four: Morning

You've been moving since daylight, when you woke and finished off the last of the reptile eggs. Progress is still slow as you pick your way down the middle of the streambed where necessary and work your way through the vegetation on the banks wherever possible. Today is the first day since you left the village four days ago that it is not raining. The first hours of morning were still dark with the gray gloom of the endless twilight beneath the canopy, but now you are elated to see a few filtered rays of sunlight streaming through the dense foliage, lifting your spirits as your stomach growls and the open wounds on your feet ache.

The joy of seeing the sunlight is short-lived, however, when you realize it is coming through the canopy from a high angle to your left as you move downstream. Without the compass that was in your pack, you can't be sure, but morning sun coming from that direction indicates that the stream you are following is flowing in a southerly direction, away from the ocean. That can't be right. You know the Kamoa, and ultimately the larger Essequibo, both flow through Guyana's interior in a northerly direction to empty into the Atlantic. If this stream is flowing south, it may be a tributary of one of the large rivers that drains into the Amazon River! Is it possible that the guides led you unknowingly across the divide between the two river basins? If so, there's no way of knowing which river this stream leads to, or how far it flows before a village or any other sign of human habitation will be found. You stop and sit beneath a giant tree to think. It would be foolish to go back upstream and try to find your way to a different drainage. You have to follow the rule of jungle navigation and stick to the path of the stream you're on. But can you go on like this, traveling on foot on a journey that may be 100 miles, or 300, or even more before finding a settle-

REAL LIFE | *Lost in the Jungle: A Harrowing True Story of Survival*

Walking out of a jungle wilderness by following a stream or river sounds straightforward enough—after all, 17-year-old Juliane Koepcke did it with no special equipment or experience (page 38). But if you read the account of a more recent jungle castaway's ordeal in his attempt to follow a river to civilization, you realize just how lucky Ms. Koepcke really was. Yossi Ghinsberg recounts his terrifying experience of being lost and alone in the Bolivian rain forest in his book *Lost in the Jungle: A Harrowing True Story of Survival*.

Ghinsberg's narrative is a classic example of how easily modern travelers can find themselves in dire straits if they have not assiduously done their homework before venturing into a wilderness as unforgiving as an uninhabited rain forest. Trusting the knowledge of an "experienced" trekker they had just met, Ghinsberg and two other travelers blindly embarked on an adventure into the jungle. Within days, the party had a bad falling out and eventually split into two pairs traveling in opposite directions. Ghinsberg and his remaining companion decided to go on as they had originally planned and travel by balsa raft down a remote river to a village

ment? Your feet are getting worse all the time, and you know there is a limit to how far they will carry you.

Day Four: Evening

Respite from the rain was short-lived and you are still pushing your way downstream through dripping foliage as the twilight deepens with the approach of another night. The stream has broadened some, the ground becoming less rocky and much

miles away, from which they planned to catch a plane back to civilization. They encountered terrifying rapids early in the journey, forcing Ghinsberg's companion to jump for the safety of the bank. Unable to follow suit, Ghinsberg nearly drowned when the out-of-control raft took him over a waterfall. By the time he was able to swim to the bank, Ghinsberg had been swept miles downstream through a whitewater canyon, hopelessly separating him from his friend.

Ghinsberg's situation deteriorated day by day, as he had little food or equipment and severe problems with his feet from rotting and peeling skin that made it impossible to remove his socks. He endured endless insect bites, a frightening nighttime encounter with a jaguar, flash floods, and bogs that he sank in to the waist and could barely extricate himself from. He lived on rotting fruit, bird's eggs, minnows, and anything else he could find until he eventually reached an abandoned camp on the river. The friend who had been on the raft with him had survived and returned with a guide in an outboard-powered canoe to search for Ghinsberg, even though the local authorities said it was pointless, as no gringo could survive that long in the jungle. The other two men in the original party disappeared without a trace and were never heard from again.

muddier along the banks. You have been hoping to find another sandbar like the one you spent the previous night on, but you have no such luck. When it gets too dark to travel, you have no choice but to huddle at the base of a huge tropical hardwood tree, leaning back against one of the enormous, finlike roots that rise several feet above the ground to form its support in the thin rain forest soil. You've found nothing else to eat today, and so you finish the last bits of beef jerky and all but a quarter of the protein bar. Tomorrow you will have to make a serious effort to find more food, and you resolve to look for grubs or anything else remotely palatable to keep up your strength for traveling.

Day Four: Midnight

You leap to your feet with an involuntary scream as you fling yourself out away from the tree roots into pitch blackness, flailing your arms wildly and dancing and shaking to make sure there is nothing on you. A moment ago, in a brief period of fitful sleep, you thought you were dreaming when you slowly became cognizant of something moving across your arm and chest, a long, slow, sliding movement of something smooth and cool, like a rope being pulled across your body. The blind panic you felt as you returned to full wakefulness and realized it was a snake gave you an adrenalin rush so powerful you are now shaking uncontrollably as you stand frozen in the dark jungle night, wondering where the snake is, what kind it is, and if there are others.

You're afraid to take a step for fear of stepping on it, and you don't dare sit back down, much less try to sleep. You reach into the pocket of your soaking-wet pants to find your one butane lighter. You've kept it dry by wrapping it in the bag the beef jerky was in. With a flick the tiny flame illuminates the area around your feet, and you feel a little better knowing that at least the snake is not that close. You don't dare burn the lighter more than a few seconds, as it's the only one you've got. Besides, its light is pathetically insignificant in this immense blackness.

Day Five: Afternoon

You've been pushing downstream as steadily as possible all day. The rain has returned in a slow but relentless downpour during the afternoon, but glimpses of the sun in the morning hours reinforced your suspicion that you are traveling south, likely following some remote tributary of the Amazon. If you can reach that great river, you know you will find people, but it's impossible to know how far you will have to walk to get there.

The terrain the stream is flowing through has leveled out some. This makes for easier going in one sense, as you are not climbing over rocks and around waterfalls and other obstacles, but now you frequently have to cross the waterway when there is no way through the thickets on one side or the other. The banks are becoming muddier and swampier. You've seen several snakes along the way today, most of them species you could not identify. The only food you've found was some wormy, half-rotten fruit on the ground beneath a tree laden with more that you had no way to reach. You risked eating it only after catching a glimpse of some small brown monkeys feeding on it high in the canopy. You also found some immature green plantains, but they are hard and inedible raw, and impossible to cook without a pot to boil them in or hot coals from a slow-burning fire to roast them. You don't even bother to try, considering how soaked everything on the forest floor is.

Day Six: Morning

Stumbling along the stream that is now a small river, nearly delirious with pain from biting flies and the sores and raw flesh on your feet that make every step an ordeal, you come to a small, clear-running feeder stream and stop to wash your face and rest. Something shimmering beneath the surface catches your eye, and you realize the little brook is teeming with schools of some kind of small fish or minnows. They scatter when you try to grab them, but upstream a few steps, you find you can corner the school in a shallow pool and using both hands to scoop, you are able to splash large amounts of water along with many of the minnows up onto the surrounding mud. These are pure protein and you are ravenous from the strenuous trekking. You eat the smallest ones whole and gut the larger ones first with the Swiss Army knife. Repeating the process, you are able to catch enough to temporarily satisfy your hunger.

After eating the fish you are feeling better as you start walking again, until you suddenly drop to the ground screaming in pain. You brush a large black ant off your upper arm, incredulous at the sensation like a hot needle piercing your flesh that its sting has caused. You've been stung by bees and wasps before at various times in your life, but never have you felt a sting or bite even close to this. It's almost as if you've been shot in the arm, and you scramble fearfully away from the bushes you had been pushing through before more of the ants can get on you.

You've heard of the dreaded bullet ant that is found in the South American rain forest, and you suspect that's what has stung you, as the pain does not get any better. The bullet ant by all accounts has the most potent and debilitating sting in the insect world. From what you've read, you're in for a good 24 hours of intense pain, but at least it wasn't something worse, like a snake bite that you could not recover from. You try everything to get some relief from the pain, including compressing wet jungle mud against your arm, but still you are in agony and your traveling is done for the day, as you are feeling nauseous and cannot even move your right arm.

Day Seven: Morning

The most intense pain from the bullet ant sting lasted some six hours before gradually subsiding through the night. You barely got any sleep because of the arm and because you now are terrified of encountering more bullet ants. But despite the fact that the pain still lingers, you know you can't remain here any longer and must push on downstream.

Your feet are in terrible shape with blisters that won't heal and are now open and infected, oozing pus that sticks to your single pair of near-rotten socks. Washing them is all you can do, though you have no idea how much worse you may be making the infection by exposing it to the stream water. The expensive leather and Gore-Tex boots that were new when you started the trip are now falling apart at the seams, as are your only other articles of clothing, your cotton-canvas trousers and long-sleeved shirt. Nothing can survive the constant forces of decay in this greenhouse humidity, and you take this as a warning sign that if you stay in one place too long here, the jungle will swallow you up as well. By midmorning you are moving again, still clutching at your right arm and ducking past low-hanging branches in an effort to avoid brushing against them.

Day Seven: Evening

You are still following an everwidening river through a jungle that seems endless and impossibly primeval. You have not seen one trace of human existence or passage along this route until now, so you stare in disbelief when you come across a small palm tree near the bank that has been cut down with some kind of sharp tool and split open at the crown to get the edible heart. It's not the work of an animal, as you can clearly see blade marks on the wood that were probably made with a machete or axe. The split wood has turned gray from exposure and a search of the muddy soil nearby reveals no footprints or other sign of man. But even though weeks or months may have passed since a human was here, your spirits are lifted because at least you know someone *has* passed this way. The daylight is nearly gone

so you decide to spend the night by the cut-down tree.

The pain in your arm is slightly better, but by no means gone. You have found nothing else to eat and hunger is gnawing at you as you stare at the cut tree and wonder who it was that passed this way on this impossibly remote stream. You know that nomadic Indian hunters still roam parts of this wild rain forest, and you realize that this small sign of human activity does not necessarily mean you are close to anything resembling civilization. A hunting party ranging many days from the nearest village could have passed this way months ago and may never come here again.

Tense Negotiations in La Mosquitia

Flying over the expansive rain forests of the Mosquitia region of Honduras and Nicaragua, I stared down through the windows of the Cessna 182 at the carpet of green stretching from horizon to horizon and wondered what it would be like if, dropped in the middle of that vast jungle, I had to get out on foot.

A week later, my canoeing partner and I found ourselves in tense negotiations with our Miskito guides over payment for their services. It was only once the guides had led us 30 miles from the nearest village that they decided

Day Eight: Noon

All morning you have been forcing yourself to continue on, certain that people live somewhere farther downstream on the river you are following. Several hours of walking have revealed nothing to indicate their presence, however, until now—when you come upon the framework of a primitive shelter of the type the jungle Indians use for hunting camps. A little further downstream, you find more evidence of people in the form of a tree stump where they probably cut the log for a dugout canoe. You are elated that there is more evidence of a nearby village, but you are still growing weaker and are having a hard time walking at all as your feet are in agony with every step you take. If not for these encouraging signs that you might reach a place inhabited by other humans you know you would find it difficult not to simply give up. You simply don't have the strength, the skills, or the knowledge to prevail here, and the lack of sufficient food is wearing you down. The jungle just goes on and on, seemingly without limits, and one lost human wandering through it on foot is as insignificant as a small boat on a vast ocean.

to start the negotiation, four armed men against the two of us. We considered what would happen to us if they chose to take all the gear and money we were carrying and leave us stranded. But fortunately for us, their intentions were good, and they were satisfied with a little extra money and small gifts such as flashlights and tarps. Few people from outside the tropics who are not acclimated to the conditions would be able to survive more than a week in the unforgiving jungle environment without ample gear and supplies. It's a test most never have to face, but it's not out of the realm of possibility if your sense of adventure leads you to the planet's wild rain forests.

Day Eight: Evening

You are about to stop for the night when a strange smell wafting through the normal scents of leaves, rain, and rotting vegetation catches your attention. Smoke! The smell of smoke can only mean one thing. It can't be far away, as there is little breeze on the forest floor beneath the canopy. You push on with a final burst of enthusiasm and hear voices speaking a strange language from a camp on a riverside sandbar ahead. You are saved! It doesn't matter who these people are or how remotely they may live. They are people and, at this point, that's all that matters.

TOP TEN TIPS FOR MAKING IT OUT
OF THE JUNGLE ALIVE

1. **Start moving immediately.** Most people want to follow the "stay where you are" rule of thumb and wait for rescue when they are lost in the wild. Unfortunately, under the dense canopy of the remote jungle, you're more likely to die waiting than be spotted by a rescue plane or stumbled upon by hikers. Instead, you need to find your bearings, come up with a plan you can stick to, and hike your way out of trouble.

2. **Follow water downstream.** Unless you have a compass, you shouldn't count on maintaining a directional bearing in the jungle. Instead, let the water guide you out. In the jungle, most streams you find will eventually feed into rivers. And as rivers get larger they're sure to lead to human settlements.

3. **If you find a river, use it.** In the choking vegetation of a tropical forest, a wide, swift-flowing river is the equivalent of a natural autobahn. Rather than attempt to push through on foot, take advantage of the current to float downstream on a simple raft of logs and brush lashed together with vines.

4. **Walk or float, but don't swim.** While rafting out of a jungle is often a viable option for escape, swimming is not. Even if a river or lake looks like the easiest way to circumvent the dense underbrush, avoid swimming at all costs. Tropical bodies of water are often rife with crocodiles, piranhas, anacondas, and other deadly predators that will take advantage of any meal that comes along.

5. **Use nighttime hours for rest, not travel.** Before the sun goes down, find an open area to rest for the night. Even if you can't sleep, the long break will help conserve energy for the next day. In addition, traveling at night is disorienting and particularly dangerous, as snakes and other nocturnal predators come out to hunt after dark.

6. **Collect your water from above.** Never drink water from a stream, river, or pool. Jungle groundwater is brimming with horrific parasites and diseases. Instead, collect your water from rain using

bromeliads or other large leaves, or cut open cut open large woody vines or lianas if you have a machete or sharp knife.

7. **Protect your skin.** Even the smallest scrape can turn into a life-threatening infection or provide a perfect opportunity for a debilitating parasite. Cover your body with clothes and watch out for sharp rocks and twigs.

8. **Keep your feet dry and protected.** Jungle rot, an aggressive fungal infection, causes the skin on the feet to flake off, making travel painful and difficult. In addition, blisters and open cuts will not heal under the moist conditions, so keep your feet well padded to avoid developing blisters.

9. **Watch your step.** Travel carefully. A snake bite, or even a bad insect bite or sting, can turn a dire situation into a guaranteed-deadly one. Watch where you step and where you place your hands as you walk through underbrush.

10. **Eat forest insects and fruit to keep your energy level up.** Strenuous jungle hiking can burn as many as 600 calories *each* hour. If you want to survive, you'll need to keep your energy intake high. Insects are high in protein, while fruit is high in calories.

CHAPTER THREE
CATEGORY 4

The last light of the day is fading from twilight to full darkness, but visibility in the horizontal rain was already so bad that you hardly notice. The wind-driven drops sting like pellets when they hit your body, so you stay down below deck in the cabin, wondering how much longer the dozen or so heavy nylon mooring lines securing the sailing yacht to the mangrove trees that surround it will hold. Your cousin and his wife look worried, and they've been doing this for nearly 10 years. Your wife and daughter are terrified as the 35-foot vessel is slung first in one direction then the other, stretching the web of lines like rubber bands as wind gusts of over 140 miles per hour slam it unmercifully. How did a family of tourists on vacation from Ohio end up aboard a sailboat in the Florida Keys, trying to survive a Category 4 hurricane?

A Summer Vacation Nightmare

Beads of sweat slide down your face as you sit in your car in the stifling humidity, windows rolled down and engine switched off to save the precious gallon or two remaining in your nearly empty gas tank. You look at your wife beside you for some encouragement as the endless line of vehicles ahead remains at a standstill. In a desperate attempt to top off your fuel tank, you've fallen into this procession and with every hour that passes, you realize your chances of getting back to the mainland from this far down in the Florida Keys before the hurricane strikes are getting slimmer. On the one highway connecting this string of low islands to the rest of Florida, those who do have gas are jammed in a slow crawl, bumper to bumper at less than five miles per hour. You had no idea how bad the traffic could be during such an event and realize you should have listened to your cousin, who has been here for years. Your 10-year-old daughter in the back seat is complaining about the heat and just wants to go home. But Ohio is a long way from the Overseas Highway, and a Category 4 hurricane is barreling right through the slot between Cuba and the tip of the Florida peninsula, heading straight for Key West.

Road Trip to the Keys

It's the second week of August and the last two weeks of summer vacation before your daughter goes back to school to start fifth grade. An expensive vacation is not really in the budget, but you've got a free-spirited younger cousin who lives aboard his sailboat with his wife in the Florida Keys, where they are both sailing instructors. They've been begging you to bring the family down for a visit and they promise to show you the sights and take you sailing, fishing, and snorkeling in the clear waters surrounding the Keys. It was supposed to be a low-budget trip, costing you only gas and food money, but after you arrived your wife didn't like staying aboard the boat, which was moored in a popular liveaboard anchorage along with many other cruising boats. Your cousin's boat, though 35 feet long and seaworthy enough to go most anywhere, felt cramped and hot down below, especially with five people on board. There was no shower, which meant you had to take a long dinghy ride across the anchorage to use the marina's public facilities, and the marine toilet on board the boat had to be manually pumped after each use. Your wife wasn't happy with the arrangements at all, so the three of you spent the next few nights in an overpriced motel room nearby.

Before you left Ohio to drive to the Keys, you voiced your concerns to your cousin that it was hurricane season. He assured you there was nothing to worry about, as most of the big storms occur later in August or in September or October. This had been an unusually active season, he said, with quite a few named tropical storms already, but the Keys always got lucky. They hadn't been hit by a major hurricane in all the years he'd been there. His assurances put your mind at ease. After all, he was the expert, living in the islands and dodging storms on his boat. All you knew about them as resident of Ohio was what you saw on the news when a big one like Katrina made landfall.

Day One: Thursday, 8:00 AM

Your concerns about hurricanes seem justified near the end of your vacation when you are starting to think about the long drive home on the coming weekend. A tropical storm named Jasmine that had formed in the Atlantic days before has now moved just north of the Caicos Islands, and has been upgraded by the National Hurricane  Center to a Category 1 hurricane. Jasmine is forecast to move through the central Bahamas in the next 24 hours, and several projected tracks are in disagreement as to where it will go after it passes through that island group. Most computer models show it going into the Florida peninsula north of Miami, but one less likely path also brings it farther south, on a course that would take it straight to Key West and then into the Gulf of Mexico beyond.

When your cousin and his wife come to shore to join you and the family for breakfast before the day's planned adventure, you express your concerns to him. He assures you that the storm will mostly likely miss the Keys. It seems they always do, he says. Something about the winds and currents keep them

REAL LIFE | *Living in Denial: Hurricanes Never Hit Here*

When it comes to hurricanes, most residents of coastal areas seem to have a short memory. Either that or they live in denial of the facts even though history clearly shows what can and has happened in the past with regard to these fearsome storms. People tend to think back just a few years, pointing out that the most recent hurricanes always seem to turn away from their area at the last minute. This gives them a false sense of security and an excuse to do little to prepare. Despite all the death and destruction from hurricanes they see on the news every time one makes landfall, most coastal residents don't want to go through the hassle and expense of evacuating. They prefer to sit tight and take their chances, hoping the storm won't hit them, and saying that even if it does, it won't be as bad as Hurricane "So and So" back in "such and such" year.

This was the fatal mistake many victims of Hurricane Katrina made in 2005. When Category 5 Hurricane Camille roared through the Mississippi coast in 1969, it became the legendary "worst possible" hurricane that could be imagined. Those old enough to remember and those young enough to have only heard about it in the stories all thought the same thing: "No hurricane can ever be as bad as

away every time, and the locals have come to count on it since there hasn't been a major hit since 1935, back before hurricanes were even named. But still, he says, he will be keeping an eye on it. And just in case it doesn't turn, he has a pre-scouted hurricane hole way up in a tidal creek in some mangroves not far from the anchorage. He says the boat is stocked up and there are always storm anchors and extra mooring warps on board.

Camille." It was common to hear statements like, "I made it through Camille; I'm not leaving for this one." As a result, it has been said after Katrina that Hurricane Camille killed more people in 2005 than it did when it came ashore in 1969.

In the Florida Keys it is common to hear residents make statements to the effect that the Keys, and Key West in particular, are somehow charmed or perhaps looked on favorably by the weather gods and will not be hit. They point out example after example of tropical storms and hurricanes that either weakened or changed course at the last minute, sparing their islands with little more than some wind and rain. The problem with this way of thinking, of course, is that these people simply don't look back far enough to realize that this feeling of immunity is only an illusion. The truth is that the Florida Keys, like most populated areas of that state and other states in the hurricane danger zone, have been ground zero for hurricanes that left trails of death and destruction.

Two of these unnamed storms were particularly devastating to the Keys. The first was on September 10, 1919. At that time, it was the most powerful hurricane to hit Key West in the history of the settlement. More than 800 people were killed, many of them lost on 10 ships that were reported missing or sunk.

You're still skeptical, but you try to relax and assure your even more skeptical wife that everything will be all right. The last thing you want to do, your cousin tells her, is to drive north and get in a traffic jam with all the people who might begin evacuating the Miami–Ft. Lauderdale area soon.

Day One: Thursday, 6:00 PM

Back from another day of visiting the nearby coral reefs on your cousin's sailboat, all of you are having dinner at the marina restaurant, where most of the sailors from the anchorage are having drinks and eating while glued to the big-screen television over the bar that is locked on the Weather Channel. Hurricane

REAL LIFE | *Category 5: Labor Day, 1935*

An even stronger hurricane hit the Keys on Labor Day of 1935, and it has so far been the only Category 5 storm to hit the U.S. coast other than Camille. That Labor Day storm was famous for winds so strong that people caught out in the open were literally sandblasted to death by wind-driven beach sand. Many others were impaled or decapitated by flying debris. Of the more than 400 people killed in the Keys by the storm, 259 were veterans working on the Overseas Highway, many of whom drowned when a train sent to rescue them was swept off its tracks by a storm surge of more than 15 feet above sea level. The sustained wind at impact was estimated at the time to be 160 miles per hour, but later studies suggest it was more likely as high as 185 to 200 miles per hour. The center of the destruction was Islamorada, one of the main settlements in the middle Keys.

In the 1930s, the population of Key West was only around 12,000, and fewer than 1000 people lived on the middle islands between the southernmost city and the

Jasmine's track through the Bahamas has been wobbly and un-certain, and now there is even more discussion of the likely path the storm will follow once it hits the warm waters of the Gulf Stream and heads toward Florida. Because it has already strengthened to Category 2 status, mandatory evacuations have been ordered for the area from West Palm Beach southward to Homestead, and evacuation from the Keys is recommended, though most of the forecast tracks show the storm still passing north of the island chain.

At this point your wife is in a near-panic and insists that you should leave, but your cousin says he's been through a lot of these evacuations and that you would be worse off in the

mainland. With little in the way of reliable weather fore-casting, people who inhabited these exposed islands between the Atlantic and the Gulf of Mexico lived by their barometers—the only sure way to know when a big storm threatened. The recorded central pressure of this compact but superintense storm was 892 millibars, the record low pressure for any hurricane in the Atlantic until Gilbert in 1988 and Wilma in 2005. Tropical low-pressure systems are classified as hurricanes when their pressure is 980 millibars or lower, and the average pressure in a hurricane is 950 millibars, compared to the normal atmospheric pressure at sea level of around 1013. Any storm with a pressure reading below 900 is rare and extremely dangerous.

If a hurricane of similar intensity were to make landfall in the Keys today, the destruction it would wreak would be much worse. Although much better forecasting today would mean no one in the area would be caught without warning as many were in 1935, it's likely that a large number of the residents would ignore the warnings and choose to stay anyway.

gridlocked traffic than you would be just staying put. He's still confident that the storm won't hit the Keys, but he and his wife plan to make some preparations on the boat first thing in the morning and get it ready to move at a moment's notice if required.

Day Two: Friday, 8:00 AM

You and your family meet your cousin and his wife for breakfast at the same waterfront restaurant where you had dinner the evening before. Once again, everyone at the bar and surrounding tables is staring at the overhead TV screen, watching the latest updates and discussions of Hurricane Jasmine on

Evacuation Bottleneck

Even those who wish to evacuate because of such an approaching storm might not be able to. A glance at a map of southern Florida will tell you in an instant just how difficult it would be to travel north by road from the Keys in time to avoid a major hurricane. With some 80,000 residents and around 40,000 visitors at peak times in the summer, the Overseas Highway itself becomes a major chokepoint, as it is the only route connecting the chain of islands to the mainland. And even after reaching the mainland, those trying to evacuate would find themselves in the most densely populated part of the state, at the tip of a crowded peninsula where limited routes north could be packed with hundreds of thousands of evacuees from cities like Miami and Ft. Lauderdale if the storm is large enough to threaten them as well. Since some hurricanes can be big enough to span a large part of the peninsula—not to mention the fact that they can change course at the last minute—you run the

the Weather Channel. Jasmine is now a Category 3 storm, with maximum sustained winds of 120 miles per hour. Your cousin tells you they have been listening to the National Oceanic and Atmospheric Administration (NOAA) reports on the marine radio since they woke at 6:00 a.m. You can clearly see that he is concerned about this storm. The forecast track has been moved south by the National Hurricane Center. A strong high-pressure system from the north has moved farther south into Florida than they originally predicted, preventing the hurricane from staying on its track toward Ft. Lauderdale or West Palm Beach. But it has to go somewhere, and it is building in intensity in the warm waters of the Bahamas, fed by the currents of the Gulf

risk of driving right into the storm or not getting far enough away from its path to avoid the strong outer bands of devastating wind. It's no wonder that most residents of the Keys prefer to ride out the storm where they are rather than get into the gridlock of a mass evacuation.

But for those unlucky tourists and other non-residents with no place to go, when a mandatory evacuation is ordered, the options are few. Hotels and motels are not allowed to maintain occupancy—all guests must pack up and leave. And if the threat is from a Category 3 or greater storm, Monroe County hurricane shelters will not be opened; none are considered safe in a Category 4 or 5 hurricane because most of the land in the Keys is just a few feet above sea level. Officials instead prefer to get as many people as possible to better shelters on the mainland. The authorities have a hard time getting the long-term residents off the islands, but the vacationers have little choice but to get forced into long lines of traffic or loaded on the last planes and buses off of the islands.

Stream. If the meteorologists are correct, the middle section of the Florida Keys is right in Jasmine's path.

Your cousin tells you that they have decided to move the boat to their hurricane hole, even though he still expects that this one will somehow turn and miss the Keys like they always do. But if they don't move now, it will be too late, as other boats will possibly occupy their spot or block the entrance to the small mangrove-lined tidal creek he had so carefully scouted out in his hurricane planning. He and his wife both suggest that the three of you should come along with them, but your wife is having none of that. She insists that you must pack the car and

The Storm Surge Is the Killer in Major Hurricanes

The storm surge generated by powerful hurricanes is one of the most misunderstood aspects of this meteorological phenomenon. Misinformed, overexcited TV journalists compare the surge to a tsunami, leading people to believe that it comes in like a powerful wave sweeping away everything in its path. This is an inaccurate analogy, as tsunamis are generated by undersea earthquakes or landslides and are, in effect, shockwaves traveling through water that can be moving at hundreds of miles per hour. A hurricane storm surge is the effect created when a hurricane pushes enough water ahead of it that it builds up on the shallow shelf found just off the coast in many seashore areas, raising the sea level by a few feet to more than 20 feet in some cases. The effect is worsened if the surge coincides with the high-tide cycle.

On top of the damage that would be caused by flooding alone because of this rise in sea level, the fierce winds that

leave now, convinced that leaving now is the only choice. The officials are calling for all non-residents to evacuate immediately, and word is a mandatory evacuation of the Keys will be ordered later that day if the storm continues on its projected path. When that happens, you will lose your motel room because the management will be forced to close it.

Day Two: Friday, 10:00 AM

You are all loading the last of your bags into the trunk of your family car, having vacated the motel room amid the frantic buzz and rush of all the other guests stuck in the same predica-

accompany a hurricane will of course generate tremendous wave action, which is what does the real damage. Far offshore in deep water, these wind-driven waves can be 50 or more feet high. When the surge  comes inland, waves of 5 to 15 feet are often raging on the crest of it, breaking in whitewater fury and destroying everything in their path. Much of the wave damage is caused by the fact that the rise in sea level (storm surge) renders protective barriers like natural reefs, man-made jetties, and sea walls useless as the sea rises enough to submerge them, allowing the waves to smash unimpeded into shoreside structures such as roads, bridges, homes, and other buildings. A large percentage of the deaths in a hurricane are drownings caused when someone is swept away in the storm surge or trapped inside a building by it.

ment. There is an ominous feeling of impending doom in the air, even though the skies are still sunny and the wind is nearly calm. Your T-shirt is already wet with sweat in the Florida humidity as you close the trunk and make sure your daughter is secure in her seat belt in the back seat. When you start the engine it occurs to you that you should have thought to refill your gas tank the evening before, but your cousin's dismissive attitude about the storm caused you to put that thought aside. The fuel gauge reads just under a quarter of a tank—not enough to get to the mainland if there are delays like you've been hearing you should expect. Getting more gas has now become your first priority.

Under Surge, Under Siege: The Odyssey of Bay St. Louis and Katrina

Those who have not seen firsthand the aftermath of the storm surge from a major hurricane like Katrina cannot comprehend the destruction it leaves in its wake. In her book *Under Surge, Under Siege: The Odyssey of Bay St. Louis and Katrina*, Ellis Anderson, who survived Katrina in her home in the hard-hit Mississippi Gulf Coast town of Bay St. Louis, describes her first impression of what was left of this old waterfront town. She likens it to what one would expect to see in a war zone after a bombing. In the Bay St. Louis and Waveland area, where Katrina's surge was at its greatest, it reached a height of 35 feet, leaving behind destruction unprecedented in 300 years of recorded history there. By comparison, Hurricane Camille, which was called a 100-year event, had a maximum storm surge of 27 feet.

Anderson was one of those betting on the outcome based on Camille. Her property had not been flooded in

Day Two: Friday, 1:00 PM

After almost three hours of sitting in a barely moving line of traffic at the gas station nearest the motel, you find out that so many cars ahead of you have gotten their maximum allowance of 10 gallons of fuel that the station's underground storage tanks have been pumped dry. There will be no tanker truck coming to refill them, and every other station on the island has the same traffic jam of waiting vehicles trying to top off their fuel tanks. Without the air conditioner—which you can't run because you are nearly out of gas—the heat in the car is intolerable. While not inching the car forward little by little, you and your family have been standing outside like everyone else. Now your hopes

1969, according to the realtor who sold it to her, so she felt safe in staying for Katrina. After all, the forecasters were predicting 20 to 22 feet of surge, with a slight chance of 25 feet, and her house was on one of the highest points on that part of the coast.

But once she was committed to staying, there was no chance of changing her mind and leaving. She watched helplessly as the storm surge first came over the street in front of her house, then over her yard, and then inside the house. Whole trees rushed past the house like kayaks caught in whitewater rapids. Neighbors she barely knew arrived at her door by boat, seeking refuge from homes closer to the waterfront where there was no chance of surviving. The house was high enough to be spared the fate of most structures within a half mile of the beach from Waveland to Gulfport—that of being swept completely off their foundations along with everything in them to end up as mountains of rubble that would take years to remove.

of getting off the islands and out of the path of the storm have been dashed. The drivers who do have fuel are crawling along the highway in the direction of the mainland at a pace that will take hours to cover 100 miles. You've heard word from others in line with you that all the public buses in the islands are full, packed with those tourists and residents alike who are evacuating but do not have their own cars. A rumor is spreading that some unscrupulous taxi drivers from Miami are offering to come down and pick up evacuees for $500 per person. Some people are walking down the highway with their bags, trying to thumb a ride. You're starting to wish you'd never dreamed up

Swept Away by Raging Waters

After Katrina passed, unbelievable reports from the survivors started coming in. In the city of Waveland, the police force remained at their station to be in position to assist citizens when the storm was over. Since the brick-walled headquarters building was situated almost two miles inland, they felt safe. But once the water started rising, it filled the building within an hour, literally flushing the officers out into the storm. Fifteen of them clung to a flimsy tree outside the station, hanging on for dear life against the current for three or four hours.

Over 30 miles to the east, in Biloxi, Hardy Jackson and his wife, Tonette, had already evacuated their children, but chose to stay in their house. Jackson's home was just a block from the beach, and when the surge came, it forced its way into his home with a thunderous roar, quickly fill-

this so-called vacation and would rather be back at work in your office than dealing with this nightmare. There's no use getting in the endless line of traffic on the highway without enough gas to get off the islands, so you call your cousin on his cell phone to see if he has any better ideas.

Day Two: Friday, 4:00 PM

Getting off the island in your car is hopeless without gas. Your cousin has plenty of extra fuel for the auxiliary engine on board his boat—several six-gallon jerry cans, in fact. But unfortunately for you, the boat's engine is a diesel, so it won't do you any good. With no other choice than to follow his advice, you and your wife and daughter have pared down your luggage to a couple of small bags so you can walk the two miles to a beach where your cousin can meet you in the dinghy. He and his wife

ing it up before a wave nearly cut the house in two. They made their way to the attic and punched through the roof to escape. Jackson clung to his wife's hands until the current swept her out of his grasp. He found himself carried in the surge with pieces of houses and furniture all around him. His wife's body was recovered days later.

Similar stories were repeated all along this hard-hit coast. Survivors of the surge had skin ripped off their hands and sometimes cut to the bone from hanging onto treetops and other immovable objects in the current. Others had cuts and broken bones from being struck by flying pieces of houses, vehicles, and boats that became shrapnel in the 140-mile-per-hour wind. Many of those who did not survive were still being found nearly a year later as mountainous piles of debris were sorted through and removed from the streets and yards of these communities.

have finished making their hurricane preparations on the sailboat, and have it secured in the mangroves with every anchor and mooring line on board. With nowhere else to go for the night, you and your family will have to spend the night on the boat. Your cousin is still hopeful the hurricane will not make a direct hit on the area, and says that if it misses this will all have been a drill like so many he's been through before.

Your wife is horrified by the idea of getting caught on a boat in a hurricane, but your cousin and his wife assure her that it would actually be safer to ride it out moored aboard a seaworthy boat in the mangroves than in some building on land that is subject to destruction by the storm surge. All the land in this part of the Keys is only a few feet above sea level, and a major hurricane making a direct hit would generate a storm surge that would completely submerge the islands. A well-secured boat surrounded by the cushioning effect of flexible mangrove trees

REAL LIFE | *Surviving Hurricane Hugo Aboard a Yacht in the Caribbean*

In September 1989, Narendra Sethia, owner of a sailing yacht operating as a crewed charter vessel in the Caribbean, was caught on a crossing between the island of Curacao off the coast of Venezuela and the island of Tortola in the British Virgin Islands, when a radio report warned that Hurricane Hugo was heading to the Caribbean from the Atlantic. The crew put in at the nearest landfall in St. Croix and entered a lagoon with a protected anchorage surrounded by mangroves. Along with 31 other vessels in the anchorage, they secured the yacht with all the anchors, chain, and line they had on board and stripped away all loose objects from the decks.

When Hurricane Hugo made landfall in the Virgin Islands, it was a Category 4 storm. Sethia describes the

and out of the worst of the wind can rise with the storm surge, as long as there is someone on board to adjust the lines—or so your cousin says.

Day Two: Friday, 7:00 PM

With leaving the Keys in time to avoid the hurricane no longer an option and with no other place for your family to take shelter for the night, you and your wife and daughter are all on board your cousin's sailing yacht with him and his wife. The boat is moored in a narrow tidal creek surrounded on all sides but the narrow entrance by a wall of dense-growing mangrove trees at least 30 feet high. The water beneath the hull is about 8 feet deep, and the distance across the creek is some 40 feet. The network of mooring lines tying the vessel to the stoutest trees on the nearby banks and to several storm anchors in the waterway brings to your mind the image of a spider sitting in the middle

experience as "all hell breaking loose," with wind noise like a runaway freight train. The yacht dragged her anchors and even with the engine running at full throttle was unable to hold position, much less make headway. Slamming into other vessels in the anchorage, the stern of the yacht was caved in and the mizzen mast collapsed, followed by the main mast. Water poured in through a hole made by the mast, and first the pumps and then the engine failed. Sethia and the rest of the crew were able to crawl outside using diving masks and snorkels to breathe in the driving rain and crawl onto the deck and then into the wheelhouse of the steel trawler they had wrecked against. The yacht was eventually salvaged, but most boats in the anchorage were totally destroyed or sunk.

of an intricate web. Your cousin has explained that the heavy nylon lines will stretch as the boat is pushed by hurricane-force winds and that there is enough slack in them to allow it to rise

several feet on the storm surge. If the surge gets higher than that, he is prepared to loosen them further to reduce the strain on the boat's fittings to which they are cleated.

Despite his assurances, you are deeply regretting the day you made the decision to bring your family to the Florida Keys during hurricane season. The NOAA weather forecast is being broadcast constantly on the marine radio in the cabin. Much of it is nautical jargon you don't understand, with talk of latitudes and longitudes and wind speeds measured in knots. But as you sit out in the cockpit and look at the evening sky fading to darkness, you know something is changing. The first outer bands of the hurricane have arrived, with strange clouds racing across the sky from the northeast to the southwest, a portent of things to come tomorrow if the storm stays on its track.

Day Three: Saturday, 6:00 AM

You've had a sleepless night lying awake in the aft cabin bunk with your wife, who has also been awake all night as you've fretted about your predicament. In the early evening, the interior of the sailboat was stuffy and hot because you are anchored in the confines of the mangroves where no breeze can reach the ventilation hatches. Running the engine all night to power the air conditioning was out of the question because of the need to conserve fuel. Your daughter has been crying off and on during the night because of the mosquitoes that kept getting into the cabin and biting her.

But now that dawn is breaking, the air is no longer still; strong gusts from the outer edges of Hurricane Jasmine occasionally funnel down the narrow creek and cause the boat to strain against its lines. In the cockpit you discuss the situation with your cousin as he checks all the lines at their attachment points for chafe. He says that it's going to be rough day. The storm is still on track for Key West, which will put its strongest quadrant right over your location by early evening. The only good news is that forecasters are not expecting it to strengthen and are saying it could weaken slightly to just barely remain a Category 4 storm when it makes landfall. This is going to be a long day of nervous anticipation, and you just want to get it over with. The waiting is the hardest part and the incessant automated NOAA reports on the radio are just making it worse.

Day Three: Saturday, 4:00 PM

You and your family are in for the ride of your lives as the hurricane approaches landfall. Wind gusts of 80 to 90 miles per hour have already lashed through the surrounding mangroves, scattering leaves and small branches all over the decks and blowing pelting rain sideways through the air. The water has been steadily rising all morning, completely submerging all the exposed mangrove roots and patches of sand beach beneath them, and widening the narrow creek so that it looks more like a river. Out past the narrow entrance, the larger cove where some other boats are anchored is whipped by the wind into a whitewater froth of breaking chop.

Day Three: Saturday, 6:00 PM

The wind's intensity has increased to a level you would not have thought possible if you were not here to experience it. It roars through the tops of the mangroves with occasional loud pops and cracks as limbs are torn away, and it screams through the wire rigging holding the mast up with a sound so high-pitched it hurts your ears even down below in the cabin. Your cousin has been going on deck periodically, despite the conditions, wearing a diving mask and clipped into a safety harness as he crawls around the deck checking and adjusting the lines. He reports that the surge has raised the sea level at least 12 and maybe 15 feet. Many of the other vessels in the less-protected harbor have broken free of their moorings and been driven into the man-

Dodging Hurricanes on My Own Sailboat

This scenario does not in any way imply that I recommend choosing to ride out a hurricane on board a boat, no matter how well secured. It's always better to leave early and get completely out of the path of the storm if at all possible. But with proper preparations and knowledge it is possible to get through such a storm unscathed, and many have done so in even the worst hurricanes. This scenario is presented to show what could happen if you were caught somewhere like the Florida Keys with no way out and no secure place to take shelter. I was caught in the Keys aboard my own sailboat in 2001 with my then-wife and stepdaughter when Hurricane Michelle, a Category 4 storm, unexpectedly made a turn in our direction. Just as in the scenario described in this chapter, a mandatory evacuation was ordered for the Keys and no official shelters were opened except on the mainland. Motels were ordered

groves; some are piled up against each other being pounded and battered.

Day Three: Saturday, 8:00 PM

The sounds outside are even scarier in the darkness, but somehow your cousin's yacht is still holding her own in the web of lines between the resilient mangroves. His last check of the various cleats revealed that a couple of them were almost parted from chafe, but it appeared that the water level had dropped a couple of feet, so the good news is that the worst is over. You begin to have hope that you will all live through the night, and that you won't end up swimming in the darkness in the raging current of a hurricane storm surge. It even looks as if the boat

closed and taxi drivers were taking advantage of stranded tourists. We could not get off the islands or sail out of the path of danger in time, so we secured the boat in a deep, mangrove-lined creek in the way described in this chapter. Thankfully, the hurricane turned east once it entered the Gulf Stream after crossing Cuba, and the Keys were spared as they so often are. We were only raked by the edges of the storm, with winds of 70 miles per hour or so and lots of rain.

When Hurricane Katrina devastated the Mississippi coast in 2005, I secured the same sailboat in a bayou that is considered one of the safest "hurricane holes" in the area. Katrina's storm surge topped 30 feet in that area, scattering boats like mine along with much larger commercial fishing vessels over thousands of acres through the surrounding woods and marsh. Luckily, I was not on board the boat during the storm. Many fishermen who did stay with their boats in that same area lost their lives that day.

will come out mostly unscathed, which is a testament to the seamanship and experience of your cousin and his wife.

Day Four: Sunday, 6:00 AM

By the time dawn breaks the next morning, the rain has become a light drizzle and the wind just a strong breeze well under gale force. You can't see anything of the nearby town because of the surrounding mangroves, but the anchorage outside the creek entrance is a scene of total devastation. Only one other sailing vessel remains afloat and mostly intact. The others are broken and capsized hulls, or just masts sticking up to indicate where they sunk. Luckily, most of the owners were not on board, having just anchored the boats as best they could and left them there.

Judging by the height of the storm surge, your cousin is certain that the devastation on land will be even worse, and he fears there will be many dead. Those that are alive will be refugees without shelter, food, or drinking water. Some people will take advantage of the situation to loot and rob. Others will simply wait for outside help that will be a long time coming. Compared to them, you and your family are in much better shape on a well-stocked vessel with everything you need, hidden away and protected from the chaos on shore where you can wait it out until the first rescuers arrive.

TOP TEN HURRICANE SURVIVAL TIPS

1. Stay tuned to the tropical weather forecast. Don't be caught off guard during any part of the hurricane season if you live or travel anywhere these storms might make landfall. Hurricane forecasts are quite accurate with regard to the path and the intensity that can be expected. Use this information to avoid ever being near one.

2. Have an evacuation plan. If you live in an area affected by hurricanes, have an evacuation plan prepared in advance and be ready to implement it before mass evacuations of the less prepared choke the highways with traffic and confusion. Keep your vehicle in good repair and keep your fuel tank full. Don't let your possessions weigh you down or delay your leaving.

3. Have bug-out or 72-hour bag. Part of your evacuation plan should include having a pre-packed bug-out bag or 72-hour evacuation bag for every member of your family. The bag should contain essentials such as drinking water, high-energy snack foods, portable shelter such as a tarp, and a sleeping bag or blanket. You should include everything you will need to stay in a shelter, with relatives, or possibly in your vehicle or outdoors.

4. Don't attempt to ride it out. Don't take foolish chances with hurricanes, especially if you are in the storm surge zone, which can in many cases be anywhere within several miles of the coast, a bay, tidal creeks, canals, or other estuaries. Never bet on your safety based on the historical record of storm surges, as records are broken all the time. Most deaths in hurricanes are from the storm surge, rather than the wind.

5. Don't die trying to save a boat. Despite the fictional scenario in this chapter, avoid trying to ride out a hurricane on a boat unless you have no better alternative. Even with the best preparations, there are too many unknowns and other, larger vessels may drag anchor and destroy or sink your boat with you in it. Many commercial fishermen died trying to save their boats (which were their livelihoods) in Hurricane Katrina.

6. **Take shelter from the wind and flying debris.** Wind-driven debris is a killer in a powerful hurricane, with all manner of ordinary items turned into projectiles in winds over 140 miles per hour. Do not stay outdoors or go outside to look around. If you are caught outside, get in a ditch or other protected area and stay down. Stay clear of standing trees that will likely be flattened.

7. **Get in the middle of the building.** If you are caught in a house or other structure during hurricane winds, stay away from the windows and take shelter in the smallest spaces, such as a hall or bathroom in the middle of the structure. Use a mattress if possible to shield yourself from a collapsing roof or debris.

8. **Don't be fooled by the eye of the storm.** If the wind suddenly stops, you may be in the calm at the eye of the hurricane. This can last for up to several minutes depending on the size and forward speed of the hurricane. When it passes over, you can expect winds of the same intensity as before, but from the opposite direction.

9. **Don't get trapped by the surge.** If you are caught in a rising storm surge, don't get trapped in an attic with no way out. Get outside the house or building and make your way to the roof. If you are swept away in the surge, use any floating debris you can find to increase your buoyancy until you can make it to higher ground or a strong structure.

10. **Proceed with caution in the aftermath.** Hurricanes leave all manner of danger in their wake. You may encounter downed power lines that are still hot, gas leaks, and any number of sharp objects in the mountains of debris that will be everywhere. Displaced wildlife, including dangerous species like alligators and venomous snakes, can turn up in the most unexpected places.

CHAPTER FOUR
IN THE LINE OF FIRE

You try to control the shaking as you crouch behind the low wall of a jewelry kiosk in middle of the mall hallway and check one last time to make sure that a round is in the chamber of your Glock 19. Two more shots cut through the screams of fear and panic that fill the open space of the food court right around the corner. With every shot fired, you fear someone else is dead or dying. There's little time to act. You've never fired a weapon at a live target before—much less an armed and dangerous one that can and will fire back if you fail. Do you have what it takes to pull this off? With two security guards down and the police probably still minutes away, nothing stands between a deranged shooter and more helpless victims besides you—a relatively new gun owner who's not even supposed be armed inside the shopping mall. You could simply look out for yourself and stay hidden until the cops arrive, but if you do, more innocent people will die. And if you use the weapon in your hand, how will the first law enforcement officers on the scene know that you're not the shooter? Will they kill you before you have a chance to explain yourself? What events could possibly lead you to a predicament like this?

Crime Is on the Rise in Your Hometown

You live in a relatively small American city that until recent years was mostly free of violent crime. But in the last few years

there has been a series of highly publicized events—some armed carjackings and a couple of home invasions
that ended badly for the homeowners,
including a family in your own neighborhood—that have prompted you to
take a serious interest in self-defense.
Growing up in an urban environment,

you had no prior experience with firearms, but after taking a
safety course and then a defensive handgun class from a local expert, you developed a keen interest in the sport of target
shooting and began to find yourself at the range at least once
a week. After passing the required background check, you received a concealed-carry permit issued by your state, and with
a new Glock carried in an inside-the-waistband holster on your
person most of the time, you begin feeling much better about
your ability to protect yourself and your family.

11:05 AM

It's Saturday, your day off. You pull into the parking lot of the
largest mall in town, planning to make a quick trip inside to get
a trim at your regular hair salon, check out the newest releases
at the bookstore, and grab some lunch. You don't expect to be
in the mall longer than about an hour and a half. Before getting
out of the car, you reach for the Glock in its concealed-carry
holster, knowing that you should leave it locked in the vehicle.
There are signs on all the entrance doors clearly stating that
weapons are prohibited inside the mall, even with a permit. But
being new to concealed carry, you enjoy the challenge of going
all sorts of places with the gun while being keenly aware that it's
there and careful not to let anyone see it who might be alarmed.
A large part of the instruction you received in your defensive
firearms course covered concealment techniques, and you feel

confident. There's a chill in the air, and the light jacket you have on will not look out of place today.

11:10 AM

One of the two security officers patrolling the food court area gives you a passing nod as you stroll through the crowd. Dressed neatly in your nice casual clothes, you don't fit any profile that would cause a second look, and nothing about your demeanor would suggest that you're carrying one of the world's most reliable high-capacity automatic pistols. The knowledge that you are so well armed prompts you to look at other mall patrons with more than a casual glance. You wonder which of the others might also be carrying, and it's an interesting mental exer-

cise to size them up and speculate. You know that the vast majority will not be, but perhaps there's one or two, here and there. You have no reason to believe it's necessary, as you don't feel any danger in the mall. The times that the Glock is a real comfort to you are when you are pulling up alone to a drive-through ATM or locking the doors of your home at night, thankful that you have the means to protect your family, but hoping it will never be necessary.

11:15 AM

You stop by the hair salon and find that the line for walk-ins is long, so you decide to make your way first to the bookstore, the entrance to which is back the way you came, in the direction of the food court. Still feeling a little self-conscious about the gun inside your waistband, you browse through the new releases at the front of the store, careful when you reach for a book on the lower shelves not to bend at the waist, which would push the butt of the gun out and make it a visible bulge under the tail of your jacket. The more experience you get carrying the gun, the better you feel about your ability to keep it hidden. You know that few among the general public, especially shoppers in the mall on a busy Saturday morning, are even thinking about guns or the possibility that someone may be carrying one. But it's all just an exercise anyway. You feel absolutely no need to have a gun inside a shopping mall on a Saturday morning, especially one that is patrolled by full-time security guards.

Shooting Sprees Usually Happen in Places Where Guns Are Prohibited

Everyone who watches the news is aware of the relatively recent phenomenon of a deranged gunman taking innocent lives at random because of some mental illness or a feeling of being an "outsider" to society. Among the most high-profile cases of these so-called active shooters are those that occur on high school or college campuses, such as Pearl and Columbine High Schools and Virginia Tech. In almost all cases, the shooter or shooters home in on a location such as a school campus where guns are prohibited or restricted, guaranteeing a low probability that they will face armed resistance. What these killers want is a large number of defenseless and unprepared targets so they can get the highest possible body count before the shooting ends, usually when the active shooter commits suicide. In studies of these kinds of assaults, in which the shooter doesn't want money or anything else from his or her victims, it has been concluded that attempts at negotiation are of no benefit.

11:21 AM

You've found a book and are standing in line at the checkout counter near the front of the store when suddenly the normal mall ambience of voices and low background music is shattered by three loud bangs in rapid succession. Everyone in the bookstore turns to look in the direction of the food court as a piercing scream and then a loud wail follow the noise. Two more ear-splitting bangs follow the screams, and suddenly there is an eruption of panicked yelling from that direction, punctuated by another bang. This all happens in a matter of seconds, and that's how long it takes you to realize what you're hearing.

This kind of shooter does not take hostages, and also rarely surrenders or attempts to escape after the killing begins.

Other facts about active shooters show that in almost all cases they act alone (Columbine High in Colorado and Westside Middle School in Arkansas being notable exceptions). Long guns (rifles or shotguns, rather than handguns) are favored by 80 percent of them, but 70 percent carry multiple weapons to the incident, as well as hundreds of rounds of ammunition. But despite the choice of weapons and large supplies of ammunition, the average hit rate by active shooters is less than 50 percent. They also tend to fold quickly upon being confronted by armed resistance and often do not hide or lie in wait for officers, preferring to take their own lives rather than be gunned down in a shootout. Their entire plan depends on having a few minutes before police arrive to kill the defenseless as ruthlessly as possible. Because of all these factors, the surest way to save lives in such an incident is for someone not in uniform to deliver an immediate counterattack with their own weapon.

Shots are being fired inside the mall. People are screaming and running in all directions. You drop your book and rush to the entrance of the bookstore, crouching behind a bargain books display just inside the door, trying to get a glimpse of what's

REAL LIFE | *An Armed High School Principal Stops a Killer*

On October 1, 1997, a shooting rampage by a student at Pearl High School in Pearl, Mississippi, became the first of a string of high-profile school shootings that included Westside Middle School in Jonesboro, Arkansas, and Columbine High School in Littleton, Colorado.

On that morning, 16-year-old Luke Woodham stabbed and beat his mother to death in their home and then armed himself with the 30-30 lever-action deer rifle she had bought him for Christmas. He filled his trench coat pockets with ammo and drove to Pearl High School. A reclusive student who later said he was mistreated every day, Woodham went there to shoot fellow students whom he felt had slighted him, beginning with his former girlfriend and another female student, both of whom died. His onslaught took everyone by surprise, but the moment vice principal Joel Myrick heard the shots, he ran to his truck in the parking lot and loaded the Colt .45 he always kept there.

Woodham was aware that he didn't have much time before the police would arrive, and when he heard sirens he ran to his car, planning to drive to the nearby Pearl Junior High School to shoot more students. What he hadn't counted on was Myrick, who saw him trying to flee and stood in the path of the car, pointing the handgun at the windshield. Woodham crashed the car and Myrick con-

happening. What you see tightens your gut in knots of fear. Several people are down on the floor, some writhing in pain and others not moving at all. You can plainly see the two security officers you saw on the way in lying still among the fall-

fronted him, holding the pistol to his head and asking him, "Why are you shooting my kids?" Woodham responded, "Life has wronged me, sir." With the tables turned, Woodham had no desire to put up a fight and the massacre was stopped without Myrick firing a shot.

No one can know for sure how many lives Joel Myrick saved that day because he had access to his gun. In addition to students and teachers at the high school, his actions may have saved the lives of more innocent victims at the junior high, as well as those of the first police officers to arrive on the scene. And most likely, Luke Woodham himself would not have survived the day, as he would have likely died in a shootout with the cops or taken his own life as such killers so often do. As it turned out, Woodham managed to hit nine students in the attack, including two who died from their wounds. Had Myrick not been prohibited from having his weapon on his person or in his office by federal, state, and local laws, it's possible he could stopped Woodham even sooner. The rifle Woodham used was not a fast-firing semi-automatic. To hit that many students, he needed time, and in an active shooter situation, the more time the shooter has, the greater the death toll usually is. But despite having to go all the way to his truck and load his weapon first, Myrick's fearless intervention cut short the killing spree and ended it much sooner than similar incidents such as the massacre at Virginia Tech in 2007, in which 32 victims lost their lives.

en. A figure in a black overcoat is walking calmly through the chaos, some sort of rifle in his hands, aiming from the hip as he methodically shoots at the dozens of people running from the food court or crawling on the floor trying to take cover under the tables and chairs.

11:22 AM

You have to take a couple of deliberate deep breaths to control your shaking as you take in the unbelievable scene unfolding before your eyes. One of your fellow bookstore patrons, a younger man who had just paid for his magazine when the shooting started, runs past you into the open hall and straight toward the food court, screaming a woman's name at the top of his lungs. He seems oblivious to the danger in his desperation. Before you realize what is happening, you see the gunman bring his weapon to bear on the young man and fire two more shots, sending the runner sprawling on the floor. You suddenly realize that the Glock is in your hand; you unconsciously drew it from its holster. You're still out of sight behind the book display, and the shooter has turned his attention back to the people under the tables in the food court. A quick glance around you confirms that the other bookstore patrons are either on the floor or crouching behind other displays. Your eyes meet those of the salesman hiding behind the checkout counter, and you see the beads of sweat running down his forehead, his face ashen with fear as he sees the gun in your hand. You motion for him to get his head back behind the counter and you try to steady your weapon and contemplate what you are about to do. You know you have to make up your mind fast. Another shot from the rifle is fired, reminding you that people are dying every few seconds.

Your firearms training has only briefly exposed you to long guns such as rifles and shotguns, as your instructor told you a handgun was much more practical for your self-defense purposes. You know that handguns are no match for rifles in combat: The rifle has more range, power, and potential accuracy, while the handgun is designed for close-range, defensive purposes. The idea of taking on a rifleman with only a handgun is something even experienced law enforcement officers don't want to contemplate, as the handgunner is at a serious

disadvantage in such a situation. But if you don't do something, who will? A glance around at other mall patrons hiding on the floor or running into stores reveals no one else with a gun. You know the police will be coming, but how long will it take for them to arrive? Even if it is just a few minutes, the life-or-death scenario you are witnessing can't wait minutes. In this situation every second counts. You have a family at home that needs you, and you don't want to die here today. But by chance or fate you are here, armed and able to intervene, and despite the risk, you decide to act.

11:23 AM

You could walk away and save yourself, but you've made up your mind that you can't do that despite the risks. Having made this decision, you must now act quickly, but not foolishly. You know the disadvantage you have with the limited range and accuracy of your 9mm pistol compared to a rifle, and you know you must get closer if you want to have decent chance of success. It would serve no purpose to start emptying your 15-round magazine wildly in the direction of the shooter, as you would likely miss him and may end up hitting innocent victims yourself. One thing is for certain: The distance from your hiding place near the door of the bookstore to the gunman is too far. You have to close the gap, and you have to avoid being seen before you can get into position.

Active Shooter Training for Citizens

The vast majority of people who get caught up in an active shooter situation will be unarmed. If you find yourself in such a scenario, there are steps you can take to avoid becoming one of the statistics and to possibly help others as well. The first such step is to develop and maintain *situational awareness*. This means being alert and keeping an eye out for who and what is around you at all times. If something doesn't seem right, leave and call the police.

If you hear shots or see a shooter in a public place, move *away* from the scene. Anytime you are in a public building such as a mall, know where the exits are, including those marked "Emergency Only" or "Employees Only." If there are no doors but there are windows, *break them*. Use anything available to shatter the glass and get away from the shooter.

If you get trapped somewhere that has no exit, do your best to secure the door and create a barricade using furniture and other heavy objects. Then stay away from the doors and be quiet. Shooters have been known to bang on doors, pretending to be victims and begging for entry; don't open the door until the police break it down to rescue you.

If you are trapped and the shooter gets into the room you're in, don't hesitate to fight back immediately using anything you can find. If you do not, past active shooter attacks have shown that he will kill everyone in the room.

If you are armed with a gun and have taken care of your first responsibility to get your family to safety, then you

Between the store entrance and the food court there is a low-walled jewelry kiosk in the middle of the hallway. The four walls contain display cases facing out from the center, and are about four feet high, with wide-open sides from the counter-

may be able to intervene. If there is time, you or someone else around you should call 911 from a cell phone and give the dispatcher a description of the shooter and the type of weapon he is using, if known, as well as his location. Then give your own description and be sure to say that you are armed as well. When the police arrive they will confront you with weapons aimed to kill, but if you are lucky and don't do anything they perceive as threatening to them or others, they will give you a chance to surrender before opening fire. Keeping your weapon pointed down, raise your other hand in the surrender position, and yell loudly, "I AM NOT THE SHOOTER." Do what they tell you to do immediately and exactly. You can expect to be treated like the bad guy anyway, and will probably be tackled to the ground and handcuffed, but if you don't resist, you won't be shot. The details of what happened can be sorted out afterward. You should be prepared to give a coherent statement about the incident, but if you had to use deadly force, keep your mouth shut until you have a lawyer on your side.

Some organizations that offer firearms instruction now provide "active shooter interdiction" classes for civilians. Such courses teach the correct tactics for using force to stop a shooter, as well as how to avoid getting shot by the police. The idea is that the well-trained armed citizen is often in the best position first and can offer the best chance of stopping a deranged active shooter or lone-wolf terrorist operator.

tops up to the canvas canopy that forms a roof over the kiosk. You don't know if the clerk working there is inside, hiding behind the walls, or has already fled. You know that moving your position there will endanger the clerk if he or she is inside, but you can see no better choice for a position of concealment that will get you in pistol range of the killer. The kiosk is a good 20 yards from your position in the direction of the food court, and from there, you will be within about 50 yards of the shooter, if he stays there long enough.

With a white-knuckle grip on the pistol, you wait until he is focused on victims in the opposite direction. Then you bend low and sprint to the kiosk as more rifle shots echo off the walls inside the mall's closed space. You reach the low walls unseen by the shooter, but you are under no illusion that they offer any kind of safety from rifle bullets. One thing you remember that your instructor often stressed is that there is a huge difference between "cover" and "concealment." Unlike in the movies, in real life neither the walls of most buildings (such as houses and stores) nor the thin sheet metal of automobile bodies will offer cover from bullets—especially rifle bullets, which can eas-

What Every Gun Owner Should Consider

Active shooter scenarios happen fast and in the most unexpected places. The chances of there being an armed citizen who is both mentally and physically capable of stopping the shooting are slim. The shooter usually chooses a location where the likelihood of encountering resistance is practically nonexistent. The police will respond, but at minimum it will take them several minutes to arrive, and in an active shooter situation that will be too late for many of the victims, who will be shot in a matter of seconds. I am not

ily pierce such obstructions and kill people hiding on the other side. What they do offer, though, is concealment, so at least you have a chance that the shooter will not know where to aim. The helpless victims crawling under the tables in the food court are probably unaware of this and think they are going to be safer, but you know that the shooter will keep killing them until either he runs out of ammo or someone stops him.

11:24 AM

This is the moment of truth. You call out in a loud whisper to see if the clerk is still within the walls of the jewelry kiosk and hear a young girl's terrified reply. The only opening from her position within the walls is on the opposite side, facing the food court where the shooter would see her if she tried to run. It's too risky to attempt it, so you tell her to keep as low on the floor as possible and to not move, then you check the Glock to make sure a round is chambered and that the magazine is still securely locked in place. Another rifle shot and more screams remind you there is no more time for hesitation.

You steady the pistol with the two-handed grip you were taught, keeping your head as low as possible when you expose

suggesting that it is your duty as a citizen to risk your life in an attempt to save strangers—that is a personal judgment call that everyone who carries a weapon will have to make. Every such scenario is different, as are the risks and the chances of success.

As a gun owner myself, I think about such scenarios often and like many others, wonder if and how I would respond if the situation demanded it. It is a scenario none of us wants to face, but the possibility is the unfortunate reality of modern life.

yourself just enough to use the countertop as a bench rest to brace for the shot. The killer is still looking the other way, focused on his victims under the tables. In preparation to unload another fusillade of bullets, he has dropped a magazine and inserted another, racking the slide of his semi-automatic rifle. You line up the big square combat sights on the Glock, aiming for the killer's center of mass as you were taught. Head shots are just too difficult at this range and the chances of missing too great. You thought it would be hard to squeeze the trigger with your weapon pointed at another human being, but when you see the shooter raise the reloaded rifle to his shoulder, you fire, careful not to jerk and cause a wild shot. The shooter hesitates and looks puzzled. He takes a step backward, but does not fall. You fire again, holding your point of aim in the same place. This time the shooter wheels both right and left, looking for the source of the counterattack, but still not falling. Is it possible that you missed? You let go with a double-tap of the trigger, sending two more rounds toward his center of mass. This time he homes in on where the shots are coming from and you see the muzzle of his rifle raise in your direction as it dawns on you that he must be wearing body armor. Of course that's it. He would come prepared, knowing the police would be shooting at him eventually.

You hit the floor in a prone position as the rifle bullets shatter the jewelry display cases, sending splintered wood and glass in every direction. You are certain that you are going to die, along with the poor clerk trapped inside the kiosk. The rifle shots continue, one after another as bullets chew up the fragile walls. You've gotten the shooter's full attention, and you're certain that he won't stop until he knows you're finished. It's risky but you decide you have to crawl to the corner of the wall and return fire. By staying in the prone position, you might have a chance.

You risk a peek around the corner long enough to see that the shooter is now much closer, having apparently been walking toward you oblivious of the danger as he fired round after round through the kiosk walls. You're about to take one last chance by shooting back at him from around the corner when you hear more shots from farther away. The reports are different from those of the killer's rifle. As you risk another look, you see that he has turned to face the main entrance. The police have arrived! You think he is about to start shooting at them now that they have distracted him from you, so you level the Glock, this time aiming at the side of his head. But instead of pointing the rifle toward the entrance he quickly brings the muzzle up under his chin and pulls the trigger before you can fire. You are shaking almost uncontrollably with adrenaline as you lay the Glock on the floor and rise to a kneeling position with both hands high above your head. You call to the girl inside the kiosk, and hear her crying. She is alive! Both of you are unscathed because you were low enough that all the bullets passed over you.

11:25 AM

Fast-moving police officers armed with assault rifles are swarming everywhere. Several cover the fallen shooter, quickly securing his weapon while another team advances on you, rifles aimed at your head. One picks up your pistol and another locks your hands behind your back in cuffs forcing you roughly to a face-down position on the floor. But it's over, and at least you are alive. You can explain this and you know there are witnesses in the bookstore to back up your story. You may not have stopped the killer yourself, but you interrupted his shooting spree and had him distracted so that the police did not come under fire. You are thankful that you were armed, and thankful that you somehow found the courage to do the right thing.

TOP TEN TIPS FOR SURVIVING AN
ACTIVE SHOOTER SITUATION

1. **Maintain situational awareness.** Stay alert to potential danger and be aware of others around you, in particular if you note strange activity that could be a sign of trouble or instability. Someone wearing a long trench coat in warm weather or carrying a large or unusual case or bag that is out of place could be concealing a rifle or shotgun.

2. **Look for escape routes.** At the first sound of gunfire, look for your options for moving *away* from the scene, especially if you are unarmed or with your family. Take note of exits, including those marked "Emergency Only" or "Employees Only," and if there are no other options, look for glass windows that can be broken.

3. **Hide or fight if you can't escape.** If you are unarmed and trapped where there is no exit, lock or barricade yourself in a room, then stay away from the doors and be quiet. Don't open the door until the police arrive and break it down. If the shooter breaks in, fight back with everything you have, including throwing chairs and other objects.

4. **Take care of your own.** Your first responsibility is the safety of your family. If you are with family, get them out of the area and keep them safe. Don't try to be a hero by getting in a gunfight that can get you killed when you have family on the scene who depend on you for protection.

5. **Know what you are getting into.** If you are armed and decide to move *toward* the sound of gunfire to see if you can help the victims, stay concealed if possible to ascertain the nature of the event. Until you can see what's going on, you don't know if you will encounter a deranged shooter, a shootout between police and criminals or even rival drug dealers, or a full-blown terrorist attack.

6. **Call 911.** Get on the phone to 911 and give the shooter's location, description, and weapon type if you know it. Also give the dispatcher *your* location and description and be sure to let them know you are armed and will remain so as long as the threat is active.

7. **Maintain the element of surprise.** The other reason you should remain in concealment is for the tactical advantage the element of surprise will give you if you do see that it is a situation where intervening is justified and practical. You may be outnumbered or outgunned by the shooter or shooters, but they will not be expecting armed resistance from ordinary-looking citizens.

8. **Know your weapons.** Unless you are trained and practice regularly with the concealed weapon you are legally carrying with a permit, you should not be carrying it at all. Your own stray shots may hit innocent victims. Learn enough about other weapons to know their ranges and limitations so you will know what you're up against if you choose to engage the shooter, and so you will know how to use them if they fall into your hands.

9. **Don't brandish your weapon.** If you must use your weapon, do so and then keep it ready but close to your body and unobtrusive until you know the threat is over. Don't run around the scene of the shooting brandishing it openly. If the first thing the police see is your gun, and especially if it is pointed in their direction, there's a good chance they will shoot. Their individual training varies and they will be pumped with adrenaline from responding to the call. The sight of a weapon will register as a threat no matter who is holding it and why.

10. **Don't get shot by the police.** When the police arrive on the scene you run a risk of being shot before they figure out you're not the bad guy. Yell loudly, "DONT SHOOT!" or, "I AM NOT THE SHOOTER!" Do exactly as they tell you without hesitation. It can all be sorted out later, but only if you are not killed before you have a chance to explain.

CHAPTER FIVE
MODERN-DAY CASTAWAY

You carefully study the backs of the curling breakers as they crash over the line of reefs separating you from the sandy beach a quarter of a mile away. It's going to be a risky proposition, attempting to find a cut between the coral heads that you can navigate through without getting smashed against them. After paddling the short, unwieldy sit-on-top kayak around much of the fringing reef of the tiny atoll, you can find no easy passage to the beaches within the encircling coral.

At last you settle on a spot where there seems to be a gap in the breakers, indicting a narrow passage you might slip through in the kayak. You turn to look one last time at the diminishing triangle of the yacht's sail as it grows smaller on the horizon. You have no other choice. This tiny atoll, who knows how many miles from the nearest inhabited island, is your only hope of survival in this far-flung tract of the South Pacific Ocean. You take your chances and paddle hard after a series of large breakers slams into the reef.

Moving as fast as the tiny kayak can go, you almost make it through the surf line when another curling crest rises behind you and pushes the kayak at breakneck speed down its steep face. You ride it for as long as you can until it breaks and swallows you in a fury of whitewater, spinning you and the boat end over end until you come to the surface spitting seawater. You still have the paddle in your hand. The kayak and your water-proof sea bag that was strapped on the stern deck are afloat several yards away in the surge, drifting parallel to the beach. You can't catch them so you swim for the shallows. You make it ashore without injury and run down the beach to grab the kayak before it gets carried back out to sea. After pulling it up on the sand, you look around you at a lonely stretch of beach. There is nothing on this islet but sand and a low thicket of scrub bushes and grasses. The rest of the atoll looks just as deserted.

Hitching a Ride at Sea

You're in a transitional period in your life when you think some open-ended travel will help you make better decisions for your future. To keep the costs down while still visiting the exotic lo-cations of your dreams, you're following the advice you read in a book about hitchhiking by sea—that is, crewing in exchange for a ride on one of the many shorthanded yachts that can be found in jumping-off ports all over the world. After a success-ful passage from San Francisco to Hilo, Hawaii, you're walk-ing the docks with your sea bag when you see a "crew needed" notice pinned to the bulletin board of the marina office. You make your way to the slip where the yacht is docked and meet the owner's nephew and his friend. The two of them seem a bit young, maybe in their early twenties, but after talking to them, it is apparent they know something about sailing.

The nephew, who is temporarily serving as the yacht's cap-tain, tells you they are taking the boat to Fiji for his rich uncle. It's an impressive vessel—a custom South African–built cata-maran called a Gunboat 48. The nephew says his uncle just pur-chased it for nearly a million dollars. They could use one more hand to help stand watches on the 3000-mile voyage, and after feeling you out they agree to take you on board. You won't get paid, but it's a free ride to Fiji and looks like a fun boat.

Trouble starts not long after Hawaii drops astern. You discover that the nephew is a control freak who loves giving orders. He and his friend argue constantly over decisions about sail trim and navigation. Several days into the passage, things deteriorate rapidly when you sail into a line of severe squalls and thunderstorms. You take sides with the other guy, who implores the skipper to reduce sail and proceed more conservatively, but the hotheaded nephew has a racing sailor's mentality and would rather risk capsizing the big cat than slow down. He stays awake for up to 36 hours at a stretch, living on caffeine pills and adrenaline as he pushes the boat as hard as it will go.

When he and his friend are finally exhausted and the wind has lessened in intensity, they leave you at the helm while they both get some sleep. You do your best to keep the boat on course but despite your best efforts you oversteer and send the boat into an accidental jibe, causing the boom to slam into the starboard shrouds and break. You don't know what to do, so you yell for help and watch as the wind flogs the mainsail and broken boom until jagged pieces of broken carbon fiber tear a ragged hole in the sail. The nephew is furious when he comes on deck and sees what has happened. He screams at you despite your apologies and tells you that you're "off the boat."

A day later you're in your bunk down below when you feel the motion change and then hear the sound of an electric winch as the main anchor is deployed. There is a sound like thunder nearby, and it dawns on you that what you are hearing is breaking surf. You clamber up the companionway to find out what's going on and find the nephew and his friend waiting for you. Your sea bag is packed and on the deck, and a tiny nine-foot sit-on-top kayak, one of the yacht's many water toys, is tied to the foot of the boarding ladder, bobbing in the waves. A quarter mile away is a ring of small, sandy islets, some with tall coconut palms waving in the wind. You are given your bag and ordered off the boat, encouraged by the muzzle of a 12-gauge flare gun pointed at your chest.

Day One: A Speck in the Ocean

A quick walk around the small islet you've landed on confirms that there are no human footprints and no sign that any one has been here recently. This coral islet, or *motu* as they are known in much of the Pacific, is one of several that form an encircling ring of sandy beaches around the atoll's central lagoon, which is maybe a mile wide and two miles long. Between the islets, there are tidal cuts where water from the open ocean connects to the lagoon. Some of these cuts are deep and far too wide to swim in the current, but with the kayak you will be able to reach all the islets to fully explore the atoll for any sign that people have been here. One thing is for sure, this islet is not suitable for habitation or even for a temporary camp. It is low and sandy with only bushes and scrub for vegetation. On the other side of the lagoon you can see tall coconut palms on some of the islets and are relieved to know that at least you will have a source of water. It will be necessary to carry the kayak across to the lagoon and paddle over there.

Before you set out to do that though, you take the sea bag up into the shade of some low bushes and sit down to rest. You open it to get out the small hand-held GPS receiver that you bought before you began your ocean travels. The first order of business is to power it up and see just where it is that you've been put ashore. Within minutes, the GPS unit has locked onto satellite signals and you have a fix on your current position, which

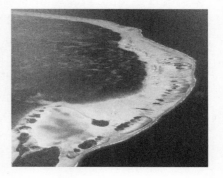

is 4 degrees south of the equator. The unit's electronic nautical charts reveal that you are on one of several small atolls that make up the Rawaki (or Phoenix) Islands in the Republic of Kiribati. The nearest neighboring island to your deserted atoll is Orona, some 58 miles to the west and also remote and uninhabited, though you don't know this for sure. The truth is that only one island in the Rawaki group is inhabited, and it's more than 150 miles away to the north. You've spent a lot of time studying maps and charts of the Pacific and reading the sailing literature, so you're somewhat familiar with these islands—at least enough to know that you're on an atoll that's not on the way to anything and that few people have reason to visit.

Day One: Early Afternoon

After getting your location while resting on the first island, you are now on the other side of the lagoon, avoiding the sun in the shade of a grove of waving coconut palms. You are both relieved

The Far-Flung Atolls of Oceania

It's fascinating to take a close look at detailed charts or satellite imagery of the vast Pacific Ocean. Aside from the well-known paradise destinations like Tahiti, Bora Bora, Tonga, and Fiji, and the sites of ferocious World War II battles that put little-known islands like Midway, Tarawa, and Guadalcanal on the map, there are thousands more islands and atolls scattered across this blue universe like dim faraway stars sprinkled in the night sky. Some of these dots in the ocean are so small and so far from their nearest neighbors that they don't even appear on most maps of the Pacific. It's only when you look closely at large-scale nautical charts or zoom in on certain areas in Google Earth that they begin showing up.

and worried to see that someone, probably islanders from another atoll in the group, has been here recently to harvest coconuts. You are relieved to know that people at least come here, as evidenced by the signs of recently cut coconut stems and some empty, husked shells lying around. The worry is that they have taken most of the mature nuts from this palm grove, leaving you with a limited supply from which to obtain water, and also leaving them little reason to return anytime soon—likely for months. Other than one small palm with a cluster of green coconuts hanging just 20 feet off the ground, the only other trees with any remaining nuts large enough to contain water are anywhere from 30 to 50 feet tall. You've seen in television documentaries how the islanders scamper up these smooth palm trees with a piece of cordage around their ankles to enable them to clamp their bare feet on the trunk, but you know from trying it that it's hard work to climb even a low palm tree

Among the most remote are little-visited groups like the Rawaki Islands, the Line Islands, and the Gilbert Islands, all of which comprise the nation of Kiribati. Many of these islands are simply too remote from larger ports where goods are available and too lacking in resources such as fresh water to support long-term human habitation, and today most of them are protected as parts of marine sanctuaries, parks, or wildlife refuges. Few of these islands feature natural safe harbors for oceangoing vessels, and as a result they are not even visited by cruising yachts, as they offer no anchorage or other attractions to justify the risk of approaching the reefs that invariably encircle them. As a result, this is one part of the world where it's still possible to become a tropical island castaway.

this way. You're hopeful there will be more easily obtainable co-conuts on one of the other islets.

You've been scrolling through the nautical charts on the GPS screen to get an idea of where you are in relation to larger islands that are ports of call for cruising yachts. You can't re-call reading about any cruising boats visiting the Rawaki group. Most of them are preserves set aside by the Kiribati government, so most of them are off-limits to visitors anyway. You realize that you could be stuck here for a while, unless those idiots on the catamaran have a change of heart and notify someone that you're here. You're sure they have no idea how serious the crime they've committed is, as it is basically equivalent to an act of pi-racy. But on the other hand, you realize it could be worse. If they did know the kind of trouble they would eventually be in, they probably would have put you over the side far out at sea, and could easily say you simply fell overboard on a night watch or

Stories That Capture the Imagination

Almost everyone is familiar with the classic tale of *Robinson Crusoe*, considered by many to be one of the greatest adventure novels ever written. The real-life inspiration for Daniel Defoe's novel was a marooned sailor named Alexander Selkirk, who was put ashore on Mas a Tierra Island, 400 miles off the coast of Chile, by the captain of the ship he was sailing on after an argument regarding the seaworthiness of the vessel. Selkirk survived in total solitude on this relatively hospitable uninhabited island that was abundant with fresh water, shellfish, edible plants, and wild goats. He was fairly well equipped with a musket, lead and powder, flint and steel, a hatchet, and other basic tools, and managed quite fine until he was picked up nearly four years later.

something—or deny that you ever came aboard in Hawaii. You can't count on anyone finding out what happened, so you know you have to take responsibility for your own survival.

You've already been through the sea bag, which you are lucky to have, and have spread its contents out on the sand to take inventory. In addition to the hand-held GPS, you have a package of spare AA batteries that fit both the GPS and an LED headlamp that you keep in the bag for reading at night. The headlamp will be useful, but you will have to use it sparingly to save batteries. One of the most valuable items in the bag is your large diving knife in its sheath. Although it would be great to have a machete, the five-inch blade will suffice to open coconuts, though with more effort than a larger blade. You've also got a small multi-tool in the bag, along with some sunscreen, a bottle of Advil, some antacid tablets, and your shaving kit with personal effects like your comb, toothbrush, and razors. The

In the great days of sailing, marooning was a common punishment equivalent to a death sentence, but more agonizing than something quick and simple like hanging or keelhauling. Condemned shipboard criminals and victims of pirates alike were often marooned on uninhabitable islands where they died of thirst, starvation, or exposure to the elements.

Other castaways have ended up on remote islands as a result of shipwrecks, and more recently, plane crashes. Still others, like Tom Neale, author of *An Island to Oneself*, have voluntarily sought out remote uninhabited islands to purposely live a life of solitude in nature. Neale's island of choice was the atoll of Suwarrow in the Cook Islands, where he took up residence on three different occasions for a total of 16 years from 1952 to 1977.

compact mirror in the kit could serve as a signal mirror. You instantly regret the fact that you gave up smoking cigars several months ago, and as a result there is no cigarette lighter to be found anywhere in your bag. Not having a means of starting a fire is going to be inconvenient, but you know there are alternative methods and you will improvise something.

The rest of the stuff in the sea bag consists of a couple of paperback novels that you're glad to have, and your spare clothing, including several T-shirts, swimming trunks, and a baseball cap. You have no shoes of any kind, as you left them down below at the foot of the bunk, but you're accustomed to going barefoot on deck and this is a tropical island, after all. The biggest limitation of not having shoes will be the sharp coral rock that is common in these islands, which will make some of the interior areas inaccessible to you.

The other major item that you know will prove helpful to your survival is the kayak. With it you can access the reef to collect shellfish and possibly lobster, and it will serve as a platform for fishing with an improvised spear. It's far too small to even contemplate using it as an escape vessel to reach another island, so you put that thought out of your mind before spending any time with it. Tomorrow you will paddle around and explore all the islets of the atoll, but today there are more pressing needs. The first is water, then seeing what possible food might be found, and then making some kind of temporary shelter for your first night's stay on the island.

Day One: Nightfall

You realize that despite the inconvenience of being marooned in the first place, you are quite lucky to be on such a hospitable island. It could be much worse if you were put ashore on some barren, windswept, and shadeless island suitable only for bird rookeries or resting places. Without the coconut palms on this island, you would bake in the sun and probably soon die of thirst, as rainfall cannot be counted on.

You collect your first "drinking nuts" from the one tree that is just 20 feet to its crown. You don't want to waste your strength or risk a fall, so rather than trying to climb the smooth trunk, you cut a long pole from a sapling in the hardwood thicket at the middle of the island and fashion a coconut-harvesting tool from it. This involves splitting the end of the pole with your knife and lashing it at a 90-degree angle to the pole with the sharp edge down, using nylon cord from a piece of fishing net you found washed up on the beach. The long pole is heavy and unwieldy, but after several attempts at maneuvering it into position, you manage to slice through the tendril holding a whole cluster of nuts. This may be safer than climbing the tree, but it is still dangerous as you must cut quickly and dash out from under the tree to keep from getting clobbered by the falling 10-pound coconuts.

Now that you have a dozen or so coconuts on the ground, you begin the difficult task of cutting away the tough outer husks to get to the shell inside. You learned how to do this in Hawaii with a machete. It's harder with the dive knife, but you eventually manage, and you'll get plenty of practice—if you can find enough remaining nuts on the atoll to keep you alive. Drinking nuts are best when they are immature, at the stage when they are so full of water that no sound can be heard when you shake them. You can live off of this mildly sweet water, though you know that it's likely to cause diarrhea until your system adapts to it.

The other abundant food found in the coconut grove is palm hearts—the tender inner stalk of the tree found at the

REAL LIFE | *Castaway: Gary Mundell, 1985*

Sometimes shipwrecked castaways are able to salvage a treasure trove of goods from the wrecked vessel before it sinks or all the contents get washed away. This was how the fictional Robinson Crusoe came to build such luxurious digs on his island paradise.

One such incident of a modern-day cruising sailor ending up as a castaway on an uninhabited atoll happened in September 1985. Gary Mundell, a solo sailor from Alaska, was almost done with an extensive cruise of the South Pacific alone on *Petrel*, his small but seaworthy Cape Dory 27 sailboat. On one of the last legs, a 2200-mile passage from Bora Bora to Hawaii, his vessel struck a reef in the middle of the night. He had been awake for 36 hours straight before turning in to his bunk at 2:00 a.m., thinking he was well past Caroline Atoll, the only land he had to worry about anywhere near the course he was steering. He could hardly have hit a more remote atoll had he been trying.

Caroline, today known as Millennium Island, is the easternmost of the Line Islands, and is considered to be perhaps the most pristine atoll in the world. Its nearest neighbor is 140 miles away. The closest mainland coast is 3200 miles to the east.

After the boat struck the reef and was rolled over on her side, Mundell scrambled out of the companionway and stared in disbelief at the outline of palm trees in the faint starlight. Quickly switching from shock to action, he worked

crown where the new fronds emerge. You can get these from the young trees that are growing up everywhere beneath the tall ones, and though it requires killing the tree, there are so many you will be in no danger of running out. This is another task that

frantically for hours to try and kedge the yacht off with his anchors, but each wave pushed her closer to shore and into shallower water. Eventually he inflated his dinghy and paddled ashore. The only sign of human life was a survey marker planted three months before.

Mundell returned to his boat to broadcast a mayday call but got no response. Though the boat was intact, there was no way he could get it ungrounded alone, so he began ferrying water, canned goods, a butane stove, sails, fishing and diving gear, and his life raft ashore to set up a camp in the coconut grove. With one of the sails stretched for a shelter, and the expensive life raft inflated for a bed, he made himself quite comfortable. He ate his perishables that included eggs, potatoes, and onions first, then began harvesting coconuts and eating the plentiful coconut crabs. He also rigged a rain catchment system and spent his days scanning for ships.

On day 50, Mundell spotted a ship emerging from a squall just three miles away. He fired off all his flares at regular intervals. He then poured kerosene over a pile of brush he had gathered for the purpose, instantly creating a bonfire, and used his signal mirror until he got a return flash from the ship's spotlight. The ship was a French research vessel that had come to Caroline Atoll to conduct biological surveys.

Mundell left the atoll with only his cap, shorts, shirt, and a belt pack. His sailing vessel *Petrel* remained on the beach where she had come to rest, a costly reminder of an unscheduled stop on an almost forgotten atoll.

would be simple with a machete, but is a lot of work hacking away with your dive knife. It's worth the trouble though; palm hearts are delicious raw. Without a fire to cook anything else, you content yourself with this simple fare for your first evening meal on the island.

Day Two: Misery at Dawn

The strong ocean breeze that swept the island throughout the day and most of the night has died down to a dead calm now, and you wake up thinking you are in hell on earth. You are being swarmed by hundreds, if not thousands, of tiny biting sand fleas (or "no-see-ums") that are attacking in fury now that there is no breeze to keep them away. They are under your clothes, in your hair, your ears, your nose, and even your eyes, and you have no way of keeping them off of you without insect netting. Their incessant biting is maddening, and you leap up from the palm frond mat that served as your bed and quickly strip off your clothes to go plunge into the lagoon. Only by ducking your head and staying under as long as you can hold your breath can you rid yourself of these persistent pests. Cursing and swearing to no one but yourself, you try returning to the beach only to be driven back into the water time after time. You're no stranger to no-see-ums, as you've encountered them while camping on beaches in the U.S., but there you could retreat to your tent or your car. This is the part of "paradise" the postcards and travel agent's brochures can't convey, you think with a grim smile, realizing that a whole lot more of these islands would remain uninhabited if not for modern methods of dealing with the insect populations.

Without insect repellent or netting, you're going to have to resort to the techniques primitive islanders in the tropics have always used. First, you will need to relocate your camp to the windward side of the atoll for the breeze, and second, you will need to figure out a way to make fire so that you can keep a small, smoky "smudge fire" going around your sleeping area. Your second day on the island will be a busy one as you set about making yourself more comfortable and looking for more substantial food. It would have been helpful if the immature young men who put you ashore had thought to provide you with more provisions and tools, as did the more benevolent Captain Thomas Stradling when he marooned Alexander Selkirk in 1702.

Day Two: A Gift from the Waves

You are now on the verge of having fire—one of the most important essentials to your comfortable survival on the atoll until you can be rescued. Although you've read about primitive techniques of making fire by friction or with flint and steel, you've never tried the former, and have no access to flint for the latter method as the rock on the island consists of only soft limestone. You know that the friction method will likely be your only option, but after trying in vain for over an hour to get a spark from rubbing two sticks together, and then attempting to twirl a spindle of dry wood against a another piece like in the drawings of a hand drill you'd seen in some survival book, you're exhausted.

Giving up for the time being, you spend most of the day beachcombing, looking through the debris above the high-tide line for anything of use. Here as on every other seashore, no matter how remote, there are various artifacts of civilization in the form of discarded trash washed ashore. There are the usual bits of poly line and rope from fishing vessels and other ships, plastic packaging and empty food containers and bottles, discarded light bulbs that somehow never get broken at sea, a boat fender, a torn life jacket, and an old plastic beach sandal. You salvage some of the line and rope for later use in building a shelter. Something else half-buried in the sand catches your eye as it glints in the sun. It's the shiny metal of an aluminum beer can. A vague memory takes shape as you walk over and pick it up. It's in perfect condition, without a dent. Then it comes back to you—a link someone sent you a couple of years ago to a video on YouTube. You can make fire with an aluminum can like this! You remember watching the video thinking you would try that sometime, but never got around to it. Now you have an urgent reason to do so and you rush back to your camp to get to work.

The method is similar to the old trick of using a magnifying glass to concentrate the sun's rays to a tightly focused spot that will ignite dry tinder. The difference is that you must use reflection, as you have no lens. The bottom of most soda and beer cans is the correct shape to make a perfect parabolic reflector. But first the somewhat dull bare aluminum must be polished to a mirror finish. The video showed this being done with chocolate or toothpaste. You have no chocolate, but there's almost a full tube of whitening toothpaste in your kit. It takes a lot of elbow grease, but by mid-afternoon, using the corner of one of your T-shirts as a polishing cloth, you have transformed the bottom of the can to a near-mirror surface.

The next step is to point the bottom of the can directly at the sun and find the point where the reflection from the parabola is most focused. You find that this is not easy. First of all, it's hard to hold the can steady enough. It is essential that the sun's rays be parallel to the can's sides and perpendicular to the bottom. You adjust it until there is no shadow but a round circle from the can's diameter. Then you move the tip of your finger in line with the reflection and adjust the distance in and out, looking for the distance where the reflection is focused in the smallest possible spot. You can see a spot and feel the warmth, but it's nowhere near hot enough to start a fire. This is going to take more work. You go back to your polishing and work on perfecting the surface even more. By the time you're done and are attempting to line it up again, the sun is getting too low on the horizon to give the intense reflection you need. You'll suffer another morning of assault by insects, but you are determined to have fire the next day.

Day Three: The Magic of Fire

By now you've found that it's nearly impossible to hold the can steady enough by hand to concentrate the reflection, so you bury all but the end of it in the sand and carefully adjust the angle. With a really bright mirror finish on the bottom now, you feel it get warm and then hot when you hold your fingertip at the right distance. Excited that you are making progress, you set about looking for the materials with which to build a fire. Driftwood is everywhere, as are the crispy dead fronds shed from the coconut palms. Everything is bone dry here on this sun-drenched island, so kindling and fuel will not be a problem. But first you need tinder, and it too can be found in the coconut grove, in the hairlike fibers of old husks and the dead fronds littering the sand. After carefully shredding the tinder, you try holding it in front of the reflector, but find out it won't work if the material is large enough to block the sun's rays. It takes a narrow strip of flammable material that is too slender to block the light. With patience and experi-mentation, you soon have smoke, and then a coal, but not instantaneous flame. You have to carefully blow the tiny coal into a flame after putting it in your prepared ball of shredded co-conut fiber and leaves. When it flares

up, you place this under a tepee-shaped pile of small kindling sticks. At last it works, and you have flames, inspiring you to dance around in a celebratory moment of joy, as you will soon be eating a variety of seafood and you now have a means of smoking out the no-see-ums and signaling any passing vessels.

Day Four: Food, Shelter, and Water

You wade ashore with the first fish you've taken from the reef—a small grouper you speared in a crevice in the rocks not far from the beach. The carefully tended fire that you've kept going all night will provide ample coals for roasting fish. Your quality of life has moved up several notches since you got it going yesterday. A hardwood pole cut from the dense scrub forest of the islet's interior serves well as a spear. You made a two-pronged forked tip by splitting the end, wedging a small piece of wood into the split, and then sharpening the two tips, which were then hardened in the flames. This makes for a crude tool, but

Sailing and Paddling Off the Beaten Track

Getting marooned on an uninhabited island may sound like a popular fantasy come true, especially if it happens to be a beautiful tropical island replete with coral reefs and sandy beaches with waving coconut palms surrounding a blue lagoon. This has been the subject of countless movies and TV programs, from old standbys like *Gilligan's Island* to reality shows like *Survivor*, and movies such *The Blue Lagoon* and *Castaway*. But if you are marooned in real life, it's not likely to be a holiday in paradise or an adventure romance on the beach.

Real-life castaway stories were once fairly common in the days of sail, when there were many uncharted or little-known islands and long-distance communication between vessels and the shore was nonexistent. Today it's not likely you'll end up stranded on an uninhabited island by boarding a passenger cruise ship or taking a commercial flight. But

the fish here are so abundant and unused to human fishermen you can get close enough to take a stab at them from above the surface. It takes many failed attempts, but once you get that first grouper, you know you'll be able to get all you want.

You're determined to keep the fire going day and night, both to avoid the hassle of having to start another one and to keep at least some smoke going at all times in case any kind of boat should pass within sight. It shouldn't be hard to do, as the beaches are littered with driftwood and the palm groves contain many dead trunks, fronds, and old coconut husks. By carefully building up a deep bed of smoldering coals protected by a high windbreak of pushed-up sand, you can go off beachcombing and fishing for hours without worrying about the fire going out. In the late evening and early morning when the no-see-ums are

if you are aboard one of the thousands of private yachts or adventurous small boats that ply the world's oceans at any given time, or if you are flying over oceans on small aircraft, your chances are much higher.

Having spent years paddling sea kayaks and sailing small, shallow draft boats that can reach islands far off the beaten track, I know first-hand how real the possibility of being marooned is. Though I've never been wrecked or abandoned on such an island without a means of leaving, I have been stormbound on tiny islands while traveling by kayak, once for almost three weeks. Any sort of serious damage to the hull or deck structure caused when landing my kayak through the raging surf zone could have left me stranded much longer, due to the inaccessible nature of the island to conventional craft. In some parts of the world, there are still islands so remote that they may not be visited by any sort of vessel for months at a time.

at their worst, adding some green brush and palm leaves increases the smoke enough to give you some relief.

Passing clouds give you hope that a rain shower will bring some relief from drinking nothing but coconut water, but all of them drift over the island without so much as a sprinkle. It's little wonder that the atoll is uninhabited, dry as it is, and you begin to worry about water, as you know there is a limited supply of coconuts remaining here. Those that are left are far too high above the ground to reach with your pole-and-knife contraption, and you realize that as much as you hate to, you will soon have to attempt to cut down one of the taller palms to get more drinking nuts.

Contemplating this and the lush green of the palm trees and other island vegetation growing here despite the lack of rain, you have another vague recollection of something you'd read or heard about Pacific atolls. With all the plant life on the island, there has to be fresh water, even if it's not on the surface. The rains that do fall on these islands are seasonal, but somehow the greenery thrives year-round. You start digging a few yards back from the beach, first with your hands and then with a spade-shaped piece of driftwood you carve with your knife. Three feet down, the hole begins to fill with water. You are

The Freshwater Lens

On most coral atolls, it is common for a layer of accumulated rainwater to lie on top of the seawater beneath. No mixing occurs in the sand, so the fresh water, which is less dense, "floats" on the salt water the way wine will float if you gently pour it into a glass of water. The weight of the fresh water pushes down on the surface of the seawater beneath it, forming the bottom of a "lens" shape. The

skeptical and assume it's salty or brackish, but when you scoop a handful out to taste it you are delighted to find that it's sweet and fresh. How could it be fresh and how much more is there?

Day Seven: Settling in to Wait

Now that you've had a week to adjust to living on the island, you have made yourself sufficiently comfortable for an extended stay, while still hoping you won't have to wait much longer to be rescued. In this time you've been able to explore the entire atoll, crossing the channels between islets with the kayak and walking all the beaches fronting both the ocean and the lagoon. In addition to exploring, you've spent a lot of your time making a more comfortable camp. One priority was to build a better shelter with a sleeping platform off the ground. Although they are harmless, you don't like the idea of one of the giant nocturnal coconut crabs climbing over you in the night, so you sleep better once you've built a crude bunk of lashed branches overlaid with a dense mat of coconut fronds. And although you don't know the technique for making a proper palm-thatched roof, you gather enough of the fronds to make a thick covering over a rude A-frame erected over the bunk. It may not be waterproof, but you still haven't seen a drop of rain anyway, and

amount of water in the lens is a balance between what is added by rain and what is withdrawn or lost. Only rain can replenish it, as there is no underground freshwater source on an atoll. This makes for a limited supply of water, but often more than enough for small populations to live on such islands. For a solo survivor marooned on such an atoll, it can be a life-saving source of fresh water.

you mainly need it for the shade and sense of security it brings. The roof also helps with keeping the area around your sleeping platform smoky enough to repel insects as your smudge fires burn through the night.

Surely one day soon, the people who came to harvest the coconuts will be back, perhaps to do some fishing. You hope it won't be long, but you know you could stay here for weeks or even months if you have to. Though you try not to think about the possibility of being stranded so long, the biggest danger in being here would be the threat of a Pacific cyclone, and you know the peak season starts in less than two months. A cyclone of any significance making a direct hit on this low atoll would ruin your day, that's for sure.

As you contemplate what you would do in such a situation, which would likely mean a storm surge sweeping over the entire atoll, you hear a distant sound that at first seems odd but then familiar as it slowly grows louder. Springing into action, you rush to the fire to heap on dry wood to build it up and then throw green palm fronds into the flames to make smoke. You are just in time as the low-flying plane cruises over the atoll and circles back for another pass, the pilot signaling with a dip of his wings that he has spotted you.

TOP TEN ISLAND SURVIVAL TIPS

1. **Avoid being swept into coral or rocks.** Whether you come ashore by dinghy, kayak, or life raft, or swim ashore from a wrecked vessel farther out, the first danger you will face is the surf zone. Many uninhabited islands are encircled by fringing reefs, which is part of the reason they are not settled. Pounding surf can cut you to pieces on coral or jagged limestone. The reef will also be populated with dangerous invertebrates like black sea urchins with poisonous spines. Make every effort to read the waves for indications of a deep channel you can slip through to avoid the reef. Gaps in the surf line where waves are not breaking are a good sign of a channel, as are deep blue colors among lighter shades of green and brown.

2. **Evaluate your resources.** Secure everything you came ashore with above the high-tide line and if possible salvage any goods floating free from your wrecked vessel or aircraft. Try to salvage anything man-made even it doesn't appear useful. Explore your surroundings for signs of human activity and look for anything of use others may have left on the island or that may have washed ashore. Many items that may appear to be litter initially could prove valuable later on.

3. **Find or make shelter.** Small islands are terribly exposed to the sun, wind, and ocean storms. Look for potential natural shelters such as caves or caverns high above the tide line, or the shade of trees. Use an upturned dinghy, a sail, or anything else you have that might shelter you. The sun will be your worst enemy, causing severe sunburn and dehydration. If you have nothing else, you can make a simple lean-to with a pole lashed between two trees with large palm fronds draped over it. Think twice about setting up camp in a coconut grove and do not hang around under clusters of coconuts—a 10-pound coconut falling 30 to 80 feet is no joke.

4. **Camp on the windward side of the island.** Biting insects will be a problem on virtually any uninhabited island. Wind is your best bet to rid yourself of them, and if you are on a small oceanic island, chances are there will be some breeze most of the time. Try to camp

on the windward side of the island if at all possible. Exposed points of land extending far out from the island's vegetation will also frequently get more breeze and could be an insect-free haven.

5. **Use sails, tarps, plastic sheeting, or anything you can to catch rain.** Rains falling on small oceanic islands may be few and far between, but occasionally can be heavy, and if you have a way to catch the rain it can quickly replenish your water supply. If you're using a boat hull or anything that's been in contact with seawater, you'll need to rinse the salt off to ensure an uncontaminated water supply; with any luck the rain will last long enough to make this feasible. Get your catchment system set up in advance so you don't miss a rain that may be your only chance.

6. **Dig a beach well.** Most coral atolls have a freshwater lens of accumulated rainwater that lies on top of the underlying coral rock of the atoll. Islands other than atolls may also have accumulations of fresh or brackish water under the sand, especially in depressions where drainage collects. To dig a beach well, start above the debris line created by the high tide and dig down through the sand— typically you will reach water within three to four feet. If the first water you find is too salty, scoop some out and let the well refill. In many cases the well will provide all the drinking water you need.

7. **Make use of coconuts.** Coconuts are another reliable source of safe drinking water. Coconut palms are found on many islands and seashores around the world in the tropical zone. As a water source, you need the mature or slightly immature green "drinking" nuts still hanging in clusters beneath the fronds at the top of the tree. If the trees are too tall or too vertical to climb, you may be able to cut down the nuts with a knife or machete on a long pole, or you may have to resort to cutting down the tree. The drinking nuts also have a layer of undeveloped coconut meat the consistency of custard that is delicious and sweet. The brown ones that have fallen on the ground will contain the denser coconut meat most people are familiar with. Young coconut palms also contain delicious palm hearts within the stem at the base of the fronds.

8. Get a fire going. There are so many other uses for fire besides warmth, including cooking, signaling, and smoking-out insects that it will be well worth your while to get one started, even if you don't have matches or a lighter. In addition to primitive friction methods, other techniques include the polished-can parabolic-reflector method described in this chapter, or concentrating sunlight using a lens from eyeglasses, a camera, binoculars, a flashlight, or possibly the bottom of a bottle. If you have batteries from a camera, flashlight, or other electronic device, you can also start a fire by using a paper clip, a piece of wire, or some other metal object to short between the negative and positive terminals.

9. Arrange SOS signals. An airplane passing overhead is your best chance of being spotted on a remote island, especially one with no safe harbors or anchorages for ships and boats that is far from any established sailing or shipping routes. Even small island governments may have a patrol plane of some sort that occasionally flies over the islands in their jurisdiction, and military aircraft from the U.S. and other developed nations also operate in far-flung areas and may pass close enough to see an SOS signal. Use rocks, driftwood, pieces of wreckage, or anything you can scrounge to arrange a large message that will contrast with the sand for the best chance of visibility.

10. Make fishing spears, nets, and fish traps. From a survival standpoint, one advantage you will have on an island compared to many other environments is an abundant and readily available source of food from the reef, the lagoon, and the surrounding ocean. Many shellfish can be collected by hand, as can crustaceans such as crabs and lobster. You can increase the variety of seafood available to you if you can fashion a simple spear. Split the tip with a wedge of wood to hold it apart. Sharpened barbs lashed on in the other direction will make it easier to keep from losing fish you manage to spear. Stakes can be driven across tidal cuts to act as fish weirs or traps, where you can funnel fish into shallow water to be speared or grabbed by hand.

CHAPTER SIX
FIRE ON THE MOUNTAIN

You are running as fast as you can, making sure your hiking partner doesn't fall behind or lose her footing as you both gasp for breath in the heat and smoke. You hear dry branches exploding and green sap sizzling as balls of flame spread through the tops of the evergreens behind you. After ditching the heavy backpacks, you had thought that the two of you could run fast enough to reach a rocky escarpment at the head of the drainage, but you underestimated the speed at which the flames could advance. The big problem is that your goal is uphill, the hardest going for you and the easiest direction for the fire to spread. You have few options, as the heavily timbered valley below you is filled with smoke and the walls beyond the wooded slopes are vertical cliffs you have no hope of climbing. The only direction of retreat is up to the head of the canyon, but you are now being overtaken by the fire and it's obvious you won't make it to the top in time. How could you end up this close to being burned alive in a remote national forest?

Day One: Dusk

As you take off your packs and look back at the steep, forested drainage through which you've climbed all afternoon, you see a thick wall of smoke in the distance, far beyond the trailhead where you began your hike from a gravel Forest Service road.

It's obvious that it must be a forest fire, but it looks far away. Both of you are from the East Coast and consequently have little knowledge of forest fires other than when they make the  news in populated areas like California. But still, it makes your friend nervous, and she suggests the idea of turning around and heading back out to the car. You tell her it would be much safer to stay here than to hike nine miles in the dark down a rocky trail. And besides, this is Wyoming, and you expect the chances of running into a bear in the growing darkness are pretty good.

After nightfall the two of you stand on the open rocks where you've pitched your tent and look at the distant lines of orange that stretch across faraway ridges like strings of Christmas tree lights. It's a beautiful sight, but frightening at the same time. You wonder what started the fire and remember the rumble of thunder you heard earlier in the day as you were preparing the packs before beginning your hike. It's impossible to tell from this distance which direction the fire is moving and how fast, but you assume the forest rangers know about it and that they are probably working to put it out even now. Your partner still thinks you should head back to the road at first light. After all, it's her new car that's parked at the trailhead, and she's concerned the fire might be headed that way.

Day Two: Sunrise

It's been daylight for several minutes, but neither of you wants to stir from your sleeping bag in the cold morning air. You've spent a mostly sleepless night worried about the fire, which you can't forget as the smell of smoke reaches you in the tent. When you do crawl outside, you are stunned by what you see in the valley below. A dense blanket of smoke has shut out most of the view that you could see last night when you turned in. It's hard to tell just where the fire is, but from the smoke, it appears that it must be near the road where the trailhead is. You yell that it's time to get up and pack the sleeping bags, even as you are already pulling up tent stakes in a rush to strike camp and get moving.

Once the backpacks are loaded and your boots are on, you wonder if it wouldn't be wiser to just keep going the other way, to the crest of the ridge and down into the next valley. But you

REAL LIFE | *Cedar Fire Victims Had No Warning*

Being inside a vehicle is no guarantee that you can escape a fast-moving wildfire, as the tragic Cedar Fire of San Diego County proved in 2003 when it claimed 12 victims who had no warning of its approach. Although some residents of this rural area did manage to drive through flames to safety, others were burned alive in their cars or inside their homes.

Started by a lost hunter in Cleveland National Forest on a Saturday afternoon, the fire moved rapidly west into an inhabited area, including the Barona Reservation and a gated community called Lake View Hills Estates. Local fire officials didn't get warning of the imminent danger the fire posed until 2 or 3 a.m. on Sunday morning and were not able to pass the warning on to most area residents in time to give them a chance to get away.

One man did narrowly escape by driving through a wall of flames 15 to 30 feet high. Jon Smalldridge had been watching the faraway glow of the Cedar Fire that Saturday evening, but wasn't concerned until his dog's barking woke up the household at about 1:30 a.m. on Sunday. Finding

already know from studying the map in advance that it's much farther to the nearest road in any other direction than the way you came, and the loop trip in that direction around to the trail-head and the car is a three-day hike. If not for the worry of the car, you might try it. If the fire reaches it before you do, you won't have a quick way out of the area and you'll lose it and all your other stuff you left inside. At the time that seems important to both of you, but you will soon come to regret the decision to head back down the canyon in an attempt to reach it.

smoke surrounding the house, he drove to nearby homes to warn other residents and watched as flames engulfed the road and then the entire hillside where there were still people who couldn't get out. His only hope was to risk driving through the flames and hope he could get through before his vehicle caught fire. He made it because he didn't hit any obstruction hidden in the fire or smoke and managed to stay on the roadway.

Other drivers were not so lucky. After the inferno passed, Smalldridge drove back into the neighborhood with his son, expecting the worst, which is what he found. In a blackened Toyota with one wheel in the ditch were skeletons of a woman and a dog. Other charred remains were nearby. He also found survivors, like a badly burned woman with flesh coming off her arms. Most of the victims, it turned out, were caught by the flames while trying to rescue relatives and neighbors. What made this fire so deadly was the speed at which it moved through the dry Southern California brush, catching residents and the authorities alike off-guard and unprepared.

Day Two: 9:00 AM

The smell of smoke is stronger the farther you descend down the trail that meanders along the course of a dry streambed winding between two steep ridges. All around you there are signs that the fire is coming your way. As you cross one open meadow, a herd of more than a dozen elk charges right past the two of you, oblivious of any threat you may present. Mule deer are on the run, too. You see them in groups of twos, threes, and fours. A black bear also makes its way past you, staying in the heavy timber but in a hurry nonetheless. The doubts you have about the decision to descend into the valley in the direction of the fire grow stronger with all these signs of the local wildlife clearing out. Reaching the trailhead in time to drive out of the fire's path seems questionable. But you reason that surely the Forest Service is on the front lines of the advancing flames, wherever that may be. You remain hopeful they can stop it before it crosses the gravel road where the car is parked.

Leave the Area at the First Sign of Fire

While the unsuspecting victims of the Cedar Fire in California (page 124) were going about their everyday lives in the apparent safety of their homes without a clue a deadly fire was bearing down on them, if you are outdoors camping or engaged in some other recreational pursuit, chances are you will see or smell smoke soon enough for it to serve as a warning. If you observe any smoke at all on the horizon, take note of the wind direction and move out of its path if you are downwind of the smoke's source. Avoid traveling uphill if the fire is anywhere nearby, and look for escape routes that will take you quickly in a direction perpendicular to the front.

Day Two: 10:00 AM

The smoke pouring upslope from the valley beneath has become so thick that you are becoming disoriented. It's hard to tell how far down the trail you've come, as everything below you is engulfed in choking smoke, limiting your horizon to just a few hundred feet. You're having serious doubts about the wisdom of going on, but your partner still wants to try to make the road and reach her car. The only alternative is to return the way you came, back up the slope to where you made camp and over the ridge above—a hard hike even if you weren't already tired from rushing back down the trail this morning. It's hard to know for sure in this unfamiliar terrain, but you think you're less than two miles from the Forest Service road and the trailhead parking lot. You decide to push on. There's just no way to tell from here if the fire has crossed the road or not.

The key to surviving a wildfire is to not let it get close enough to put you in a race for your life that you can't win. When the wind conditions are right and fuel is available, a grass fire or brushfire can spread much faster than a human can run. Although vehicles won't always save you, as was the case for some in the Cedar Fire, they can sometimes give enough shelter until the main flame front passes, and usually won't ignite or explode unless the fire is moving much slower and burning hotter. Just as Jon Smalldridge did, it is sometimes possible to drive through a flame front, provided you can see the roadway to avoid going in a ditch and there are no other obstructions like fallen trees in the vehicle's path.

Day Two: 10:30 AM

You realize the seriousness of the mistake the two of you have made when you start hearing the explosions of resin-soaked

REAL LIFE | *Young Men and Fire: The Tragedy at Mann Gulch*

Fighting forest fires has long been an important part of the work of the U.S. Forest Service. The use of airplanes alone was a huge technical advance in fighting fires and helping spot fires early, and by 1929, airplanes were being used to drop supplies to firefighters on the ground. But when parachutes made it possible to put men directly in position to work on containing fires, many fires were put out before they ever grew out of control. In 1940, the parachuting Smokejumpers were organized and became the most elite firefighting unit in the Forest Service.

In 1949, the Smokejumpers suffered their worst tragedy in Montana's Mann Gulch fire. Thinking they were responding to a routine forest fire of moderate proportions, the team of 15 landed near the fire's front lines. But what started out as a routine day's work soon turned into a race for life as the fire became an unstoppable "blow-up" and raged uphill in the gulch's dry grass faster than all but two of the men could run.

The vegetation of Mann Gulch contained all the ingredients for disaster on that hot August day. The fire started in a dense stand of Douglas fir and ponderosa pine on the south side of the gulch. This type of forest vegetation is conducive to a crown fire that burns with terrific heat, but doesn't spread much faster than a half-mile to a mile per hour. The steep slopes on the north side of the gulch, however, where the crew was working their way down to the fire, were covered

tree limbs popping in the flames and then catch the first glimpse of the fire as the trail emerges into a meadow you remember from yesterday that was about a half-hour's hike uphill from the car. On the downhill side of the grassy meadow, a dense grove

with an understory of dense bunch grass with a scattering of ponderosa pine—just the right fuel for a fire that can move at astonishing speeds, especially when traveling upslope and fanned by the strong winds the fire itself generates.

By the time the crew realized what was happening and R. Wagner Dodge, the foreman in charge, ordered them to drop their tools and run from the fire, it was already moving so fast they had little chance of reaching the rocky ridge at the top of the gulch. Some 200 yards short of the ridge, Dodge estimated they had only 30 seconds before the fire would overtake them, and that's when he did something incomprehensible to the young men on his crew. He struck a match and set his own "escape fire," and ordered them to follow him into it. He heard someone yell, "To hell with that, I'm getting out of here," and all of them broke for the ridge as fast as they could run. The flames overtook all but two of them well before they reached the top. The two survivors, Robert Sallee and Walter Rumsey, escaped death running for a narrow crevice in the rock that they spotted when the smoke cleared momentarily. Dodge also lived, surviving by lying down in the ashes of the lesser fire he built. His escape fire created a haven by burning the available fuel in the immediate area so that the main fire would pass around him.

The intricate details of how Dodge, Sallee, and Rumsey lived through a fire that killed 13 others are expanded on at length in *Young Men and Fire,* published in 1972. There was also a 1952 movie inspired by the Mann Gulch tragedy— *Red Skies of Montana.*

of spruce and fir trees has turned into an inferno that eliminates any hope of reaching the road or the trailhead. The fire completely spans the narrow, V-shaped drainage and is moving upslope while steadily burning everything in its path.

Burning a Hole in the Fire: How an Escape Fire Can Save Your Life

Wildfires in open grassy or brushy areas are more dangerous than fires in dense timber. Grass fires don't build up as much heat, mainly because they are moving so fast the flames often don't stay in one place long enough to thoroughly burn structures like cabins or houses in their path. The speed of such grass fires makes them dangerous if you get caught out in the open, because you can't outrun them and they certainly have enough heat to kill. But it is because of this speed that an escape fire like the one R. Wagner Dodge used at Montana's Mann Gulch Fire in 1949 (page 128) can save your life. The dry grass that enables the wildfire to burn so fast will also enable you to quickly burn out a hole in the fuel surrounding your immediate area. By getting rid of this fuel in advance of the approaching fire line, you take away any reason for the fire to come into this "hole" among the surrounding combustible material. In a heavy timber fire, this is not likely to work because the escape fire cannot burn fast enough to create a haven—but in timber you can probably get out of the path fast enough anyway.

Although the heat and smoke of the main fire passing so close while you are within the escape-fire area may be intense, it is better than the alternative, which would surely be death. By lying facedown you can avoid some of the heat and hopefully find enough oxygen to breathe, as any available oxygen not consumed by the fire will be near the ground.

The first reaction both of you have is that of panic, just like the frightened animals you passed all morning bolting up the drainage ahead of the fire. You both turn to look for any avenue of escape, but there is nothing but steep slopes boxing you in

How did Dodge know to build an escape fire when it was not part of any standard firefighting training at the time? In his testimony afterward he said he had never heard of such a concept but conceived it as a last resort. But there is some evidence that the Plains Indians set such escape fires to survive fast-moving prairie fires. Such an incident is also mentioned in the James Fenimore Cooper novel *The Prairie,* published in 1827. Perhaps Dodge had knowledge of this technique in his subconscious from something he had read or heard previously. One thing is certain, he had little time to act, and the fire he set did not have time to burn out a large safe area with the wall of flames bearing down on him. He later said that when the fire went over him he was lifted off the ground two or three times during an ordeal that lasted about five minutes.

How does one overcome the natural animal instinct to run away from fire even if it's impossible to run fast enough? It won't be easy, but the important thing is to try to remain calm and think clearly, letting logic and knowledge control your actions rather than fear. In a situation where you cannot outrun a wildfire, the only options for survival are to set an escape fire if there is time to burn out a safety area; hunker in place among rocks, bare ground, an area of pavement, a body of water, or other areas of less fuel than the surrounding terrain; or attempt to pass through the fire into an already burned-out area.

on both sides, and the trail back the way you came seems to be the only option. Looking over your shoulder, you see that the fire is now sweeping across the grassy meadow at unbelievable speed. And there's plenty of grass and brush all around you in the semi-open forest through which you've descended, so you

Hunker Down or Run Through: The Last Two Options

If there isn't enough time or you don't have the means to quickly ignite an escape fire (page 130), there are only two other options for surviving a fire that you cannot outrun. Like the escape fire, these options are also both desperate and you may be severely burned, but the alternative is certain death.

Hunkering down is just what it sounds like. You find closest area of scant fuel where the fire will likely be less intense when it passes over, and get yourself as close to the ground and as shielded from the flames as possible. Places to consider are rocky areas, deep depressions in the ground, marshy areas, a body of water, or a previously burnt area from an earlier fire. In developed areas, a paved or gravel road may be the best option. In the deadly Australian wildfires of 2009 that killed 173 people, survivor Mark Strubing and a companion narrowly escaped death by crawling into drainage pipe under a road on his property. Though the pipe was confined, dark, and infested with spiders and other crawling things, it had enough water in it that they could roll around a bit to stay wet as the flames licked the inside of their refuge.

To ensure the best chance of survival while hunkering down, you should lie flat with your nose to the ground while the fire is burning over and around you. Lying flat will

have little reason to believe the fire will slow down much when it reaches your side of the meadow.

You hear a helicopter passing low overhead and run frantically to try and find a place where there is an opening in the enveloping smoke, but you can't see the aircraft and you know

minimize your body's exposure to radiant heat, the invisible heat emitted from the flames that will usually kill you before the flames directly contact you. The heating of body tissues from this thermal radiation can be unbearable, but it's important to stay calm and not get up until the fire has dissipated if you want to survive. To increase your odds, cover yourself with anything that will help shield you from the heat, such as extra clothing or a fire-retardant blanket if at all possible. Don't do this with synthetic materials, though, as they can melt and cause even worse burns than if you were uncovered. Keep your face down to protect your airways and minimize smoke inhalation, and cover your face, neck, and ears with your hands, wearing gloves if you have them.

Passing through the flame front to reach the area already burned is another technique that many have used to survive wildfires. There is certainly a considerable risk involved, but survivors who picked their spots and avoided the areas of most intense flames have utilized this technique successfully. If the flames are more than about five feet in height or depth, you may not survive running through. In flames of this size or smaller, a person dashing through would be immersed in radiant heat for less than 7.5 seconds in ideal running conditions with no obstructions. To live through even this brief contact with the flames, it is necessary to hold your breath and it certainly helps to have as much protective clothing on as possible. Even so, you can expect to be burned, maybe severely.

the pilot can't see you either. Your friend suggests maybe they know about the car parked at the trailhead and are looking for you. It's a comforting possibility, but how will they find you in all this smoke with the fire bearing down faster than ever? And more smoke is pouring up the slopes of the valley, driven by the strong winds created by the fire. It's not likely there will be an opening in it anywhere short of the ridge at the crest.

You simultaneously make a decision to ditch the heavy backpacks with all your gear, keeping only your water bottles and the clothing and jackets you are wearing. Then the race begins. Knowing you can't go full-speed all the way to the top of the valley, you both fall into a comfortable lope, grateful that regular running back home has prepared you for this kind of test of endurance.

But despite your fitness level, outrunning this fire in an uphill direction is hopeless, as you will soon find out. Others

It Only Takes a Spark in the Arid West

Many temperate forest areas of the world are subject to large-scale wildfires, some of which are deliberately or accidentally started by man, while others are caused naturally by intense lightning. The American West, with its arid climate, mountainous terrain, and often-windy conditions has more than its share of big forest and brush fires. Since there is so much remote, uninhabited forest land in many of these mountainous areas, such fires can start suddenly and take recreational backcountry users by surprise. In the right conditions, a forest fire can spread faster than humans or wild animals can run, destroying everything in its path.

Anyone who has spent time traveling in the wild mountain areas of the West has surely passed through vast "burns" from prior forest fires that left in their wake a

even more experienced and fit for such situations have tried it and failed.

Day Two: 10:45 AM

As the two of you run back up the trail, you realize with a growing panic that the raging fire is gaining on you as it rushes up the drainage. Areas of open, parklike woods with plenty of open grass and brush allow it to move much faster than you would have believed possible. But farther uphill the trail winds past areas of rock outcrops and you yell to your partner that there is nothing else to do but look for shelter. It's still much too far to the place you camped last night and the ridge beyond, and it's apparent you can't reach it before the fire catches you. In desperation, you move in a direction lateral to the fire front into some jumbled boulders and frantically search for a place away from the dry grass and brush where you might hunker down. It's

wasteland of ashes and blackened stumps. These fires are often good for the environment, as they provide a chance for natural regeneration and consume decades worth of old deadfall and other forest floor litter. But if you are far from access to a road and vehicle that allow quick escape, you could find yourself trapped or overtaken by a wall of flames before you realize what is happening.

During my own wanderings in the West, I've often had to change my hiking plans at the last minute because of forest fires in the area. The last thing any sensible hiker would do is set out into the mountains when a fire is already burning and spreading. But on long trips when you're out of touch with the outside world, a summer thunderstorm or another careless campfire builder can start a fire you have no way of knowing about until you start smelling smoke.

a terrifying prospect, and you find it almost impossible to resist the urge to keep running uphill as the fire roars closer.

But the rocks provide hope, as there are large slabs of exposed outcrop that are free of grass and other vegetation, as well as boulders that might shield you from radiant heat. You  find a depression between two such boulders and quickly pile up other smaller rocks to form even more of a barricade. The heat is now so intense you can no longer stand up to it and you both lie facedown in the rocks, pulling the hoods of your sweatshirts over your hair as the fire-driven wind sweeps your position. The heat from the passing flames is unimaginable and for a few moments you are certain that you both will die and that you've made a terrible mistake by stopping. It's difficult to breathe and you gasp for oxygen, wondering if there will be enough to take another breath.

Day Two: 10:50 AM

The intensity relents and you raise your head enough to check that your friend is still alive. The fire has rushed past the rocks that saved your life and is now sweeping up the slopes above you, on an unstoppable path to the ridge. The two of you get to your feet and find yourselves blackened with ash and soot, but unburned. All around and below you the slopes of the drainage are charred black, with many isolated trees still burning and columns of smoke spiraling up from the ground in random places. There is nothing to do but to try and pick your way downhill through the smoldering embers of the burned-out area to find your way to the road. You know that the car could not have survived this intense fire, but things like that are of little significance to you now.

TOP TEN WILDFIRE SURVIVAL TIPS

1. Be aware of weather and fire conditions in advance. Awareness of danger is the first safety measure for avoiding wildfires. Before you set out into a remote area, check with the Forest Service, Park Service, or other authorities about the current fire conditions. High temperatures, low humidity, and a prior period of drought that renders undergrowth tinder-dry increase the likelihood of fire and the speed at which it will spread. A chance of thunderstorms greatly increases the danger, but remember that even on a clear, sunny day, a fire can be started by a careless hiker or camper.

2. Look, listen, and smell. If you see smoke, smell smoke, or hear fire, leave the area immediately. Don't waste precious time breaking camp or trying to save all your gear—just get out. The fastest escape routes will be open trails or roads where you can move unhindered by vegetation and may encounter firefighters or others who can assist you in evacuating.

3. Avoid running in an uphill direction. Steep slopes, canyons, chutes, draws, and narrow valleys act as chimneys for wildfires, which can spread in an uphill direction much faster than you can run. If caught in a mountainous area, try to work your way to a lower elevation or at least stay at the same elevation as you pick your route away from the fire. If you are at a lower elevation than the fire, your chances of outpacing it are good.

4. Retreat into water or a low spot, or dig a hole if there is time. Larger streams, ponds, and lakes can offer a haven from fire if there is no other alternative. Get as far from the bank as possible and submerge as much of your body as you can. Be aware of the risk of hypothermia, though, as some fire survivors have died from overexposure in frigid water. A ditch or other natural depression, or a hole if you can dig one, can also protect you from fire and smoke.

5. Hunker down in an area with the least flammable material. Other possible safety zones are bare, rocky areas, old burns with no new fuel, plowed fields, and gravel or paved roads or other man-made clearings. If you are in a forest, be aware that evergreen trees will burn much faster than deciduous trees, and areas of undergrowth and grass will burn faster than either type of forest.

6. **Use jackets, backpacks, hats, blankets, or other items to shield yourself from the heat.** Use anything you have with you or can find in the area to shield your body from radiant heat. Cotton or wool fabrics are best—synthetics can melt and cause severe burns. Above all, try to protect your face, neck, and ears. Wrapping your hair is a good idea as well, as it will easily catch fire.

7. **Stay calm; keep low and facedown to protect your airways.** If you are overtaken by the fire and forced to hunker down, try to stay calm and resist the urge to run. Your best chance of survival is to stay facedown and low to the ground, where there may be a small amount of oxygen and you can reduce the amount of smoke you inhale. The prone position also minimizes your exposure to radiant heat.

8. **Burn out a safety area with an escape fire.** If you find yourself in the path of a fast-moving grass fire or brushfire with no escape route, you may be able to set an escape fire to burn out a large enough safety area. This will work only if you can start the fire quickly and if you start it in an area of highly flammable grass or brush that will burn before the wildfire reaches it.

9. **Break through the fire front into the burned-out area.** Although it may result in serious burns, it is sometimes possible to survive a wildfire by passing through the leading edge into the already-burned area. Don't attempt this if the flames are more than about five feet high or deep. Move as fast as possible and try to pick the area of least intensity while avoiding obstructions that could trip you up. As when hunkering down, try to cover your face, neck, and ears.

10. **Stay in your vehicle if caught by a fire while driving.** Although your instinct may be to run from your vehicle for fear of explosion, many have survived wildfires by staying inside the vehicle, which gives your body some protection from radiant heat. Get down on the floorboards and cover your head and face. Tires may deflate but gas tanks don't explode easily and most fires will pass over before enough heat builds up for that to happen.

CHAPTER SEVEN
SNOWBOUND

Visibility barely extends beyond the end of the hood, forcing you to slow down to a crawl as the roadway in front of you loses all definition in a blur of white and gray. You are trying to maintain confidence in the capabilities of your four-wheel-drive SUV, but this is beyond anything you've ever imagined. Banks of previously fallen snow rise up on either side of you, and now this blizzard threatens to fill in the space between, completely burying the road. You've lost traction several times on the winding switchback route, and now realize you should have turned around several miles back. The snow is simply coming down too fast to see a way forward and piling up too deep to push through. You know you've got to give it up and go back, but the accumulated snow hides the rocks that are on the uphill side of the mountain road and makes it impossible to know where the edge of the drop-off is on the down-

hill side. Turning around here in the middle of the road, where there is no scenic overlook or passing lane, would be scary even if there were no snow. In these conditions, it's impossible. You can't go forward, you're afraid to attempt to turn around for fear of driving off a cliff or getting stuck, and it would be practically impossible to see how to back up in this snowfall on the winding mountain road. You've gotten yourself in a real fix by attempting to take this route ahead of a winter storm. What were you thinking?

Winter Comes Early to the High Country

You're visiting Idaho and Montana on a two-week vacation from your crowded home city in Southern California. You've been

REAL LIFE | *Blindly Following GPS Instructions Leads Two Couples to Danger*

With the prevalence of automotive GPS units today, drivers rarely bother with paper maps and often blindly follow the instructions given by computer-generated voices telling them where to go turn by turn. While having a GPS unit in your vehicle can be a wonderful convenience, it can never take the place of common sense and human analysis of a situation. Two incidents that occurred the week of Christmas 2009 in Oregon illustrate the potential dangers that blind faith in technology can pose. In both cases, couples traveling for the holidays in GPS-equipped SUVs took shortcuts that led them to backcountry mountain roads that turned out to be impassable due to snow.

The first couple, Jeramie Griffin and Megan Garrison, only had to endure 12 hours before being rescued. Griffin's uncle got a call saying they never arrived at the family home that was their destination, so he called a friend with a similar GPS unit and typed in the address to see which route the navigation system suggested. As he suspected, the route

looking at small parcels of land for sale in these two mountain states, thinking about buying a place for a getaway cabin or your future retirement. The search has taken you through some incredibly scenic country, but it turns out that you almost waited too late in the season to make the trip. Snow has already fallen several times at the higher elevations, and some of the listings you had found in your advance research are difficult to reach because of road closings. But your four-wheel-drive SUV gets you where you want to go, and you are not deterred from driving gravel Forest Service roads that lead into the mountains. This is what you came here for, after all, and you intend to

given was a shortcut through a section of national forest in the Cascades that was not a winter road. The uncle loaded up with water, blankets, food, and shovels and drove along the remote Forest Service road until he saw footprints, and then continued until he saw the missing couple walking up the road. The two had no food, water, or warm clothes.

The second couple led astray by their GPS in Oregon that week spent three days stranded in a wildlife refuge and wilderness area while on their way home from Bend to Nevada. Traveling along a main highway, John Rhoads and his wife heard their GPS voice tell them to take a right on a county road, and when they ignored it, the voice advised them to take a U-turn. Trusting that they were getting valid advice on the shortest route, they turned onto the small road, passing a sign that said it was "Not Winter Maintained." But since the road appeared passable, they continued on until the truck got stuck in the snow. They survived because of their obsessive overpacking, eating cold cuts, cheeses, crackers, fruit, and nutrition bars until they finally got a 911 call through and their position was triangulated from cell phone towers.

make the most of this vacation time because you won't be able to come back for another year.

Using your state maps and the mapping system in the SUV's onboard GPS unit, you have been able to find all the proper-

---

REAL LIFE | *Trying to Walk Out—a Deadly Mistake*

Not all vehicle strandings in winter storms end as well as they did in the case of the two couples in Oregon in 2009 (page 140). In January 1996, Palmer and Leah Olrun, both in their early fifties, took their two-year-old grandson Ethan with them on a multiday road trip out of their home in Anchorage, Alaska, planning to go ice fishing. They apparently left the main highway a couple days later to travel a gravel road that appeared to be well-maintained near the end, but is in reality impassable for traffic in winter. When they didn't return on the expected day, Ethan's mother reported them missing.

Two caribou hunters in the area happened down the road the Olruns had taken, noting the vehicle tracks as they drove the remote road in a four-wheel-drive pickup. They saw at least four places where the vehicle preceding them had become stuck and the occupants had dug it out and continued on. Several miles later, the hunters came to the vehicle parked in the middle of the road. It was a red Subaru station wagon. Upon inspecting it, they found no one inside, but looking around the area they discovered a large arrow and the word "HELP" stamped into the snowbank beside the road. There were two sets of tracks leading eastward away from the car.

The two men had seen no other hunters this far from the highway, but they could not be certain that the vehicle's

---

ties you wanted to look at. The most affordable ones are located quite far from any sizeable towns, and that's what you're looking for as your retreat from the city—splendid isolation. You get into trouble near the end of your trip after driving to a small

occupants were not already safe in one of the cabins they knew were in the area. They decided to return to the highway and go to Cantwell, 50 miles away, to inform the Alaska State Troopers of the whereabouts of the disabled car. Because of a mix-up with who they reported the car to, the report was not taken seriously. No immediate action was taken and it was the next day before an off-duty Trooper made the connection between the hunter's story and the missing persons report filed by the child's mother. When an Air National Guard helicopter finally searched the correct area, the bodies of the missing family were found just a half-mile from their car. As it turned out, they were also less than a mile from a lodge where they could have found help, but of course they were not familiar with the area and had no way of knowing this. Upon later inspection of their Subaru station wagon, Troopers found no survival equipment and a Thermos filled with liquid frozen solid.

If the Olruns had simply provided family members with a more detailed plan of where they intended to go, chances are rescuers could have found the disabled car much sooner after it was reported missing. Aside from that, the two main mistakes they made were traveling in winter in Alaska without proper survival gear and supplies, and leaving the relative safety of the vehicle in an attempt to walk somewhere for help without knowledge of the area. The severity of the cold they faced was made clear by the short distance they traveled before they all succumbed to hypothermia.

community near the Continental Divide to see one last listing, and then finding that there is no motel or bed-and-breakfast where you can stay after visiting the property. It's late in the afternoon, and you have a choice of driving over 100 miles back to the small city where you spent the previous night, or going on to another somewhat larger town across the state line where you can find a room. The sky has been darkening all afternoon with heavy cloud cover, but you don't know enough about the local weather to know what it means or realize the danger. The realtor who showed you the property earlier said that heavy snow was expected overnight, but he didn't ask where you were going, and you dismissed his comment without inquiring further. You know enough about the area to be aware that the roads through the high mountain passes get closed in the winter, but it's still just October, and you expect that there will be signs and any roads that would be dangerous would be blocked off to ve-

All Winter Travelers Should Be Prepared for Possible Stranding

Recreational winter travelers often end up in life-or-death survival situations simply because they are not prepared for what could happen if their vehicle gets stuck or breaks down in heavy snow or ice. Snowmobiles, in particular, can quickly get you into such a situation simply because of the ease with which they can travel great distances into remote backcountry.

Not even thinking about the possibility of having to spend the night outdoors, five men out for some "extreme snowmobiling" in the Oregon backcountry ended up burning their cash, credit cards, and wallets in a desperate attempt to get a fire going as they huddled under a makeshift snow shelter. The men, ranging in age from 26 to 39, were about

hicles. And besides, you're in a big, powerful V8 with four-wheel drive. You can go where lesser vehicles fear to tread.

Day One: Midafternoon

The route across the mountain range separating you from a nice-sized town with the promise of a good restaurant and a bed begins as a wide highway and then turns into a narrow, two-lane blacktop that winds up to the pass in a series of switchbacks. You begin reaching heavy accumulations of snow from the last two weeks as you gain elevation, and fresh snow is beginning to fall as the wind picks up and the skies darken with heavier clouds. The falling snow concerns you and you pull over at an overlook to study your map while sipping coffee bought at the gas station in the valley you just left. The fast-moving clouds are coming from the west, the direction in which you are heading. You worry that the weather will be much worse in that di-

to head for home when they decided to ride into a steep ravine deep with fresh powder. All of them got stuck there, and they then set off walking and ended up lost as they had no compass. When it became apparent that they would not get out before dark, they hunkered down in a snow shelter and began burning everything they had, which also included a 150-foot nylon rope and the titles to their machines. With over 200 searchers combing the area the next day, the five were found by midafternoon, all still alive but suffering from hypothermia and frostbite.

Had they been carrying at least one shovel between them, they probably could have dug their machines out. A basic survival kit with reliable firestarters and a simple shelter would have transformed the experience from an ordeal into an inconvenience.

rection, but you don't want to turn back, as it's getting later and you've already come this far. You're betting that you can get over the pass and down the other side before the worst of the storm arrives, but you don't know how fast snow can accumulate at elevation in a blizzard.

There's no other traffic on this remote stretch of road, but that doesn't cause undue alarm, as you've seen plenty of lightly traveled roads where meeting a car is rare in the past few days. There's no question about the route, as signs you've passed

Winter Storm Preparedness

If you are traveling in northern or mountain climates subject to severe winter storm weather, there's really no excuse for being without basic winter emergency and survival equipment. Motorists have been stranded and have died of hypothermia even on major highways in some of the worst storms. Any time you go out in a place with the potential for such conditions, you put yourself at risk of getting into a cold-weather survival scenario.

First of all, you should have snow chains, a tow rope or chain, jumper cables, emergency road flares, and a fluorescent emergency distress flag. Other tools should include a shovel for digging out of deep snow, a scraper for de-icing your windshield, and a good flashlight with extra batteries.

Ideally, your survival gear would include everything you might take on a winter backcountry camping trip, such as a four-season tent, a cold-weather sleeping bag and self-inflating insulating mattress, a reliable back-

along the way concur with the information you're getting from your GPS. You pull your SUV out into the road again, driving slowly as the wind whips and swirls large flakes of snow in all directions in front of your windshield. You can see the road ahead all right as long as you are only traveling 20 miles per hour or so, and you think driving in this is really nothing to get worked up about. The roadway is still easy to make out, and you're getting good traction as long as you keep a check on your speed and use four-wheel-drive.

packing stove and plenty of fuel for it, fire-starting tools and material designed to work in wet conditions, plenty of high-calorie food, and drink mixes like hot chocolate, along with a multiday water supply. With this kind of gear, you could remain comfortable even without your vehicle. Most people will not be this well-equipped, but it's not hard to gather some of this as a basic winter car kit, at least a blanket or sleeping bag, fire-starting tools, and some food items. If you can start a fire or you have a stove, you can melt snow for drinking water. (Don't try to eat snow directly, as it will only decrease your core body temperature as your body heat melts it.)

In almost all cases, you should stay with your vehicle if you are traveling in one. The vehicle will give you some protection from the wind, though unless you can run the engine, it won't provide much warmth. You will still need to keep your body moving to maintain your circulation and body heat, and you should use anything you can find in the vehicle for insulation if you do not have adequate clothing. This can include the seat covers and foam cushions inside them, which you can cut or tear out to wrap around your body and especially your extremities to prevent frostbite.

Whiteout

The higher you climb up the pass, the heavier the snowfall becomes. You realize you are in a real storm now as an accumulation of several inches buries the pavement in front of you and  your visibility is reduced to about 50 feet beyond the windshield. You slow down and come to a stop. There's no way to visually ascertain how much farther it is to the pass where you can begin descending to a lower elevation, but the GPS has topographic maps as well as street maps, so you switch views on the screen to see where you are in relation to the pass. Looking at the contour lines, you realize that it's farther than you thought. The snow is coming down heavier than you've ever seen before, and for the first time you have serious doubts that you can reach the pass on this road. Looking back in your rear-view mirror, you wonder about going back down. The way behind you is obscured as well. You decide that the only sensible thing to do is go forward until you reach another scenic overlook, then do a U-turn and head back down the way you came. Putting the transmission in gear, you feel the traction slip as you push forward into the teeth of the blizzard. The road leads to another hairpin switchback and then climbs steeply. You're starting to get scared now, thinking about the drop-off beyond the shoulder, which in this whiteout appears only as a gray abyss with the edge ill-defined beyond what you can still see of the road. You wish you could head back down immediately, but it's much too risky to back up here, and you can't simply stop, or you'll be snowed in for sure.

Crawling forward in the lowest gear, you inch the big SUV up the mountainside, pushing a path through snow as deep as the front bumper. Around the next switchback you come to a snowdrift several feet deep, and the falling snow has reduced visibility to the end of your hood. Going forward is hopeless. You put the transmission in park and try not to panic as you wonder what you will do next. It won't be long until dark, and the snow shows no indication of letting up anytime soon. You're going to be stuck here for the night and possibly buried under several feet of snow if it continues to fall at this rate.

Day One: Nightfall

You switch off your engine to give it a rest from idling and to save fuel. The heater has been working well and the interior is warm enough that you are in no immediate danger. Despite that, you are worried about what will happen next, now that you know you are stuck here for the night and possibly much longer. The snowdrift in front of you that blocked your passage farther up the mountain is growing deeper by the minute. You attempted to reverse back down the road to someplace you could turn around, but gave up after just a few yards. It was simply too dangerous. Then an effort to turn around in place by inching forward and back resulted in all four wheels spinning on the slick pavement until you managed to get stuck for good. Despite the four-wheel-drive, you realize you're not going anywhere without help. Snow piles up around you so fast that you decide to open the doors while you still can and attempt to scoop and kick it away so you will have a way to get in and out. You walk to the rear and do the same at the rear bumper, clearing it away from the exhaust pipe so the engine can breathe when you start it back up for heat.

The air outside is so cold it takes your breath away. You know you can't survive out there without shelter and proper clothing, which you don't have. The vehicle is your only hope. You just wish you had thought about the possibility of being stranded beforehand. If only you had a sleeping bag or heavy blanket, and a Thermos of hot coffee or tea, and some hot food, this would not be so bad. As it is there's nothing but half a bottle of water and a bag of potato chips you picked up at the store where  you bought the now-empty cup of coffee. It's not pleasant to contemplate how cold and hungry you're going to get if someone doesn't come along tomorrow to get you out of here. You tell yourself a snowplow will be coming to open up the road, but what you don't know is that this is not a road the locals use in the winter, so it will be forgotten until spring, which comes late this high in the northern Rockies.

Back inside the vehicle, you start the engine again, letting it idle while the heater blows full blast. You regret that you didn't top off the gas tank when you stopped for coffee before leaving the valley. Though the fuel gauge was at the halfway mark then, it has dropped with all this idling and driving up the mountain in low gear. You will have to make it last until help arrives, so you resolve to only run the engine in short increments to keep the interior warm. And you'll have to go out periodically to keep the snow from building up around the exhaust pipe. It will be a long, cold night.

Day Two: 2:00 AM

It's getting cold again inside the SUV and the chill wakes you up from a short nap. You reach up to turn on the dome light. Looking at your watch, you realize it's been almost two hours since you started the engine. Snow is evidently still falling outside; you cleared off the windows the last time you went outside, but now they are covered again. Dreading the icy wind, you push the door open to go clear the snow away from the exhaust pipe again, then hurry back inside to turn the ignition key. To your dismay, the engine sluggishly turns over a few times, and after that the only response you get from the starter is a clicking sound. The battery does not have enough juice to start it. Could it be that the battery was already weak and the extreme cold simply killed it? You can't believe this is happening, as you thought you could depend on your relatively new vehicle not to let you down at a time like this. Without a means of heating the cabin it won't be long before the temperature inside the vehicle drops to about the same level as outside, though at least you will be protected from the body-heat-sapping wind.

Digging through your luggage, you put on extra layers of clothing, including socks, pants, and shirts, and wrap your head and your hands in extra T-shirts, underwear, and towels. If only you had a blanket! Crawling into the backseat, you curl into the fetal position with your bags around you and on you. Your only wish at this point is for dawn, and the hope of clear skies and sunshine shortly to follow. If the sun comes out, you know you can stay warm enough during the day, but how will you get back down the mountain? You know nothing about winter travel on foot except that snowshoes or skis would be required, and of course you have neither, nor would you know how to use them if you did.

Day Two: Daybreak

You are almost afraid to move for fear of shifting the extra clothes and bags around you and losing more body heat, but sleep has been impossible and you spent the last two hours shivering and waiting for daylight, which at last arrives. You push one of the back doors open, having to kick it with both feet shove away the snow piled against it. The sky is gray and gloomy, but at least it's no longer dark and only a light snow is falling, smaller flakes swirling in a breeze that has abated greatly since the evening before.

Your immediate priority is to get warm, and to that end you will stop at nothing, and as you have been lying there in the

REAL LIFE | *How One Woman Survived on a Frigid Mountain with No Equipment*

In April of 1976, Lauren Elder lived through both a small plane crash and a winter survival ordeal in California's Sierra Nevada. She had set out with friends Jay Fuller and Jean Noller in a single-engine Cessna to fly to Death Valley. The plane crashed against a steep granite incline near the crest of a mountain, leaving Lauren with a broken arm and gashed leg. Her companions were hurt worse, with Jean unconscious. Lauren and Jay were able get her out of the airplane, where they tried to protect her against the cold. All of them were dressed for a warm spring day at much lower elevations—unprepared for a night above the snowline. Jean died of her injuries before nightfall, and Lauren salvaged everything she could find in the plane for a fire. Even in the daytime sun, the temperature had been near freezing.

She used the airplane's 12-volt cigarette lighter to start a fire with scraps of paper and the cardboard carton from a case of beer. Then she crawled under the plane and filled an empty beer bottle with gas from the leaking fuel tank and poured gas onto the rocks to keep the fire going. Realizing how hot the rocks in the fire were getting, she hit upon the idea of getting them hot enough to work as radiators. At first Jay helped her, but as he grew weaker with hypothermia, he let the fire go out.

With the aircraft's battery now dead, the lighter no longer worked and Lauren could not restart the fire. She car-

cold the past two hours, you have been thinking and scheming, trying to come up with a plan that will save you. Your conclusion is that you have no choice but to sacrifice your vehicle to the cause of survival. After all, it is insured and can be replaced.

ried the still-hot rocks to the aircraft and crawled inside the small tail section. By putting the rocks near her feet, back and head, as well as holding one in her hands, Lauren felt comfortably warm for the first time.

She called to Jay to come inside and bring more rocks, but he ignored her and climbed into the aircraft's front seat. Later as she huddled in a fetal position with her warm rocks, Jay crawled and thrashed. When dawn came and revealed fresh falling snow, he thought it meant no rescuers could come looking for them. After desperate fits of yelling, pounding, and kicking, he died, leaving Lauren alone. She took off Jay's warm socks and put them on her feet. Now the sun was out, and what Jay had thought was a blizzard was nothing but loose snow blowing in the wind.

She decided the best course of action was to try and reach a lower elevation, which required her to climb to the crest of the ridge they had crashed on and work her way down the other side. She climbed across a nearly vertical icy crust, punching through it with her hands and feet to keep from falling. Eventually she reached gentler slopes where she could sit down and slide on her bottom until she was able to walk. She finally staggered into the town of Independence, California, late the following night.

Lauren Elder survived because of her will to live and her realization that she had to retain her body heat to survive the first night. Jean Noller's autopsy revealed that she died of brain damage and hypothermia, and Jay Fuller's death was also ruled hypothermia and hemorrhaging from internal injuries.

Your life, on the other hand, cannot, and you know that you will freeze to death if you don't find a way to warm up and attract some attention to your plight at the same time.

Using a pair of scissors from the grooming kit in your travel bag, you rip open the fabric covering the rear seat and start pulling out chunks of foam cushion. Then you cut up the carpet from the floorboards and drag this and the foam outside, kicking out a hole in the snow on the roadway a few yards behind the vehicle. You then open the rear hatch and remove the cover from the spare tire compartment, dragging the spare tire and wheel to the pile as well. The next step is to take the tire iron from the tool kit and crawl under the rear of the vehicle. Your hands are so cold you can barely make them work, but you are determined to carry out your plan. You locate the bottom of the fuel tank, which is made of tough plastic, and jab the end of the tire iron into it. But it just bounces off, making you furious and even more desperate. There's no way the blunt end of this tool will penetrate it. You crawl back out from under the vehicle and

Cold Will Kill You Fast

Every winter in northern or high-mountain regions, motorists attempting to travel or get home in advance of a severe winter storm are caught unprepared by heavy snowfall and impassable roads and are stranded in their cars, where they risk freezing to death. Many people underestimate the dangers of such storms, especially if they are outsiders to these areas and unfamiliar with severe cold or with winter travel in mountain country, where roads through many high passes become impossible to negotiate in any vehicle.

Hypothermia is a killer that doesn't take long to do you in. Getting stranded without adequate shelter or the knowhow to improvise it will not be a long, drawn-out situation

retrieve the scissors from inside. Digging in the snow beside the road, you locate a baseball-sized rock that will serve as a hammer and crawl back under the tank. This time, by holding the point of the closed scissors against the plastic and pounding with the rock for all you're worth, you manage to jab a small hole in the tank and are rewarded with a stream of gasoline that spills across your clothing.

Crawling back into the vehicle, you dig frantically through your scattered luggage until you locate a book of paper matches that you took with you from one of the motel rooms you stayed in during the previous week. Then you take the empty coffee cup from yesterday and crawl back under the vehicle to catch a cupful of the spilling fuel. You pour the gasoline onto the pile of seat fabric, cushions, and the spare tire, then fumble with the flimsy paper matches to get one lit. Match after match fails in your numb, clumsy hands, until you are down to the last half dozen in the book. You cannot risk ruining the last of them, so you put your hands inside your shirt, rubbing them vigorously

like some of the scenarios in this book. You won't be concerned with finding food, or probably even water, as you will die before even the first 24 hours have passed.

Most stranded-motorist situations could have been avoided by paying better attention to weather reports and just staying put when winter storms threaten. But just as people ignore the threat of hurricanes despite the known dangers, they will also venture out in the face of a blizzard with the same "it won't happen to me" attitude. Secure in the comfort of a heated automobile, it's all too easy to be oblivious to the dangers outside and to ignore the thought of what could happen if the vehicle becomes inoperable in severe winter conditions.

against your body to get the blood flowing again so you can use your fingers. This time you tear off three of the paper matches together, holding them in a tight clump as you rub them across the striking surface on the book. Finally you get a flame, which you put immediately into the gasoline-soaked foam. Flames flare up immediately, forcing you to roll backward, covering your face, but now you have a heat source! You squat as close as you dare, reveling in the warmth, which increases to intense heat when the rubber of the spare tire catches fire.

The burning tire creates a plume of black smoke, and after warming your hands and feet enough to regain full function, you are determined to take advantage of the visibility potential the smoke offers. The snow has stopped falling and the sky is clearing, so you set to work with the jack and lug wrench to remove the four wheels from the SUV. You also remove the rest of the seat covers, foam, and carpeting, knowing you need to keep a fire going as long as possible in hopes of attracting attention. Looking down in the valley far below, you can see the small town you left yesterday and scattered ranches in the surrounding countryside. Someone will surely notice black smoke coming off a freshly powdered mountain after a blizzard of that magnitude. In the meantime, you will stay warm, even if it means burning everything you have.

TOP TEN WINTER STORM SURVIVAL TIPS

1. **Monitor weather forecasts and do not travel during winter storms.** By staying aware of current and forecast weather conditions, you can avoid getting caught in most winter storms. The biggest storms can paralyze an entire region, shutting down all travel. But mountain areas, especially at higher elevations, can generate their own weather and you should be aware of the potential for isolated storms even if the overall regional forecast is good.

2. **Travel during the day and inform others of your route and destination.** If you must travel in winter storm conditions, try to get where you're going in daylight hours when temperatures will be higher and visibility better. Make sure to inform friends or relatives of where you are going and what time you expect to be there, and provide details of the route you expect to take.

3. **Stay on main roads and avoid backroad shortcuts.** Stay on well-traveled highways and roads that are more likely to be maintained for winter travel and patrolled by emergency vehicles. Avoid secondary roads and especially remote backroads. Don't put all your trust in GPS navigation systems, as the routing information in the software has no way of taking into account winter road conditions.

4. **Keep a winter survival kit in your vehicle.** Winter survival equipment kept in your vehicle should include a shovel, a windshield scraper, a flashlight and extra batteries, a battery-powered radio, water, high-energy snack food, matches, extra clothing, sleeping bags or blankets, a first aid kit, a pocketknife, a tow rope or chain, jumper cables, emergency road flares, and a fluorescent distress flag.

5. **Stay inside the vehicle if trapped by the storm.** If you get stuck, try to pull off the roadway if possible, turn on your hazard lights, and hang your distress flag from your antenna. Stay inside the vehicle unless you see an occupied building close by where you know you can take shelter.

6. **Run the engine for short periods of heat.** Run the engine and heater for 10 minutes each hour to keep warm. Partially open a

window on the downwind side of the vehicle while running the engine to prevent carbon monoxide poisoning. If you are doing this in deep accumulating snow, you should also periodically clear snow from the exhaust pipe to prevent carbon monoxide buildup.

7. **Keep yourself moving.** Even in the confines of a vehicle, you should exercise frequently by vigorously moving your arms, legs, fingers, and toes to keep blood circulating and maintain body heat.

8. **Watch for signs of frostbite and hypothermia.** Frostbite is damage to body tissue that occurs when that tissue is frozen. Early signs are a loss of feeling and a white or pale appearance in extremities such as fingers, toes, earlobes, or the tip of the nose. Initial signs of hypothermia include shivering and an impaired ability to make decisions. Fatigue, lethargy, slurred speech, stumbling, incoherence, and disorientation are all symptoms. If you notice these symptoms, warm the affected person by starting with the body core, using your own body, dry clothing, or a warm blanket. Do not warm extremities first, as cold blood driven to the heart can cause heart failure.

9. **Drink fluids to stay hydrated; do not eat snow.** Drink plenty of water and other available fluids to prevent dehydration, but avoid alcohol. Avoid eating snow unless you can melt it first, as it will reduce your body temperature.

10. **After the storm, make yourself visible.** After the storm has passed and you can safely exit your vehicle, increase your visibility to searchers by stomping out an SOS in the snow or arranging rocks or tree limbs to attract rescue aircraft that may be surveying the area.

CHAPTER EIGHT
BROKE DOWN IN THE DESERT

The sun is beating down with midday intensity as you return from your walk a short distance down the dry gulch and look at your disabled machine still lying in the pile of rocks where you broke it. The silence around you is ominous and you've never felt so small as you contemplate the predicament you've gotten yourself into.

There was no sign of water in the stretch of dry riverbed you just walked. You look at the distant brown ridges of the desert mountain ranges surrounding this parched valley and think that there probably isn't another human being anywhere within your circle of vision. It's as if you are the only person on earth and you wonder how you will have the strength to walk out of this place along the dusty track that brought you here. It would be difficult even if you were equipped with good hiking boots, a backpack, and a supply of water. But with stiff riding boots and barely a day's supply of water left, you know you are in trouble. There's no indication that another vehicle has been this way anytime recently. Few could travel the route that brought you here anyway, and this time of year even those inclined to do so would likely stay home. How could you have ended up stranded in a desert 25 miles from the nearest paved road?

Day One: Sunday, 9:00 AM

You've been riding for less than a half hour since breaking camp, picking your path among the boulders and clumps of cactus as you follow a seldom-used jeep trail across an expanse of a desert valley between two barren mountain ranges. You haven't seen another person since you rode off the pavement of the nearest highway the day before yesterday. The route has led across numerous arroyos and dry gulches, and now you've come to the steepest one yet. Large rocks are jumbled together in the bed of a dry river that looks as if it hasn't seen water in ages. You stand on the footpegs of the tall KLR 650 dual-sport motorcycle to get more control and to enable yourself to pick a better line through the rocks. It takes finesse and balance to keep the bike upright as you carefully ease off the clutch and give it enough throttle for the back tire to get a grip and maintain traction in the loose stones.

You reach the bottom and hit an area of deep sand, forcing you to gun the engine to keep the bike from sinking and getting stuck. Near the other side you reach rocks again before you can let off the throttle in the sand, and the front wheel lifts abruptly over a boulder before the bike slams back down on top of it, landing squarely on the plastic skid plate under the engine. The sudden stop causes you to lose your balance and fall to one side into more rocks. It's not the first off-road spill you've had, and your helmet and protective riding gear save you from more serious injury than a bruised right shoulder.

You pull your leg out from under the machine and start to dust yourself off before trying to right it. That's when you are shocked to see motor oil running into the dry sand at your feet. The inadequate factory skid plate that you knew you should have replaced before this trip allowed the oil drain plug to absorb all the impact of the bike's landing on the big rock. The stream of leaking oil is coming from a crack in the aluminum crankcase into which the oil plug is threaded. You stare help-lessly as the black fluid runs into the sand. There is nothing in your toolkit that can fix this without outside help, and no way to improvise anything; you know you won't be riding out of here. You take off your helmet and squint in the harsh sunlight beating down on you. Without the sound of the motor, there is nothing but silence in an emptiness that surrounds you for as far as you can see.

Looking for Adventure: Exploring the Desert on a Dual-Sport Motorcycle

You're new to the Southwestern environment as a recent trans-plant to Reno, but the more time you spend in Nevada, the more fascinated you become with the wide-open spaces of the des-erts and mountains nearby. After looking at the available op-tions and doing some research, you decide that the best vehicle to take you out into the remote places you want to see is a dual-sport motorcycle. This type  of motorcycle is equally at home on the pavement, eating up Interstate miles to get to an area of interest, or negotiating rough jeep trails, fire roads, and single-track in the backcountry.

You chose the venerable Kawasaki KLR 650 for its simplic-ity, relatively low cost, and great reputation as a do-it-all bike for this kind of adventure. Since buying it you have been in-creasing the range of your weekend trips, studying maps and reading guidebooks about the surrounding country to find new places to explore. You are particularly interested in visiting old ghost towns, abandoned mines, and other remnants of the Old West, of which there are no shortage of in the Nevada desert. As your confidence increases, you find yourself riding farther and farther off-road—far enough that even before you have a mishap you know that you could get yourself in trouble. But though it would be safer to ride with a partner or a group, you prefer

REAL LIFE | *Skeletons Found 13 Years After German Tourists Disappear in Death Valley*

The disappearance of four German tourists in Death Valley illustrates how deceptive the dangers of the desert can be to those who are not prepared or do not have local knowledge of the severe conditions there. The party consisted of a 27-year-old woman and her 4-year-old son, and the woman's 33-year-old boyfriend and his 10-year-old son. They checked out of a Las Vegas hotel on July 22, 1996, and drove to Death Valley in a rented minivan on a day when temperatures reached as high as 120°F. The last trace of them was a note they left the next day in a guest box at an abandoned mining camp where they spent the night before driving off the pavement on a dirt road near the remote Panamint Range. It was not until October 23 that the van was found stuck in a sandy ravine in a roadless area far from any established routes. A beer bottle that was apparently from the van was found a quarter-mile away, but there were no tracks to indicate which way the occupants had gone beyond that point. The area was combed by searchers from law enforcement agencies, but no trace of the missing Germans was found.

In November 2009, two off-duty mountain rescue workers from Riverside County were exploring a previously unsearched area in the vicinity based on a theory they had formulated about the case. They reasoned that people unfamiliar with the area might have tried to walk to a remote military base some 11 miles away. Thinking such a base would be the same as in

going alone for the peace and solitude and the freedom to set your own pace. You brush up on desert survival skills by studying books on the subject, and you always carry extra water, some food, and basic emergency equipment.

their home country, with razor wire and guards patrolling the perimeter, the Germans attempted to hike to it in the withering heat and never made it, which on this weapons testing ground was unmanned, roadless, and rarely visited.

The rescue workers' theory proved correct, and when one of them came upon a wine bottle far off any regular hiking route, he then noticed pieces of bone in the sand around him, and further searching led to vertebrae and a human skull. A more thorough search was then organized and more bones were found in the area, which indeed was between two and four miles from the desolate boundary of the China Lake Naval Weapons Testing Center. The bones have since been identified as those of the two adults. So far, the whereabouts of the children remain a mystery.

These hapless tourists with little understanding of the vastness and harshness of the Death Valley environment never had a chance of traveling that far on foot in the direction they had taken. Few experienced hikers would attempt it. But this is a case where the often-repeated advice of staying with your vehicle would have done them no good either. The driver of the van made a fatal mistake when he left the road in a two-wheel-drive street van with no local knowledge and nothing but an inadequate tourist map. Staying there with little supplies or water would have been fatal as well, but had they been more familiar with the nature of large military bases in the western U.S., they might have tried to walk back they way they came rather than strike out across trackless desert to a desolate, unmanned bombing range.

When you finally have a three-day weekend free, you plan an even bigger adventure and leave before daylight on Friday to ride some 90 miles north to a remote mountain range in the Black Rock Desert. The area is for the most part inaccessible and completely uninhabited. You plan to ride into this desert wasteland on an all-dirt route that leads to a seldom-visited ghost town. The going will be rough and slow, so you plan on camping for two nights in the desert, probably at the ghost town. You study the terrain in advance on Google Earth and program the route into your handlebar-mounted GPS unit. You are confident you can find your way, and when you at last turn off the pavement to begin the adventure, you are stoked with excitement for what lies ahead. It's still early when you get to

Extreme Heat Impairs Judgment

Heat exhaustion is much like hypothermia in the way that it impairs judgment and causes people to make irrational decisions and take actions that make their situation worse. Symptoms can include hallucinations and a feeling of euphoria in the early stages before you lose your ability to travel. In the extreme dry heat of North American deserts like Death Valley, and many similar deserts throughout the world, the lack of humidity can mask the danger of the environment because the victims don't realize how hot it really is until the effects of heat exhaustion have already begun to kick in. People unfamiliar with such environments generally have no idea how much water is required on a daily basis to keep the body hydrated to a safe level. Once they begin to get dehydrated, they may already be too weak to take the appropriate action to do something about it.

the turn-off, and you don't plan to ride back onto the asphalt of the highway until sometime Sunday.

Day One: Sunday, 11:30 AM

Back at the disabled bike after a short reconnoiter down the dry gulch, you begin unloading your stuff from the metal panniers mounted on either side of the rear rack so you can take inventory of what you have and try to formulate a plan. Your biggest concern is water. Since you planned to be back to the highway sometime this afternoon, you don't have much left after spending two nights camping in the desert, carrying all the water you could manage on the bike for your drinking and cooking needs. This morning as you were breaking camp and loading up, you

The reality is that if you were stranded in the desert on a hot summer morning without shade or protective clothing and had no water, you would likely not live until sunset. In temperatures as high as 120°F, you would sweat away as much as two gallons of water by afternoon. At that point, your body is drawing on water stored in fat, tissues, and blood, and by then you would be feverish and delirious until death came from circulatory failure.

For humans to survive in the desert environment, it is essential to have sufficient water, but the amount needed can be drastically reduced if you have protection from the sun during the day and keep movement to a minimum, doing any necessary traveling and other activities at night, when temperatures are much lower. The key to reducing the body's water loss through perspiration and evaporation is to keep yourself fully clothed and to remain as calm and inactive as possible in the heat of the day, taking advantage of any natural shade you can find, no matter how scant.

refilled your three-liter Camelbak hydration pack with the last of the water bottles scattered throughout your gear. It would have been enough and then some under normal circumstances, but now you realize it's only enough to last about one day if you don't exert yourself. You're going to have to find more, and soon. But the question is, where? The only surface water you've seen all weekend was a stagnant pool in the bottom of an old cistern back at the ghost town. It was too deep to reach even if you had wanted to, and at the time you thought a person would have to be mighty desperate to even want such a foul-smelling concoction. But the one-time residents of that town would have been glad to get it. Ghost towns throughout the arid West are remnants of failed settlements that suffered from a constant shortage of water in an environment hard for human life.

Now you're alone in a place few dare to venture, especially this time of year. You have seen no vehicle tracks other than your own, and you doubt that conventional strategy of waiting by your broken-down vehicle for help applies in this situation. You didn't tell anyone exactly where you were going, just a brief mention to your coworkers that you were going on a motorcycle camping trip somewhere in the deserts to the north.

You power up your mobile phone to confirm what you already know: You are much too far from a road to be within range of any cellular towers, and thus you have no signal. If you can't call for help and you can't have any reasonable expectations that someone will come along before you run out of water, what can you do? You know for certain that you don't have enough water to walk 25 miles through the desert heat to the highway. Even if you travel only at night when temperatures are down it will still be risky.

Day One: Sunday, 12:00 Noon

You are more than a little frightened as you contemplate your situation from a small patch of shade under an overhanging boulder near your disabled bike. You've moved your gear and supplies out of the direct sun as well, and you scroll through the topographical maps on the GPS unit that was mounted to the handlebars, looking for anything that might be closer than the two-lane highway you were riding back to.

This patch of Nevada desert you've gotten yourself stranded in is a quarter-million-acre swath of mixed National Forest Service and BLM land, though "forest" hardly describes scrub brush and desert vegetation with a scattering of pinyon pines. The few "roads" that penetrate it are just unauthorized rocky tracks and off-road vehicle trails like the one you've ridden in on. There are no human inhabitants any closer than the highway, and from the beginning of the blacktop it's a long way to the nearest ranch and even farther to a town. But what your GPS shows you is that from the point where you are broken down, the dirt track you were following is not the closest route to the highway. The track follows the easy terrain of the valley floor, and you know from your odometer reading that it's approximately 25 miles that way to the highway. The distance as the crow flies, however, in the direction that the dry streambed winds down from the hills, is just a tad under 18 miles—still a long way and over uncertain obstacles.

One thing you know for sure is that you can't walk out of here in the heat of the day, and to even start walking this time of day would be suicide. But based on the lack of other traffic you've observed, and the condition of the dirt track you've traveled in and out of the area on, you know that waiting for someone to come along is equally risky. Since it's Sunday and most people have to be back at work on Monday, if someone doesn't pass this way today, chances are good no one will all week. You've got to do something to save yourself, but any movement will have to wait until sunset or nearly sunset. Should you try to make your way back along the track the 10 miles or so to the ghost town, where at least you know there is *some* water, no matter how distasteful? Or should you attempt the much longer trek out to the pavement, where someone will eventually come along in a vehicle? The other option is to follow the dry wash uphill, still moving in the direction of the highway, but with hope of finding a spring or a low place where you might dig for water. Going uphill along the dry creek bed will take you into an area of sandstone ridges at the flanks of the mountain range. Pinyon pines, junipers, and bushes and grasses on the slopes in that direction indicate there must be some water, but can you find it before you die of dehydration? You know this is one of the most important decisions you've ever made in your life, and if you don't make the right one, it could be your last. You've got all day to think about it, as there is nothing you can do but lay low

REAL LIFE | *Motorcyclist with Broken Ankle Tracked Down After Four Days*

Jeremy Cox of Prescott, Arizona, found himself in a similar situation involving a dual-sport motorcycle when he rode out from his home into Prescott National Forest to scout an area he planned to hunt in during the coming deer season. Cox left on a Saturday morning without telling his girlfriend his travel route, and without a cell phone or GPS. When he didn't come home that night, his girlfriend reported him missing and a search team began looking in a rugged area of rocky dirt roads and trails. It was not until Tuesday afternoon, the third day that he was missing, that the searchers discovered motorcycle tracks and a search-and-rescue tracker began the job of following and deciphering his the confusing trail.

In the meantime, Cox had been stranded with a badly broken ankle, unable to ride or walk. He was attempting

in the shade until the brutal sun sinks low on the horizon to give you some relief.

Day One: Sunday, Late Afternoon

The sun is finally low enough that the rocky banks of the arroyo are casting long shadows, enabling you to move around a little. You've had time to consider your options, and you've ruled out trying to hike 25 miles of dirt track to the highway with only the small amount of water you have left. If there was a chance of encountering other travelers en route, it might be feasible, but that probability is slim, and the stiff motorcycle boots you are wearing are too heavy and uncomfortable to make that kind of trek in one night. The only other footwear you have with you is a pair of light-duty river sandals you brought for wear-

to ride up a steep, rocky hill when his tires slipped on the stones and the bike fell on him, smashing his ankle into a rock. In this hostile, arid terrain he was in serious trouble. He ran out of the water he had with him by the second night, and the only thing that saved him was the fact that he was in a free-range cattle grazing area and he was able to hobble to a cattle tank where he found water. He also found prickly pear fruit growing near the tank and ate that, as he had no other food. He resolved to stay near the tank and await rescue, spelling out "SOS" on the ground and laying out his white helmet and riding jacket where it could be seen from the air.

The tracker following Cox's trail reached him shortly after noon on Wednesday, four days after he rode into the area at the beginning of his ordeal. Had he not been lucky enough to crash near a source of water, he certainly would not have lived to tell about it.

ing in camp—hardly any better for long-distance desert hiking where thorns and sharp rocks are everywhere. But even if you had comfortable hiking books, you know you would still have to break the journey to the highway up into two nights of walking, with another day in between spent laying up in the shade. Without more water, it's a hopeless proposition.

Going back to the ghost town will reward you with the stagnant cistern water, but after considering this option, you wonder if you would be any better off there. It's still in the middle of nowhere and you saw no signs of recent visitors. It could be days, weeks, or months before someone visits it again, and other than the limited amount of water you saw, there are no resources there to keep you alive. And the 10-mile hike back there is no piece of cake either. You're willing to attempt it if your new plan fails, but only as a last resort. You know you have to have water first, and then you have to get back to the asphalt if you ever want to be found.

REAL LIFE | *A Motorcycle Adventurer Who Didn't Make It*

Things did not turn out so well for former champion UFC fighter Evan Tanner, who rode out into the desert east of his Oceanside, California, home on a motorcycle camping trip to hunt for lost treasure and take a pilgrimage to solitude. The 37-year-old man was found dead just a few days later. His troubles apparently began after his motorcycle ran out of gas. When he didn't return on the day he told his friends to expect him, a call was made to the Sheriff's office and search-and-rescue teams scoured the area near Palo Verde where he was supposed to be, enduring temperatures up to 114°F. When they found his camp but no

The new plan that you've decided on since you've had a chance to examine your surroundings in the cooler late afternoon light is to head up the arroyo at least as far as the base of the hills, where you hope you will find water. If you can locate a sufficient source to fill all your containers, then perhaps find something to eat, you can make the trek cross-country to the closest point of the highway by traveling at night at a relaxed pace that would not turn into a death march in the desert heat.

Signs of life that were not apparent when you first broke down and were so stressed out about your predicament are now everywhere around you as the sun begins to sink behind the faraway range bounding the valley to the west. Birdcalls ring out from the dry bushes and sagebrush along the banks of the arroyo; you see blackbirds, quail, and doves, and high overhead, a large hawk riding the updrafts. In the sandy bottom of the dry creek bed, you see the tracks of a variety of small animals, from rabbits to some kind of doglike prints, probably

sign of Tanner, a U.S. Marine helicopter joined the search. Flying just two miles from where his equipment was found earlier, they spotted Tanner's body. Apparently the heat, which ranged from 115 to 118°F the day he ran out of gas, impaired his judgment, leading him to attempt to walk out and eventually succumb to the punishing desert sun.

Before leaving on the trip, Tanner claimed in a blog entry he posted to have spent a good deal of time doing research and collecting supplies for his journey, which was to be a big escape from civilization that he was really looking forward to. He wrote that he was planning to go so deep into the desert that any failure of his equipment could cost him his life, and as a result he studied and bought what he concluded was the best gear.

fox or coyote. With all this animal life, you reason that there has to be water. You've read a lot about the history of the West since moving out here, and one thing that always stuck in your mind were the tales of the legendary Apache warriors and how for years they eluded capture in defiance of the entire U.S. Army by traveling light and fast over some of the most hostile desert terrain on the continent.

The Apaches were masters at finding hidden water, and you remember reading how they could find pockets of trapped rainwater and snowmelt in rocky hills and mountains where there

Follow the Wildlife to Find Water in the Desert

The desert environment is defined by the scarcity of water, but despite this almost all desert areas are inhabited by plants and animals that require at least some water. By knowing a bit about desert insects, birds, reptiles, and mammals, you can often find their hidden sources of life-giving water. It also helps to remember that water flows downhill and seeks the lowest level.

Anywhere you find damp soil or sand is a good place to dig. In dry streambeds, this will mostly be in the outside of bends under the concave bank of the outer curve, the same part of the stream that would be deepest if it were flowing with surface water. Indicators of subsurface water in a dry wash include an abundance of green plants, especially those that require lots of water such as cattails, cottonwood, or willow trees. Dense clouds of flies swarming over a spot usually indicate that water can be found by digging there.

The presence of ants and bees is also a certain indicator of water. Bees are rarely found more than three or four miles from fresh water. If ants and bees are going in and out of a hole in the crotch of a tree, there's probably a hidden

are no surface streams or springs. This thought gives you hope, and the presence of so much wildlife confirms that this desert cannot be as much of a wasteland as it seems at first glance.

Day One: Sunday, Sundown

Before leaving the disabled motorcycle in a quest to find water, you decide that it would be a good idea to leave a note with the bike, explaining what happened and stating your intentions, just in case someone should chance along the remote track and see it. You have a pen and a book about Old West ghost towns

reservoir of trapped rainwater there. Find out by dipping a long piece of grass or a stick in the tree and mopping the water out with bits of cloth tied to a stick, or suck it out directly with a hollow straw or reed.

Doves, blackbirds, and other grain and seed eaters are a reliable indictor of water. If you see them flying low and swift late in the day, they are flying to water. On the other hand, carnivorous birds (hawks, eagles and owls) get most of the moisture they need from their prey, and are not reliable water indicators.

If you see frogs or salamanders there is almost always water nearby. Mammals also need water at regular intervals, though many that are found in the desert can travel long distances between drinks. Animal trails do not always lead to water, but fresh tracks of grazing animals such as deer that lead downhill late in the day will sometimes take you to water. Some of these sources will be natural rock basins and pockets that trap rainwater and snow melt, sometimes holding it for months. By carefully studying the terrain for areas of sandstone cut by water runoff you can usually find such hidden water basins.

that has a few blank pages in the back, so you tear one of these out and leave your message in the waterproof map case that was attached to your tank bag. At least if someone does come along, they will know where to look for you.

Since you were camping, you have all the necessary gear to sleep comfortably outdoors, but unfortunately you have no easy way to carry all of it. The metal panniers bolted to the bike did a great job of carrying all this stuff and your toolkit while riding, but you have no large backpack or duffel bag. You have to sort it out and take only the essentials. This includes your compact sleeping bag in a nylon stuff sack, the rainfly from the tent to rig as shade, a water- and windproof riding jacket that will keep you warm in the desert night, a pocketknife, your GPS receiver, and a couple of disposable butane lighters for starting a fire. You have a camp stove and cookware as well, but you only brought a couple of cans of beans and some instant rice packs, which you already used during the two nights at the ghost town. You leave the stove with the bike, taking your Cam-

How to Get Water from Desert Plants

In the seemingly waterless desert, water can be obtained from plants, including dew that can be mopped up from grasses and other low-growing vegetation. The easiest way to collect it is to use rags or articles of clothing to sponge it up in the early morning before the sun evaporates it and squeeze it into a container. Other plants contain water in their roots, stems, or leaves. Tree roots near the surface in gullies and other low areas can be pulled up and cut into short lengths to drain out the moisture. Some desert plants such as the barrel cactus have large amounts of water, but it's very difficult to get without a good knife and lots of hard

elbak, two empty one-gallon jugs, and three empty one-quart Nalgene bottles. The only food you have left is a pack of peanut butter crackers, a candy bar, two overripe bananas, and a few almonds. You eat the bananas and almonds, and then take a good, long drink of water from the Camelbak to keep yourself hydrated before you set out walking. All the gear is bundled up in the tent fly, which you've slung over your shoulder like some kind of desert hobo. By now a nearly full moon is rising over the open desert country, making it quite easy to pick your way among the rocks.

Day Two: Monday, 3:00 AM

With a nearly full moon lighting your way, you've found it surprisingly easy to pick your way up the dry gulch in the cool night air. The lower temperatures are a great relief and now that your body is not assaulted by the heat, you are feeling better about your chances of getting out of this alive. But you still have seen no water or even mud in the creek bottom. In places there are so

work—you need to cut the cactus into sections and mash the pulp to squeeze out the water.

Water can also be evaporated from plants by placing leaves and stems in clear plastic "transpiration" bags and putting them in the sun. The water drawn out of the plant material will condense on the inside surface of the plastic and run down to the bottom, where it can be collected. Any type of clear plastic bag can work; the key is sealing it tightly to prevent water loss through evaporation. You can make a solar still from a sheet of clear plastic stretched over a hole about three feet wide by 18 inches deep. Use green plants to line the hole under the plastic to increase the amount of water condensed by the still.

many jumbled boulders, you have to scramble up the side and walk along the top bank. It's not like following a trail, but so far, so good, even though the stiff boots are not conducive to walking at a swift pace. But you don't want to overexert yourself anyway, so with frequent rest stops and scouting around for water, you estimate you've covered six or seven miles since sunset.

Day Two: Monday, Dawn

As the sky lightens in the east, your worries and fears begin anew, as you still have found no water. It is essential that you find water before the sun gets high enough to heat up the desert floor; otherwise you will have to spend another entire day resting in the shade with only a quart left from your original supply. You stop and put down your gear, climbing a small ridge on one side of the wash for a better view. Wet grass on the slopes dampens your boots and the cuffs of your pants. It's dew! Heavy dew saturates the knee-high grass, and you immediately kneel and

The Desert's Irresistible Lure

The deserts of the world have always been particularly forbidding and dangerous places to travel across, mainly because of the risk of getting stranded in the middle of a barren wasteland where water is scarce and temperatures can range from scorching heat to extreme cold. Paved highways with substantial traffic and services en route cross many once-formidable deserts, but despite the encroachment of civilization, there are still plenty of vast expanses of trackless and little-traveled desert—including many in the American West.

Because the desert is intriguing and hauntingly beautiful in many unique ways, it is an enticing destination for adventurous travelers seeking its wide-open spaces in much

wipe your hand across it, licking the moisture from your fingers. Morning dew is a
water source you had forgotten about. Now
you head back to your gear to get a T-shirt
and an empty water bottle. By mopping the
shirt through the grass and wringing it out
as hard as you can, you are able to slowly
collect enough water to quench your im-

mediate thirst without having to deplete your remaining supply. But the sun is coming up, and the dew will soon evaporate.
It doesn't take the place of finding a real water supply, but it's
certainly better than nothing.

Your trek has now taken you within a mile of the steep
slopes from which the dry streambed runs. There's time to look
for water there before it gets too hot, so you push on without
wasting the little time that remains before you will have to seek
shade. Larger boulders broken off ages ago from the slopes up-

the same way the sea calls to mariners. I have often found
myself drawn to desert areas and out in these expanses of
sky, sand, rock, and sparse vegetation, I get much of the
same feeling of independence and solitude I get when sailing alone on the sea. Many types of rugged four-wheel-drive
vehicles, ATVs, dune buggies, and off-road motorcycles can
quickly get an intrepid desert traveler far off the beaten path
into areas where few humans ever go. Such travel calls
for total self-sufficiency. You'll need tools and ability to use
them to make both minor and major repairs, as anything mechanical is subject to failure. But sometimes the failure can
be catastrophic and impossible to repair in the field, leaving
the desert traveler no option but to try to walk out or to stay
put and hope for rescue.

hill are piled up in the streambed. Some are as big as a bus. Spotting strange markings on one, you at first think you're seeing graffiti, but then you recognize the simple drawings as ancient petroglyphs. There are lots of them, indicating that people at one time either lived here or spent considerable time in the vicinity. On the ground you find broken bits of pottery and sharp shards of flint, the byproduct of Stone Age tool manufacturing. Surely there is water nearby.

Day Two: Monday, Midmorning

Above the site where you found the petroglyphs, you are combing a series of sandstone ridges at the head of the arroyo, looking for the water pockets that you are certain must be there. As the sun climbs higher and begins to heat the bare rock around you, it's beginning to look like you're going to have to give up

for the day and look for some shade. You climb just a bit higher, working your way up an eroded ridgeline where you can see a wide shelf just a bit further uphill at the base of a steeper slope. Your hunch is correct and when you reach the shelf you find a landscape of pockmarked sandstone with several deep, crater-like holes in the surface. Some are glistening with the reflection of water! It's just the kind of place where rain and snowmelt from the previous spring would run off the slopes above and collect in pools. There is enough water here to drink your fill and top off all your containers. You taste it first and find it clear and pleasantly cool. This will be the ideal place to spend the day in the shade of the rocks and plan your next move.

Day Two: Monday, Dusk

With your Camelbak full, as well as the two one-gallon containers and the three one-quart Nalgene bottles, you are ready to move out. Foraging around the area in the vicinity of the water pockets in the late afternoon, you found an area with lots of blooming yucca plants and made a meal of the fresh flower petals, which are loaded with carbohydrates. You found the yucca flowers not at all bad-tasting, and though bland, they at least give you a feeling of being full and replenish your energy for traveling. Now, as you stand on the ridge looking in the direction that the GPS shows as the straightest line to the highway, just 11 miles away, you see a moving light making its way across the horizon and realize you are looking at the headlights of a distant vehicle traveling the lonely highway. Though it is still far and you have a heavier load slung over your shoulder, the water you are carrying gives you confidence that you can make it.

TOP TEN DESERT SURVIVAL TIPS

1. **Always inform someone of your plans.** Inform a reliable person of your desert travel plans, including your destination, route, and expected time of return. If the destination is a remote off-road location, provide GPS coordinates. Also include a description and the license plate number of the vehicle you will be using.

2. **Carry a compass, a GPS, and detailed maps.** Don't drive off the pavement to explore remote dirt roads and jeep tracks with a regular road map or tourist map of public lands. Always carry detailed maps of the area you intend to explore, along with a compass and a GPS receiver. Ideally the GPS unit will be loaded with topographical maps of the area. Consider carrying a SPOT satellite GPS messenger or satellite phone in case you get stranded.

3. **Don't travel into a desert with less than one gallon of water per person per day.** This is the minimum amount you should carry for desert travel. You will need more if you are hiking or doing other strenuous activity, especially in the hotter months. Always have at least five extra gallons in your vehicle to allow for breakdowns and delays.

4. **Stay near your vehicle.** A vehicle is more easily spotted from the air than a person on foot. The vehicle can provide shade in the daytime and protection from cold and wind at night. It also offers fuel for starting fires—burning tires create black smoke that can be seen for miles—and mirrors that can be removed and used for signaling.

5. **If you are on a road, stay on it.** If no one knows where you are and you are in an area so remote that you must attempt to walk out, do not travel cross-country unless you know for certain where you can find help and how far away it is. If you are guessing, stay on the road or stay put. Desert terrain that looks flat and easy to cross is often convoluted with dry washes and other obstacles that make for rough going. Your chances of meeting another person are far greater even on a remote dirt road than out in the wasteland of a desert wilderness.

6. **Use available shade or erect shade from what you have.** Get out of the direct heat of the sun anywhere you can. Use the shade of rocks or cliffs or your vehicle; open doors or hatchbacks or erect shade from tarps, blankets, spare clothing, or seat covers. Don't sit or lie directly on the ground in full sun, as it will be much hotter than the air. If you are in a flat, featureless desert, try to dig out a narrow pit to get below ground level and out of the sun.

7. **Wear lightweight, light-colored protective clothing.** Choose clothing appropriate to the desert environment before you begin your adventure. This should include long sleeves, long pants, and a wide-brimmed hat. Light colors are best. Keep your clothing on and keep your head covered to keep your body temperature down and prevent sunburn.

8. **Retain body moisture.** Avoid unnecessary or stressful activities that cause perspiration. Stay in the shade, and if you have no water, do not talk, eat, smoke, use salt, or drink alcohol. Keep your clothing on to prevent the evaporation of water through your skin. Keep your mouth closed and breathe through your nose. The Indian trick of keeping a small pebble in your mouth will ease your thirst.

9. **Do not ration water.** If you have water, drink what you need to stay hydrated. Rationing water will not prolong your life, as small sips will not be enough to prevent dehydration. But don't gulp the water down; swish it around your mouth and swallow each mouthful slowly.

10. **Know where to look for water.** Water can sometimes be found by digging in the inside of bends in dry washes and arroyos, at the heads of canyons, or at the bases of hills. Standing pools of water left from infrequent rains or snowmelt can sometimes be found in natural rock basins. Look for animal tracks converging in the same direction. Look for green vegetation and especially water-indicator plants, such as cattails, cottonwood, and willow trees.

CHAPTER NINE
ADRIFT ON
THE HIGH SEAS

Since sundown a couple of hours ago, you have been amazed by how bright the glow of man-made lights appears on the far horizon to the west. You long to be there, safe and secure in the nearly solid line of urban development stretching from Miami to Palm Beach. In every other direction there is nothing but empty sky and water, broken only by the occasional speck of light from a distant freighter or fishing vessel. All have been much too far away to see you and your friend, drifting north in the current of the Gulf Stream in a 21-foot open boat. The current is strong, bearing you to the north parallel to the Florida mainland at a speed of four knots. The console-mounted GPS receiver tells you that you are now 31 miles from the coast and steadily being pushed farther away by a westerly wind that has been increasing all day. All the GPS can do is tell you where you are. Either of you would trade a dozen of them for a single VHF radio with which you could call for help, but you have nothing but two cell phones—worthless this far offshore where they are unable to pick up a signal from the towers on the mainland. How could you end up adrift so far from land in an open boat with no provisions?

A Spur-of-the-Moment Plan to Go Offshore Fishing

You've come to south Florida with your best friend to escape the winter cold and participate in some of the beachgoing, drinking, and other festivities happening in Ft. Lauderdale during the week of Spring Break. A few days of partying were enough and you both are ready for something different. You have an uncle with a fishing boat who lives just to the north in Boca Raton, and you decide to call him up and ask if he can take the two of you fishing. Unfortunately, he is out of town on a business trip and says with apologies that he won't be back until after your vacation. Your friend still wants to see the boat, and since you have nothing better to do, you drive to your uncle's house and walk around back to where he keeps the 21-foot Mako docked in a canal that connects to the Intracoastal Waterway. You've been out on this same boat several times with your uncle on previous trips to Florida, when he taught you a bit about saltwater fishing and occasionally let you take the wheel.

Already drinking beer by noon, the two of you step aboard and relax in the fishing chairs, talking about what it would be like to be reeling in a big one out in the Gulf Stream. The temptation is too great. You dig into one of the tackle storage compartments and find that the spare key you remembered is still there. There are also several rods and reels on board, and a huge assortment of artificial lures. Life jackets and a fire extinguisher are present, as well as the console-mounted GPS chartplotter and fishfinder combo. The VHF radio has been removed for some reason—maybe your uncle took it in for repair. But both of you have cell phones, so that's

not a deterrent. You take the two gas tanks and empty cooler to your car and head for a convenience store to load up on fuel, beer, and ice. You're going fishing—and what your uncle doesn't know will never hurt him.

Day One: Late Afternoon

The two of you have a blast. You speed out to the impossibly blue waters of the Gulf Stream and troll artificial lures around in circles, going through the first 12-pack and then shutting down the engine to drift and listen to the stereo. It's a great way to spend the afternoon. You went so far out that the tall condominiums and hotels along the beaches turned to hazy gray outlines and then disappeared. Your buddy thinks it's the coolest thing ever—he's never been out of sight of land before. There's no one else around, just the occasional distant ship or other fishing boat, but nothing like the crowds of small boats you passed closer to shore on the way out here.

The sun and all the beer have conspired to make you both hungry, and while you have a couple of bags of chips and pretzels to snack on, you start thinking about dinner. It will take the rest of the remaining daylight to make the 18-mile run back in and then motor through the canals and get the boat docked and cleaned up. You break down the fishing rods and stow them in the holders, then open another beer and turn the starter key. The engine turns over but doesn't start. You turn the key and hold it down again, listening as the starter spins the motor without firing. The battery is obviously good, but there's something else wrong, either a fuel problem or something electrical. You know little about outboard motors, other than to check to see that the fuel line to the tank is connected and that gas is getting through it. The 200-hp Mercury outboard is as old as the boat, which is at least 20 years, but you don't recall your uncle ever having a problem with it.

You keep trying until you notice the battery getting weaker and decide to give it a rest. Thoughts of getting to a restaurant shortly after dark fade into the beginnings of frustration. At this point all this seems like nothing more than an inconvenience. Surely someone will come along—the Coast Guard or some other fishing boat—and either give you a tow or help you start the engine. But your friend is not as comfortable out here as you are. The boat is rocking in the chop stirred up by a strong offshore wind. You look at the chart displayed on the GPS and see that your current location is 20 miles offshore from the inlet where you entered the ocean earlier that afternoon. And while the boat seems to be sitting still, in reality it is in the grip of one of the world's mightiest ocean currents, the Gulf Stream, and is clipping along to the north at a rate of four nautical miles per hour. You turn off the receiver to save battery power, hoping you will have enough to get the engine started when you figure out what the problem is.

Day One: Sunset

With the engine cover removed, both of you stare helplessly at the lifeless hunk of metal hanging off the transom that is your only means of getting the boat back to shore. There's an owner's manual and basic toolkit on board, but beyond checking that fuel is getting to the carburetor and removing and cleaning the spark plugs, there's little else you know how to do. The engine still won't fire, and now you've run the battery down to the point where it doesn't have the strength to turn over. There's an emergency pull rope in the tool-kit, but trying to hand-crank the big unresponsive engine does nothing but wear you both out.

You've gone through all the storage compartments in the boat looking for anything that will help you, especially the emergency signaling kit that you know your uncle keeps on board. You remember him showing it to you on previous trips and remember that it contains a flare gun, day and night flares, smoke signals, and a signal mirror, but to your great disappointment, you cannot find the bright orange bag that contains the kit. Why would he have taken it off? Was it because the flares were expired and he was going to replace them? Or perhaps he took the flares and radio with him on a fishing trip aboard a different boat? At this point, the why doesn't matter, but you are starting to realize you really screwed up taking off on this half-cocked fishing trip without his permission and without having sense enough to check that all this stuff was on board.

With nothing else to do, you both open another beer and watch as the sun sinks in the direction of the mainland. Twilight is a short transition and soon the last light fades away, along with your hopes of getting back to shore anytime soon. It's going to be harder for any other boat to spot you out here in the dark, and it's a bit unnerving to think about drifting around out here all night. The indigo blue of the Gulf Stream has turned to oily black, and a 21-foot open boat seems awfully small to be bouncing around on the swells of the open Atlantic.

Day Two: Shortly after Midnight

The two of you have been talking for hours about what you're going to do to get out of this predicament. Your friend gets so upset with his non-functioning cell phone that he throws it into the sea in disgust, cursing the carrier and the high monthly bills he's been paying. But you both know you made a big mistake coming out here with nothing but your cell phones. For hours, you've seen distant lights of freighters moving north and south in the straits between Florida and the Bahamas, but none are anywhere near close enough to see you, even if it were daylight. The boat has running lights, but with the weak condition of the single 12-volt battery that powers everything electrical on board, you both decide it would be wiser to leave the lights off as long as there are no vessels close by. You'll keep a sharp lookout through the night, and if you see something nearby, you can then power up the lights and hopefully be seen.

Despite the fact that you are off south Florida, and less than 25 miles from the end of Grand Bahama Island, it's unbelievably chilly out here in an open boat in the middle of the night. The constant 15-mile-per-hour breeze over the water makes it feel much cooler than it really is. Of course, you didn't bring jackets for a sunny day of fishing in the Gulf Stream. Both of you are dressed the same: T-shirts, shorts, deck shoes, and baseball caps. Why would you have thought to bring anything else? There's no way to get any warmer on the open boat, other than to crouch down low beneath the gunwales to get out of the wind. You stay down until you can't contain your worry any longer and have to turn on the GPS to see where you are. Looking at the charts earlier you both realized that the northwest-ernmost islands of the Bahamas were about the same distance away as the Florida mainland. You have hopes that the westerly breeze will push the boat across the straits, where you'll drift ashore on some Bahamian beach. But without a sail, no amount of wind can push you in a straight line across the impossibly strong current of the Gulf Stream. Averaging three to four knots and more than 30 miles wide in the Florida Straits, the Stream is so powerful it carries warm water across the North Atlantic that defines the climate of Western Europe. A disabled boat caught in its clutches between Florida and the Little Bahama Bank has little chance of making landfall before being carried north of the islands and into the open Atlantic Ocean.

Day Two: Noon

The chill of the night has been replaced by broiling subtropical sun that beats down on you with unrelenting intensity in a now-calm sea. With no wind to push you farther east, you are in

REAL LIFE | *Drunken Misjudgment: Wolfgang Bunjes's Three-Day Dinghy Ride to Venezuela*

Cruising the Caribbean on his 31-foot catamaran, *Double Trouble,* Wolfgang Bunjes ended up adrift at sea in an open dinghy while trying to return to his floating home from a dock less than 100 feet away. The factor that turned a five-minute row into a three-day ordeal of survival at sea: Wolfgang was drunk after a night of shoreside partying during Carnival in Trinidad. In his inebriated state, he managed to miss his boat while rowing through the anchorage and soon he was drifting out into the Gulf of Paria on a night that he later described as "damn windy."

It didn't take him long to sober up when he discovered that the little plastic oars he had on the eight-and-a-half-foot plywood boat could do nothing to move him against 20 to 30 knots of offshore wind. He gave up fighting it and let the boat drift, sure that a passing boat would find him come morning. But by sunrise the winds had carried him even farther offshore and no boats could be seen. Waves broke over the dinghy, carrying away one oar. His sole possessions were now one oar, a towel, and what he was wearing—a T-shirt, shorts, deck shoes, and a money belt containing $300.

He watched as the island of Trinidad faded from sight. He hoped that a ship would pick him up, but also reasoned that he would eventually drift to land. To speed up this drift he made a crude sail with the towel and oar. During the

the grip of the Gulf Stream and are being carried inexorably to the North Atlantic. A brief power-up of the GPS to check your position shows that you are north of latitude 27, with part of the Little Bahama Bank still some 20 miles to the east, a direc-

ensuing night he partially quenched his thirst by licking the dinghy's floor when a brief shower passed. Cold and wet, he shivered under the towel until the next morning.

His spirits sank until later that afternoon, when he saw trees on the coast of Venezuela several miles ahead. The coast he was approaching was the danger zone of a vast river delta where shifting sandbars and strong currents created fierce breaking seas. A big wave capsized the dinghy at sunset, and after he crawled back in and bailed it out, another one rolled it again. This time the wind swept it away in the darkness before he could swim to it. He shed his shoes and money belt to help him stay afloat, fighting to keep his head above water in the breaking waves. At last he felt his toes touch bottom. Before daylight on the third morning, he staggered through the surf and crawled up on the beach of Cotorra Island, in the Pedernales River delta.

The island was uninhabited, and he was there 12 hours before by chance a passing Venezuelan Coast Guard vessel saw him lying facedown on the beach. Back at the anchorage where he had left his catamaran, it wasn't until two days later that his friends noticed he was missing and alerted the local authorities. Wolfgang was lucky; other boaters in the same situation have disappeared without a trace. These incidents with dinghies often occur when a crew is trying to return to the yacht on a windy night. Most small dinghies, especially inflatables, don't row well, and if a finicky outboard picks the wrong time to fail, it can be fatal.

tion you have no way of going. In a few more hours, you will be completely north of the banks and the closest land other than Florida will be the west coast of Africa. This part of the Florida peninsula curves away to the northwest, so every mile you travel north you are also being carried farther from the U.S. mainland. Since dawn, you have seen several fishing boats on the far horizon. Plenty of big sportfishing vessels make the run between Florida and the Bahama banks to fish, but the only ones you've seen were specks on the horizon. You both realize how small you really are out here. If only you had flares or a VHF

Adrift in an Open Boat—A Survival Scenario That Happens Again and Again

People get into these open-boat survival situations on a regular basis, mostly because of inexperience, poorly maintained equipment, or simply bad judgment. Because of bad luck or circumstances, others with good seamanship skills end up in sea survival ordeals after their ship or boat goes down, leaving them adrift on a life raft. Most of this chapter deals with those in the former category who blissfully head out into the ocean for a day of fun or fishing and then find themselves farther offshore than they bargained for.

In many cases, the people involved have no prior boating experience or knowledge of the sea or navigation, yet are able to rent a small boat, personal watercraft, or sailboard while on vacation at the beach. Not all rental companies enforce restrictions on how far offshore such novices are allowed to venture, and before they realize what is happening, they are caught by wind or current, or set adrift by mechanical failure. In the case of rental craft, the customers are usually rescued in time when the owners of the opera-

radio, you could have gotten the attention of more than a dozen passing vessels by now; as it is, you're invisible.

At this point, your new concern is your water supply. Yesterday's beer is now down to six 12-ounce bottles. Water was the last thing on your mind when you went to the convenience store to load up on ice and beer. Now the only other liquid you have is about thee or four gallons of water from the melted ice in the cooler. You pick out the dissolved beer bottle labels floating around in it and treat it like your most precious possession—which it is. It will keep you alive for now, but if you are not rescued soon, you're going to run out. It's a scary propo-

tion realize they are overdue. But when the inexperienced purchase their own craft and go out without telling a responsible party of their plans, the result is often more serious.

All boaters should recognize that when they head out onto open seas, they are entering the largest and wildest wilderness left on earth. Going to sea is something that should never be approached casually, and anyone who plans to drop the horizon astern had best be prepared to be self-sufficient with regard to all systems that keep the boat afloat and operational. This means having redundancy of systems—for example, a good set of oars to back up an outboard on a dinghy, and spare parts for motors and other systems, along with the tools and know-how to install them. Even well-equipped and experienced mariners should recognize the possibility of problems or emergencies that the crew cannot deal with on their own, and carry appropriate communication and signaling devices to get outside help if needed. With today's technology, there's little excuse not to have the means to get out a distress signal to the Coast Guard or other rescue agencies.

sition, and heat of the midday sun makes you realize how inadequate this small supply really is. Since midmorning it has been beating down on you out of a clear blue sky, and without the large bottle of sunscreen that you share between you, you would both be cooking in its rays with nothing to protect you but shorts and T-shirts.

Day Three: Morning

The winds are nonexistent to light and variable and have been through the night and since noon yesterday. There doesn't seem

REAL LIFE | *Three Mexican Fishermen Survive an Epic Ordeal at Sea*

One of the most amazing stories of survival at sea in an open boat unfolded when three Mexican fishermen who had long been given up for dead turned up some 5000 miles away near the Marshall Islands in the Western Pacific. The men were all from the town of San Blas on the Pacific coast of Mexico, from where they had set out along with two others on board an open 25-foot boat with twin 200-horsepower outboards. Accustomed to the hardships of the sea in an open boat, they left on October 28, 2005, to fish for shark, planning to be out a few days and taking enough drinking water to last that long. They had no radio or other modern safety equipment, which was the way they always worked. Strong offshore winds pushed them farther out than they planned, and then the engines broke down, putting them at the mercy of the currents and prevailing winds in that region that make it so easy for boats to sail westward to the South Pacific. Soon after it became apparent they could not return to land, two of the five men on board the boat jumped overboard and were lost.

to be a chance of getting blown to land, unless some strong wind from the east comes up and blows long and hard enough to push the boat back to Florida. You are now well north of the Bahamas and north of the normal routes of sportfishing and pleasure yachts crossing back and forth between Florida and the islands. Ship sightings have gotten less frequent—just a couple of northbound freighters far away to the west, somewhere between your position and the now-distant mainland.

There is still water in the cooler, but the supply is down to half what it was yesterday. You each had a beer in the evening, and

Toughened from their everyday lives, which already included hardships at sea, the three remaining men survived on rainwater and the fish and sea birds they managed to catch. They never doubted their survival, and kept their faith by taking turns reading the Bible to maintain their spirits and praying together, despite periods of up to 15 days without food. Over nine months later, on August 9, 2006, they drifted across fishing routes used by tuna vessels and were spotted by a Taiwanese trawler between the Marshall Islands and Kiribati.

Similar incidents have been widely publicized in recent years, perhaps because many impoverished fishermen in developing countries have abandoned traditional sailing craft and switched to outboard engines, which are prone to breakdown. In 1988, five Costa Rican fishermen were found adrift in the Pacific five months after their engine failed. In 1996, a 67-year-old Japanese fisherman survived for 46 days after his motor failed, and in that same year a villager from Papua New Guinea was rescued after drifting five weeks with his brokendown motor. This story is repeated time and time again to remind anyone who will listen that relying on a single means of propulsion in the open sea is not such a good idea.

you've finished up the last of the pretzels and chips you brought for snacks. Now you are getting seriously hungry, and both of you are fishing, trying a variety of artificial lures from your uncle's tackle boxes—but so far there hasn't even been a nibble.

Day Four: Noon

Dark clouds are building on the horizon to the south, and just in time. You're down to the last of your water and the promise of rain is all you have. The two of you are hardly talking to each

REAL LIFE | *Adrift: Seventy-Six Days Lost at Sea*

Even those who go to sea in well-found oceangoing vessels sometimes find themselves adrift and at the mercy of wind and currents. Ships and yachts sink all the time, capsized or broken up in storms, or from hitting floating debris and even whales. Many survivors of such incidents have written of their adventures, but none have described what it's like to be alone on the ocean in a battle for survival as eloquently as Steve Callahan did in his gripping narrative *Adrift: Seventy-Six Days Lost at Sea.* Callahan was sailing a small boat solo across the Atlantic when, in the dark of night, six days out of the Canary Islands, he heard a loud crash followed by the sound of water rushing into his wood and fiberglass hull. The water came in so fast he was waist deep in it by the time he got out of his bunk. He had only seconds to make it to the deck with his emergency gear and pull the cord to inflate his life raft before the boat sank to the level of the cabin. He remained tethered to the boat until it disappeared completely, marking the beginning of a more than 1800-mile journey in the tiny inflatable raft. His life from that point on consisted of distilling water by the spoonful with an emergency still, fighting off sharks, eating

other at this point. Each of you blames the other one for the predicament you're in, but your short tempers and bad dispositions are the result of the onset of dehydration and the hunger you both are feeling. Your efforts at fishing have been utterly fruitless. The ocean seems empty and lifeless. There are no sea birds, no fish visible beneath you, and nothing jumping out of the water. You haven't seen a ship in almost 24 hours. The emptiness and isolation is wearing on your nerves and you're beginning to doubt that you'll get out of this alive.

raw fish, and broiling in the tropical sun between frequent storms that threatened to drown him.

Callahan describes all this in vivid detail in his book, as well as what was going on in his mind through all those long days and nights spent so close to imminent death. The raft was practically self-destructing with leaks from tears and abrasions, while all along, sharks circled it and rubbed against the rubber bottom beneath him like hungry vultures waiting for the right moment to strike. Still, he fought for his survival, improvising a spear to take the dorado that followed the raft and using a makeshift sextant constructed from pencils to keep track of his drift rate and approximate position. On the night of his 75th day in the raft, he noticed a glow on the horizon and the following morning sighted green islands rising up out of the sea. Shortly afterward, three men in a fishing boat spotted him, and he learned that he had made landfall at Guadeloupe, in the West Indies, just a short hop from Antigua, his original destination in the sailboat that he lost.

Callahan survived, but just barely. His account describes an epic struggle of determination and resourcefulness in a situation where few would find a glimmer of hope.

Day Five: Sunrise

The storm clouds that built up yesterday around noon blew over your drifting boat without relinquishing a drop of rain. Beneath darker clouds on the horizon to the north, the sky was streaked with heavy sheets of falling rain punctuated by occasional strikes of lighting. All you could do was watch helplessly until the skies cleared and the intense sun returned.

But this fifth day dawns cloudier than any you've seen since you've been out here, and it seems inevitable that it will rain soon. It had better, because there is no more water. Your friend is ranting about how he doesn't see what it would hurt to drink

REAL LIFE | *Starvation and Cannibalism at Sea*

For as long as men have sailed the world's oceans, there have been accounts of famished survivors becalmed, cast adrift in life boats, or washed ashore on desolate islands with no remaining provisions, slowly dying of starvation. In such desperate circumstances, there have been numerous incidents of survivors who had no other alternative than to eat the remains of their less-fortunate shipmates. In most of these cases, the survivors resorted to this when weaker members of the party expired on their own, but in some of the more gruesome stories, lots were drawn among the living, and the loser was sacrificed for the good of the rest.

In his book *In the Heart of the Sea: The Tragedy of the Whaleship Essex*, Nathaniel Philbrick describes in great detail the ordeal of a group of unfortunate sailors cast adrift in open boats after their ship was destroyed in the Pacific Ocean by a whale. It happened in a remote stretch of the Pacific, east of any tropical islands; the year was 1820

just a little seawater, to alleviate his thirst, but you talk him out of it, for now at least. You don't know much about sea survival, but you at least know that drinking salt water will only make things worse and hasten dehydration and death. You point out that rain is bound to fall soon, and he seems pacified for now, but you're worried because his attitude has worsened considerably and you're afraid the influence of it will rub off on you, though you're trying hard to remain positive. You know that attitude plays a huge role in an ordeal like this, and if you give up hope, you are doomed. Compared to what some sea survivors have lived through, you haven't even begun to suffer yet.

and the men were at sea in the small boats some three months, trying to make their way to the west coast of South America. After running out of the meager rations they had with them in the boats, they had no alternative but to eat those who were weaker and died of starvation first. In one boat the last two survivors ate every scrap of flesh from the bones of the dead, and then smashed open the bones to get the marrow, which contained the fat they so desperately needed. Aboard the other boat, long separated from the first, lots were eventually drawn among four survivors and a teenaged seaman named Owen Coffin drew the unlucky piece of paper out of a hat. He accepted his fate with resignation, laying his head across the gunwale so that he could be dispatched with a pistol.

Some of the men from each boat were eventually rescued, though those who made it through the ordeal were little more than skeletons themselves. None of them would have lived had they not eaten the flesh of their companions.

Day Five: Afternoon

Just as you'd hoped, the dark skies at the beginning of the day have not cleared and now a steady rain is pelting the sea around you and washing the encrusted salt from the decks of the boat and your bodies. You open the lid of the cooler and prop it at an angle that will funnel rain in, then begin bailing out the water collecting on the floorboards to get rid of the salt that's mixed with it in the beginning. The rain shows no sign of letting up for a while, so you are able to clean out the bilges of the boat, leaving an uncontaminated surface for collecting fresh water. By the time the rain stops just before dark, you've both drunk your fill and managed to scoop up enough clean, life-giving

An Emergency Flare I Happened to Notice

Despite all the advances in boat design, equipment, and knowledge of the inherent dangers, many who venture out on the sea find themselves in life-or-death struggles, often because they place too much faith in the technology designed to make them safer. A common mistake is venturing far from land on small open boats with no other means of propulsion than outboard engines, and without adequate provisions or shelter to aid in survival if a mechanical failure occurs. The scenario presented in this chapter, of a disabled open boat adrift on the high seas, is repeated over and over again in many variations wherever inexperienced mariners have access to outboard-powered boats or water toys such as Jet Skis or WaveRunners.

I was personally involved in one such incident while kayak camping on a remote beach on the island of Culebra, which lies nearly 20 miles east of Puerto Rico. While cooking my rice for dinner as the afternoon sun was nearing

water to fill the entire 48-quart cooler. You are now set for days as far as water is concerned, but there is still nothing to alleviate your hunger.

Day Seven: Morning

You are awakened from where you are sleeping on the floor of the boat near the bow by a strange sound and open your eyes to see a gull-sized seabird of some species you are not familiar with perched on the gunwale. The bird is obviously exhausted from a long flight over water and has landed on the boat for a rest. At first you are half-asleep and glad that your boat could be of help to another weary pelagic traveler, but then your stomach growls and your hunting instinct kicks in. Here is food, de-

the horizon, I saw a single flare arc through the sky in the direction of the mountains on the main island. I couldn't see the boat from which it originated, but fortunately there were some local guys camping a half-mile away who had a fast, outboard-powered fishing boat. I ran to them for help and soon we were speeding in the direction of the flare.

Five miles west of Culebra, we spotted the boat in distress. It was a 20-foot open fishing boat with twin outboards. The young couple on board had set out from Fajardo, planning to visit Culebra for the day. The woman was clad in only a bikini, and the man in nothing but swimming trunks. They had no VHF radio and had used their last flare when the second outboard failed after the first one had given out halfway across. They didn't seem particularly alarmed, as they expected someone to tow them in to port, but had their flare gone unnoticed, the prevailing currents would have sent them into the open North Atlantic during the night, ending any hope of reaching land alive.

livered to you without asking. All you have to do is be careful not to frighten it away. You glance at your friend out of the corner of your eye, while still keeping the bird in view. He is sleeping soundly, which is a good thing, as he might make noise if he were awake. You ease inch by inch across the bilge, sliding on your bottom and trying to make your movements as inconspicuous to the bird as possible. It is looking at you, but doesn't show any sign of being alarmed. Moments seem to take hours as you gradually work your way within reach. When at last you are sure you cannot miss, you shoot out your arm and manage to grab the bird by one scrawny leg just as it opens its wings to take flight. It puts up a struggle and tries to get at your hand with its pointed beak but you quickly smash its head against the fiberglass and awaken your buddy with a shout. Breakfast!

The two of you share the fresh blood and then divide everything that is left, wasting nothing. When you are done, nothing is left but feathers, feet, and the head, and these you will put to use as fish bait.

Day Nine: Afternoon

Since the good fortune of the bird landing on the boat, little has changed in your empty world of sea and sky. There has been no more rain and you wonder if there will be any before your water supply runs out again. There have been no ships in two days, but on several occasions you've seen the contrails of jets high overhead, way too high for any of the occupants to see anything as small as an open boat drifting in the blue vastness 30,000 feet below.

The bottle of sunscreen that is protecting you both from severe sunburn is running low as well. Soon it will be gone and with it the only protection you have from being cooked in the subtropical sun. You can no longer get a fix with the GPS, as there is not enough juice left in the battery to run it. You can't know for sure, but you assume you must be a couple hundred miles out in the Atlantic by now, and wonder if the drifting boat will ever be found, even after the two of you are dead.

Staring into the emptiness to the northeast, wondering how far it is to Europe, you are startled by your friend's sudden exclamation as he sits trailing a fishing line over the stern. You are sure he must be hallucinating when he screams, "A SHIP!" but you turn to look to the south anyway. What you see when you do cannot be real, and you wonder how you could both have the same hallucination. It's a three-masted, square-rigged schooner, and it's heading right at you from less than a mile away. If it remains on the same heading, it will either hit you or pass very close. You watch as the hallucination draws close enough that its reality becomes undeniable. You are both waving your life jackets; you see crewmen on the deck pointing and then watch as the antique wooden vessel is hove-to and a boat is lowered from davits at the stern. The ship is real, all right, and when the longboat crew reaches you, you learn that it is en route from the Virgin Islands to a wooden-boat show in Mystic, Connecticut. Because you happened to drift across her rhumb line on this empty tract of ocean, the two of you will be sailing to New England as well.

TOP TEN TIPS FOR SURVIVAL AT SEA

1. **Be prepared before leaving the dock.** Don't go boating without a reliable VHF Marine Band radio transceiver, flare gun with day and night flares, smoke signals, and signal mirror. Better yet, also include a 406 MHz satellite EPIRB (emergency position indicator radio beacon) transmitter or a SPOT satellite messenger. Don't rely on cell phones, as they are not marine communication devices. Carry extra drinking water, food, sunscreen, protective clothing, first aid supplies, fire extinguishers, emergency fishing equipment, and an emergency desalinator.

2. **Don't go offshore on a poorly maintained vessel.** Make sure the hull, decks, and hatches are structurally sound and watertight. Check engines, props, electrical systems, sails, and rigging, and carry the necessary tools and spare parts to make any emergency repairs that might be needed. When you go to sea, assume that you are on your own and outside help is unavailable. Prepare to be self-sufficient.

3. **Don't go offshore on watercraft intended for protected waters.** Personal watercraft such as Jet Skis and WaveRunners are intended for recreational use in protected and near-shore waters. Some of these have engine compartments that cannot be accessed while afloat in deep water and especially in rough conditions. Many small boats are likewise unsuitable for trips far from land. Know your vessel and its capabilities as well as your own before heading far from land.

4. **File a float plan.** Inform a trusted friend or family member or the Coast Guard of your intended route and destination before heading out. You greatly increase your chances of being found by rescuers if someone knows that you're out there in the first place, that you're overdue to return, and where you were supposed to be traveling to and from.

5. **Stay aboard your vessel.** If your boat or other watercraft is disabled or damaged, don't abandon ship for a life raft unless it is sinking or on fire. Your chances of survival and of being found are

far greater on a larger boat than on a raft. Even if your vessel is capsized but still afloat, you are better off clinging to the bottom of the hull than drifting in a life jacket. If you have a life raft, you can tether it to the capsized hull.

6. **Do not drink salt water.** Resist the urge to drink seawater regardless of how long you've been without water. The salt in seawater will draw upon water stored in the body's cells and begin a vicious cycle of increasing dehydration and thirst that will be broken only by death.

7. **Drink the water you need.** People have died with water still aboard while trying to ration it too stringently. Your odds are better if you store it in your body and focus your attention on procuring more from rain, condensation, or fluid from marine life.

8. **Reduce your body's water loss.** Water evaporates through the skin. Keep your body protected from the sun and wind, and avoid unnecessary activity. Avoid eating if you have little or no water, as digestion depletes the water in the body.

9. **Make an effort to catch fish.** Fish are often attracted to drifting boats and rafts. If you have no hooks, improvise spears, grapples, or hooks from wood split from seats or other parts of the boat. Line can be made by unraveling canvas. If you have water, you can utilize every part of fish caught for food; the blood is salty and should not be consumed unless you have plenty of water. Fish eyes and spinal fluid, on the other hand, contain a high percentage of water.

10. **Look for other food sources.** Most seaweed is too tough to eat raw, but some varieties can be eaten if you have plenty of water. Usually seaweed is more useful for the small edible animals it contains. Patches of drifting sargasso weed and other seaweeds can be shaken in the boat to reveal tiny shrimp, crabs, and small fish hidden in them. In addition, all seabirds are edible; they often have no fear and will land on a boat or raft where they can be grabbed or snagged with a hook.

CHAPTER TEN
TRAPPED ON
THE 13TH FLOOR

In your half-asleep, half-dreaming state you think that your alarm clock is going off and it's time to go to work. But as consciousness returns, you know that can't be right because you are on vacation, and setting a wake-up alarm is the last thing on earth you would do this week. The sound doesn't go away, though, and it's much louder than any alarm clock anyway. You suddenly realize what you're hearing. It's not an alarm clock at all, but a fire alarm!

You throw off the covers and leap out of bed, flipping on the lamp beside you. Your first reaction is to go to the window and see if there's any way to tell what's going on. You see two cars with flashing blue lights speeding into the condominium parking lot 13 stories below. Sirens can be heard in the distance, but the building's fire alarms are so loud you can't tell if you're hearing the police, the fire department, or a combination of both. Whatever it is, this is real, and you've got to get out fast. But you don't want to run out into the hall in your underwear, because if there is a fire, it would be best to have some clothes and shoes on, so you decide you can spare the few seconds it will take to dress. You grab the only pair of long pants you brought on the trip and pull them on, followed by your tennis shoes and a cotton button-down shirt. Leaving everything else but your wallet and your passport, you head for the door to make a quick exit, confident that you can run to the stairwell at the end of the hall and get to the street in record time. But when you open the door just a few inches, you are shocked to find the entire hallway filled with thick, choking smoke. You can't even see the door ad-  jacent to yours on the other side, much less the other end of the hall where you remember the stairwell is located. You slam the door shut and retreat into your room coughing, your eyes burning from the acrid fumes. Trying to run through that stuff would likely take you out before you could even reach the stairwell, and you don't know that it's not full of smoke too. You're in quite a predicament. How could you end up trapped on the 13th floor of a burning building?

Escaping Winter with a Beach Vacation in Mexico

You've come to Mexico a few weeks after Christmas for a much-needed vacation from work and to escape the winter snow at home. A great deal on a one-week condominium rental at a Yucatan resort was too enticing to pass up, and the view from your unit is fantastic, overlooking the emerald-green water of the Caribbean. The view is the best part, however, as you soon discover why the rate was so cheap. Compared to newer developments in this popular resort destination, this building is a bit run-down and neglected, but there's so much to do on the beach and in the water that you don't let it bother you. You mainly need the condo as a place to sleep and shower; the rest of the time you're on the go anyway.

It never occurred to you that there was any danger in staying in the building just because it wasn't as posh as some of the others, but now as you cough to clear the smoke from your lungs, you wonder how the fire got started and how big it is. You aren't sure what kind of fire department there is in this resort town. Even if they are as efficient and professional as the one back home, which seems unlikely, you know it will take some time before they can help you get out. First of all, you have to try to keep the smoke out of your unit. You grab a bath towel and

REAL LIFE | *Risky Escapes Are Often the Only Way to Survive*

Time and time again, fires in multistory buildings put people in desperate situations that will cause them to take extraordinary actions to avoid being burned alive. Many jump to their deaths before the flames can reach them, but some survive falls that should have killed them, and others climb down all or part of the way on ropes hurriedly cobbled together from bedsheets, towels, clothing, or other items. A firefighter friend I spoke with, Lieutenant Scott Finazzo of the fire department in Overland Park, Kansas (a suburb of Kansas City), has seen firsthand how desperate people will become. He says that fire department personnel have to use caution when placing tall ladders near a victim hanging from a window, because the trapped person will often leap for the ladder before it is securely set, endangering the rescuers as well as themselves.

In a 2004 motel fire in Greenville, South Carolina, smoke filling the building killed six occupants and forced many others to jump out of windows or climb down their

soak it with water, then roll it up and shove it hard against the bottom of the door, sealing the crack between door and carpet. Then you look at the bedside clock and see that it is 2:01 a.m. just before the power goes out and the room goes black.

2:03 AM

You can see enough to move around inside the bedroom now that you've yanked the curtains down away from the window and ambient light from other nearby buildings and the street lights below filters in. Beyond the living room area of the condo, sliding glass doors open onto a concrete balcony that faces the

bedsheets to escape the five-story building. Those who perished were found on the third floor, where they collapsed from smoke inhalation while trying to get down the hall to the stairs. Terry Letterman was one of those who climbed down using a rope made of knotted sheets. He later stated that he didn't have time to be scared or to stop to consider the risk he was taking.

A similar fire on Christmas Eve, 2003, in a newly opened 10-story motel in Payatta, Thailand, trapped many foreign tourists on the upper floors and the roof. Some used sheets to climb down, and others managed a daring crossing from a balcony of the burning building to the balcony of an adjacent hotel using a ladder as a bridge between the two buildings. An American guest at the hotel named William Koerber was trapped on the tenth floor but managed to climb down as far as the sixth floor before some window bars he was clinging to gave way, sending him plunging the rest of the way to the ground. Witnesses were certain that he had fallen to his death, but he suffered only a few broken bones in his feet, legs, hips, and pelvis.

beach. You've spent each morning since you've arrived there, drinking coffee and looking out over the sea. Now the balcony is your only retreat from the room—an outdoor place where you can go to get away from the smoke and where you can see much better than in the dark interior.

2:04 AM

You're on the seven-by-ten-foot balcony, leaning over the four-foot-high metal safety rail to see if you can tell what's going on in the other parts of the building. Midway across the wall of the building, which is 10 units wide, you see smoke pouring from several windows on the 10th floor. An orange glow emanates

REAL LIFE | *The Odds of Surviving a Jump Are Not Good*

If you're trapped in a burning building, jumping should always be a last resort, especially if you are higher than the third floor. While some people have survived jumps or falls from much greater heights, once you're higher than about 30 feet, the odds are against you. Even a jump from the third floor can result in serious injury or death, depending on how you land and what you hit on the way down or on the ground. If you have no option other than jumping from a second- or third-story level, try to first hang at arms' length from the balcony or window ledge and then drop, to at least decrease the distance you fall by the length of your body.

Some building fires have resulted in horrific death tolls from people leaping to their deaths. In a 1911 factory fire in New York that killed 148 workers, mostly the girls and young women employed there, the victims jumped from the eighth, ninth, and tenth floors in groups of twos and threes, many hitting firemen on the ground trying to catch

from within the building, and at this point, there is no doubt in your mind that this is a major fire. People are running through the parking lot far below, many pointing up and staring. More sirens fill the air and you realize there is more commotion around on the other side of the building at the front entrance, which you cannot see from your balcony vantage point.

You know that there is no point going back to try and reach the stairs. You would probably die of smoke inhalation, and from what you've seen, it's clear that the fire is lower down in the building and the stairwell may be impassable anyway. You look back down over the balcony rail. It's a vertical drop of at least 130 feet to the concrete below. There are no external fire

them with nets. Falling from that height, the nets couldn't even slow them down, and several of the firemen were killed in what was described as a rain of bodies. Just a few minutes after the fire broke out, 53 people were lying dead on the pavement. The elevator made one trip to the ground floor before it stopped permanently, and later another pile of more than 25 bodies was found in the elevator shaft—victims who opened the doors on the burning floors and either jumped or tried to slide down the cables. An hour after the last of the girls jumped, one survivor from the ninth floor was found among the bodies on the street, but she died later from her injuries.

In an incredible act of desperate heroism, three male employees of the factory made a human chain of their bodies, swinging across a narrow alleyway to an adjacent building. A witness who survived said that several people escaped by climbing over the men's bodies, but then too many people crowded on at once, and all three men and those crossing fell to their deaths.

escapes—the building is much too modern for that. The only breaks in the smooth stucco facade of the building are the balconies like the one you're on. They are inset so that the openings are flush with the outside walls. Leaning over, you can see railing of the next one, which is one floor below you. It appears to be about 10 feet from the top of your railing to the top of the one below—too far to climb, as there is no place to put your feet

Why Elevators Are a Bad Idea in a Fire

Elevators are normally the fastest way up or down inside a tall building, but during a fire there are several reasons why the elevator is a poor choice for an escape route.

Mechanical failure: An elevator is a complex mechanism that can break down for many reasons in the abnormal conditions caused by a fire. Although some modern buildings have emergency elevators designed for use in a fire, any elevator can fail.

Increased exposure: If you are waiting to escape from a fire by using an elevator, you may have to wait too long for it to reach the floor you're on, increasing your exposure to fire or smoke. Also, automatic elevators travel between floors in response to pressed buttons both in the elevator car and in elevator lobbies. Because this operation cannot be cancelled once a button is pressed, it is possible for an elevator descending from floors above a fire to stop at the floor of the fire and open its doors automatically, exposing the occupants to smoke or fire. The elevator car may even get stuck there if the heat melts the wiring or the call buttons on that floor. More

and nothing to grab hold of other than the steel rails at each balcony overlook.

2:05 AM

You feel your way in the dark back to the entrance door to check it for heat. Touching the inside of it briefly with your hand, you find that it's not hot yet, so there's no fire out in the hall, but you

modern elevators are designed to prevent this from happening by automatically calling the elevator car to the designated egress floor (ground floor) when an alarm goes off, unless the alarm comes from that floor.

Crowding: Large numbers of people trying to crowd into an elevator may prevent the doors from closing, and for safety reasons, modern elevators will not operate until the doors are fully closed.

Chimney effect: The elevator shaft can act as a chimney in a high-rise building, carrying deadly heat and smoke to the passengers of the elevator even if it continues to function. The heat in the shaft can also burn out the electrical cables that supply the elevator car and cause it to stop between floors, where rescue through the escape hatches may not be feasible because of the heat.

Stairwells can also act as chimneys, but emergency stairwells are built with heavy doors that are supposed to be kept closed at all times to prevent this from happening. A properly built emergency stairwell will have no flammable material or interior decoration on the walls. Although it may take a long time to reach the ground from a tall building using the stairs, many survivors have done so, even from the World Trade Center in the September 11, 2001, terror attacks.

don't know how much time you have. You go back into the bedroom to look through your things and then into the main living room. You have a crazy idea, but you don't know if you can find what you need to make it work. If only you had a rope! Why did you not pack  a nice 200-foot rock-climbing rope in your suitcase?, you ask yourself, finding the humor in answering your own question with "Why would you?" But there has to be a way. It's just not that far down to the next balcony, and from there, not any farther to the next, and the next....

You run back out there hoping but not really expecting to see some kind of rescue device—a supertall fireman's ladder or a cherry-picker bucket, even a helicopter, perhaps. But instead what you see, to your horror, are the bodies of two people on the sidewalk just to the south, near the midpoint of the building. A crowd of onlookers points and yells. You hear screams, and you look as a man and woman climb over the rail of a balcony just a few units away on the 11th floor. They jump together, hold-

Don't Delay

Whether you attempt to use the elevator, stairs, a fire escape, or a more unconventional method, the most important key to surviving a burning building is to act without delay. Researchers have concluded that more than half of those who survived the September 11 attacks delayed evacuating because they wanted to gather more information about what was happening before leaving, taking between 1.5 and 2.6 times longer to begin evacuating than others who acted without hesitation. This caused congestion in the stairways that prevented many from getting out, even

ing hands as flames shoot out the window behind them, leaving them nothing but the grim choice they made together. Time is running out and you know you would jump, too, rather than be burned alive. But you don't want to die here. You've seen a movie about escaping prisoners that gives you an idea. It may be a big risk, and you may fall, but you can't think of another option.

You rush back inside and drag out the heavy fabric drapes you jerked down from the window when the power went out. Then you make your way to the kitchen and find a sharp knife. The drapes are only about seven feet long and won't work as they are. The material seems sturdy enough—it takes strong sawing action to get a rip started, and then you can split the fabric vertically. There are two six-foot-wide pieces. Splitting each into three strips gives you six two-foot-wide sections that are narrow enough to twist at the ends and tie together to increase their length. The fabric is bulky and hard to force into a knot, and you lose about three feet for every connection of two strips, as it takes a bulky square knot to join them securely. You're also losing precious time, and the minutes tick by as you wrestle with

though the towers were less than one-third occupied that day. This is human nature and is hard to overcome, especially when faced with an unprecedented event of such magnitude, but many more of the victims might have survived had they acted more decisively.

The fact is that the World Trade Center disaster was a deliberate act that caused a lot of fear and uncertainty about what would happen next, but most building fires are accidents and the fire itself will be your main threat. Don't delay by trying to figure it out. The cause of the fire and the extent of the damage is not your concern. Get out and do it fast, while helping others around you if at all possible.

the knots. But when you're done, you have a makeshift "rope" of drapery that is just over 25 feet long. There's a lingering doubt in your mind as to whether it will be strong enough. You trust your knots, as you're good at tying them, but you're not sure if

Extreme Measures: New Equipment for Skyscraper Evacuation

Although a surprising number of survivors escaped the World Trade Center on September 11 by using the stairs, the world watched in horror on live television as many other desperate souls jumped out of windows as high as the 106th and 107th floors to avoid being burned in the fires caused by the jets crashing into the buildings. Not long after this event, products started showing up on the market for skyscraper escape when conventional means are nearly impossible.

Despite the risks of jumping with a parachute in an urban area, Executive Chute, a maker of parachutes designed for skyscraper escape, was overwhelmed with inquiries from potential customers right after the World Trade Center attacks. The company received hundreds of orders shortly after launching its product, which is a round parachute designed to carry the user straight down, unlike the rectangular chutes used by recreational skydivers. The parachute opens automatically to full inflation in 1.9 seconds when the user's weight triggers a static line that is designed to be clipped to a desk or doorknob in the room being evacuated. Though the descent rate is fast, at 1000 feet per minute, the deceleration has proven to be acceptable for a high survivability rate. The designer says this rapid descent rate is necessary to get a jumper to ground fast and help prevent lateral drift into other buildings and objects. The Executive Chute sells for about $1000.

the fabric will hold your weight or rip crossways as easily as it did when you split it vertically with the knife. It certainly seems stronger than the bedsheets they used in the movie, though. You also wonder if you have the strength to make such a climb.

If you prefer not to trust your fate to a small parachute and all the inherent risk of what is essentially BASE jumping without any training, another company called Rescue Reel offers a device that lets you lower yourself Batman-style from a window as high as 1000 feet. The device consists of a plastic housing containing 1000 feet of Kevlar-reinforced cable with an anchor on one end and at the other end a harness you sit in much like a rock-climber's or window-washer's. The reel features a centrifugal braking system that controls the rate of descent, allowing you to evacuate at the rate of about two seconds per story. The Rescue Reel is just now ready to be introduced to the market at an expected introductory price of about $1500.

More elaborate systems have also been devised and tested, including a system of pods that can be lowered from roof storage down the side of a building to allow rescue or counter-terrorism personnel to ride up the building and evacuees to exit from windows at each level.

For those who reside or work in buildings too tall to jump from but not so tall as to require such elaborate escape technology, it may be wise to invest in a simple means of safe descent, such as a rope ladder or a climbing rope on which you can descend using rappelling gear. For buildings between three and ten or so stories high, this could be a viable and inexpensive option, provided you are sufficiently fit to use such equipment and have the proper training.

You know you could have done it with ease back when you were a kid and climbed trees all the time, but your climbing muscles haven't seen that kind of use in many years.

2:15 AM

Ten minutes have been consumed making the rope. You check the door again and find it warm. The temperature inside the unit is rising. The fire is certainly on your floor on the other side of the hall and perhaps within the hall itself. You realize you may only have seconds before it bursts through the floor beneath you. It's time to go.

Back on the balcony, you see that more people have jumped, but so far there are no bodies on the sidewalk directly below you. That's a good sign that means the fire has not reached the

Consider What Could Happen Wherever You Go

As we saw in Chapter Six, fires are scary enough at ground level and out in the open, where there are usually multiple avenues of escape. But the idea of being caught inside a burning multistory building with fire between you and the ground is truly terrifying. If you are too far up to exit through windows and climb or jump to safety, or the building is too tall or too modern for exterior fire escapes, there are few options—most involving elevators or stairwells inside the building. Escaping such a building along with hundreds or perhaps even thousands of other occupants in a situation where panic is sure to break out is no easy feat, even if you are intimately familiar with the building. It would be even more daunting for a visitor with no knowledge of the layout. Most people who live and work in such environments barely give the danger a second thought. Those of us with active imaginations who think about survival scenarios

units beneath you on this corner of the building. Maybe those below you got out. Now it's time for the scary part, when you must take the leap of faith in the strength of the rope and of your arms, and climb over the edge in an attempt to lower yourself to the next balcony.

The steel railing that spans the opening above a stucco half-wall is made of two-inch-diameter pipe. The ends disappear into the stucco and cement on either side. You can only hope that they are buried far enough in the casement that they won't pull out with your weight. You lower one end of the drapery rope under the rail and pass the midsection of it over the top, lowering the other half so that it is divided evenly, the two ends dangling some 12 or 13 feet below, well past the top of the next railing. You can't tie it to the railing, as you would then

wherever we may travel see it differently, though. Just as the urban dweller who rarely visits the woods may be unduly apprehensive about bears, when I go to the city and find myself in tall buildings, I can't help but think about fires and earthquakes.

But despite the obstacles to getting safely to ground level, many people have escaped from seemingly impossible burning building scenarios—including, of course, the World Trade Center towers after they were struck with airplanes on September 11, 2001. As in any survival situation, a bit of knowledge of what to do can make all the difference, and the accounts of survivors are good source of that knowledge. And if you spend a lot of time in high-rise skyscrapers and you really want to be prepared for anything, the lessons learned in the September 11 attacks have spawned new inventions that can give you additional options (page 214).

have no way to retrieve it and it's only long enough to get you down one story at a time. Instead, you must grasp both halves evenly, keeping it centered on the rail while you climb down, until you can get over the rail onto the next deck below and then pull one end to free it and bring it down to you. You know the method works because you did it with a rope as a kid when lowering yourself from the branches of tall trees.

2:16 AM

You wipe the sweat from your palms and place them both on the steel pipe rail, fingers facing inward to the balcony and one hand on either side of the centered rope. This is the tricky part, and your heart nearly stops as you swing one leg over the rail to straddle it, then center your weight over your palms as you bring the other leg across and lower yourself down to arms' length. You try not to think about the 130 feet of empty space between you and the hard cement below. The two strands of the rope are now right in front of your face and running down below your body. You have to let go with one hand and grab them both, and to decrease your chance of slipping, you lock your

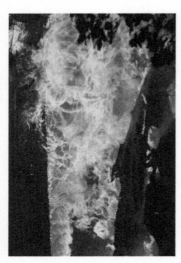

ankles around the two strands. That part goes well, but you know that once your second hand is off the rail, your entire body weight will be on the rope and it will either save you or it will fail and you will die.

You take the chance and make the grab. As soon as you are committed, you waste no time moving down. It's holding, and you hear no ripping sounds. It only takes a few hand-over-hand moves with your feet providing backup until you are low enough to put both feet on the next rail below you. Moving your hands down the rope until you are in a squatting position, you can now jump over onto the deck of the 12th floor balcony.

2:17 AM

From the 12th-floor balcony you pull one end of your makeshift rope so that the other end goes up and over the rail above you, allowing you haul it down onto the patio where you are standing and get it in place for your descent to the next floor. Time is running out. Just a few units over, flames are licking the side of the building from the 11th and 12th floors. Either the unit behind you on the 12th floor balcony was unoccupied, or the occupants escaped or perhaps succumbed to the smoke in the hall. The sliding glass door is shut, and when you push on it, you discover it's locked as well. That's a relief because you have no way to help anyone anyway, and there's no time to delay.

You quickly check the knots in the drapery rope and make sure there are no tears in the fabric. Going over the rail the second time is not as hard as it was the first time now that you know the rope will hold you.

2:18 AM

When you clear the rail and step down onto the 11th floor balcony, you are almost overcome by the heat. The glass is broken in the sliding door and the part of the unit nearest the hall is in flames. Turning your face away from the radiant heat, you yank the rope down from above and get it set so you can go over the rail before the withering heat causes you to lose consciousness.

One more floor down and you are on the 10th floor. It's still approximately 100 feet to the ground. But you don't feel the heat at this level, and there are no flames through the open balcony door. You wonder if the occupants of this unit got out, and you feel they must have, because if the fire started midway down the building on the 10th floor, they would have had time to reach the stairwell after the alarm went off and before smoke filled the hall. You decide it would be wise to go down another level or two before attempting to re-enter the building.

2:19 AM

This time when you go over the rail, you hear the drapery fabric rip as you are about halfway to the 9th floor balcony. The fear that grips you takes your breath away as you carefully continue down in a desperate attempt to get to safety. It wouldn't matter if you fell now or from the full 13 stories where you started—you would be just as dead. But the drapery holds and you make it to the deck of the 9th floor balcony, shaking uncontrollably. As you pull the rope in, you see that the tear that started when you first heard it rip has run nearly halfway across the width of one of the drapery strips. Just a few more inches and you would have been gone. But now you're below the fire. You use a patio chair to break the glass door and enter the unit. It's empty, but there are unpacked suitcases and scattered items on the floor indicating someone left in a hurry. You will have to find you way in the dark, but you are below the flames and the smoke, and confident you can find your way down the stairwell.

TOP TEN TIPS FOR ESCAPING A BURNING BUILDING

1. Know the layout in advance. You should make an effort to know the layout and the exit options for any building you spend time in well before a fire emergency occurs. Even on a one-time visit to a new building, take a minute as you enter to make mental notes of the locations of exits, elevators, and stairwells. In a fire you may have to find them in the dark or in thick smoke.

2. Have a detailed escape plan. If you live or work in a multistory building, you will have plenty of time in advance of an emergency to formulate a detailed plan of action that includes primary and secondary escape routes. Know where the fire alarms are and make sure that they are maintained and working properly. Participate in organized fire drills in advance if possible.

3. Check your escape route for obstacles. Know in advance if there are security bars or other obstacles that will prevent you from escaping through a window. If your plan involves going through a window that cannot be opened fully, keep something close by that you can use to break it if necessary.

4. Climb or drop if feasible. You will most likely survive a jump from three stories or less. You might break and ankle or leg, but it will be better than dying from smoke or flames. Climb as close to the ground as possible, and hang from a ledge and drop rather than jump to decrease the freefall distance by a few feet.

5. Consider investing in an escape device. If you live or work in a tall skyscraper with few options for a quick escape in an emergency, investigate new technologies in building-escape devices, such as reels and parachutes. While such devices may be expensive and frightening to use, they present an alternative to death in certain situations where there is no other reasonable means of escape. A simpler and cheaper option to consider if you are between three and about ten stories up is a climbing rope or rope ladder.

6. React quickly. As soon as you become aware that there is a sign of fire such as the sounding of alarms or the smell of smoke, react quickly and decisively. Don't wait to see what is happening or it may be too late to implement your escape plan.

7. **Avoid elevators.** Resist the urge to use an elevator when caught high up in a multistory building. The elevator could stop on the floor that's on fire or get stuck between floors. An enclosed stairwell inside the building or a fire escape on the outside is a much better bet for reaching the ground floor.

8. **Check doors for heat.** Always feel doors with the back of your hand before you open them. The back of your hand is more sensitive to heat than your palm, and if you get burned, it's better not to burn your palm so you can still grab things. If a door feels hot, there may be flames on the other side.

9. **Cover your mouth and nose.** Use a shirt or towel to cover your mouth and nose to help filter your air and reduce smoke inhalation. Wet the material in advance if possible. Smoke inhalation kills most building fire victims before the flames reach them.

10. **Stay low and crawl.** Staying low and crawling on your hands and knees while moving to your exit will also help reduce smoke inhalation. If there is any available oxygen, it will be close to the floor, while the thickest smoke will fill the upper area of a room.

CHAPTER ELEVEN
MAULED BY A BEAR

You scream in terror and pain as teeth puncture your left shoulder with crushing force. The bear bites hard and then releases you to bite again, getting closer to your neck. You cover your face and throat as much as possible with your other hand as the bear tears at the flesh of your shoulder and upper arm. As it bites down harder, you punch at its face and gouge at its eye with your right hand and try to kick at it and push it away with your knees and feet. The bear has you down on your back, gripping your upper body with its forepaws and straddling you with its hind legs. You hear its deep, savage growls as it tastes your blood and ignores your seemingly futile resistance while it continues to tear at your left shoulder with determination, leaving your right arm free to fight back. At this point, you realize this bear intends to kill you and eat you. It was not a defensive or reactionary attack, and the bear did not leave you alone after knocking you flat and delivering the first bite to your left arm as you tried to go into a submissive position. Fighting back is your only chance, but how are you going to defend yourself against several hundred pounds of muscle, tooth, and claw? How could you end up in this nightmare to begin with?

A North Woods Canoe Trip
You look forward all year to an early fall paddling trip in the Boundary Waters Canoe Area along the border of Minnesota and

Ontario. It's your first time there, but your more experienced friend has mapped out a route sure to take you far from the path of most other paddlers visiting the area. The route leads north of the border and involves overland portages between lakes, assuring several days of the solitude and good fishing you both came here to enjoy. The place has lived up to its promises: It is a North Woods delight, with thousands of jewel-like lakes sprinkled through millions of acres of evergreen forest. You've seen far more wildlife than fellow humans, and along the way you've photographed moose, black bear, and bald eagles.

Your friend has spent years paddling these waters and dismisses your concerns about the large bear population of the area. He says that as long as you keep a clean camp and hang your food out of their reach at night, the black bears that live there are unlikely to come close to people. You are still apprehensive, as this is the first time you've seen bears in the wild,

REAL LIFE | *Fighting Off a Vicious Black Bear Attack*

In September 2010, Bellevue City Councilman John Chelminiak was savagely mauled by a black bear while spending time at his vacation cabin in central Washington. While his wife and daughter were at the cabin, Chelminiak was out walking the family dogs when he heard a rustling in the brush and the exhalation of a bear before it launched right into him without provocation. He ended up wrestling with it to try and keep it from taking him to the ground. Each time he went down he got back to his feet because he felt he had to fight for his life to survive. The struggle turned into a horrendous battle in which Chelminiak remembers hearing the sound of the bear's teeth grating across

even from a distance. You would feel better about the situation if you had at least one gun between the two of you, but taking a firearm into Canada presents far too much hassle, and without a hunting license it's nearly impossible. After the first couple of nights of camping along the evergreen-forested lakeshores of the route, you begin to relax a bit and start to sleep better as thoughts of bears in the night get pushed to the back of your mind by the fun you're having in the daytime.

his scull as it bit him on the head. He kicked and punched at the bear and at some point the attack stopped, leaving him badly injured and soaked in blood. He made his way to the cabin, running up the driveway and yelling "bear" and "call 911." Thinking he was dying, Chelminiak collapsed until he heard his wife yelling for him. She stayed with him and kept watch for the bear in case it returned while they waited for an ambulance to arrive.

Chelminiak lost his left eye but was expected to recover from his other injuries. He was able to hold his own against the bear because it was a relatively small female, weighing only 148 pounds, and in poor condition, as was discovered when wildlife officials tracked it down and shot it. The attack was obviously motivated by hunger and was predatory in nature.

Day 3: Late Afternoon

Your friend enjoys fishing much more than you do, so on the third day, at the most remote lake you'll visit on the route, you tell him to take the canoe out and say that you would rather spend the afternoon doing some hiking and exploring. You take your camera and follow an old path that leads even farther north, connecting this lake to another one some two miles

REAL LIFE | *Bear Attacks Are Increasingly Common*

Perhaps because they are hunted less by man today, or because more people venture into remote territory and encounter bears that are unfamiliar with humans, the number of fatal bear attacks in North America has increased in the last two decades. From 1900 to 1990, there were a total of 40 fatal bear attacks recorded, while from 1990 through the end of summer 2010, 54 known fatal attacks have occurred. Of those 54, brown and grizzly bears were responsible for 27, and black bears accounted for 26, with one death caused by a polar bear. These numbers, of course, are but a fraction of the total number of incidents involving attacks or confrontations, as most are not fatal.

Many of the recent fatal attacks by black bears have been predatory in nature. Some examples include 31-year-old Dr. Jacqueline Perry, who was attacked along with her husband while they were kayaking and camping in a provincial park in northern Ontario. The bear killed Dr. Perry before her husband was able to drive it off by stabbing it with a knife. In Tennessee, a female black bear and her yearling cub killed a 50-year-old hiker named Glenda Ann Bradley in May 2000 in what was the first recorded bear attack fatality in Great Smoky Mountains National Park. The bears had

away. Before leaving, you use the camp axe to cut a stout hiking staff from a hardwood sapling. You don't really need it for walking, it's just that you feel better being "armed." A big stick is better than nothing, at least in your mind.

You reach the other lake and sit on the shore enjoying the solitude until the afternoon sun gets low enough to cast long shadows and you decide it's time to head back to camp. You

partially eaten her and had to be driven away from the body when searchers found her.

In 2006, a six-year-old girl was killed by a black bear in the nearby Cherokee National Forest. The mother was visiting a waterfall with her daughter and two-year-old son when a black bear grabbed the small boy. The mother hit the bear with sticks and rocks, causing it to drop the two-year-old, but it then grabbed the little girl in its mouth and ran into the woods with her. The woman's screams drew other hikers in the area, and eventually they found the bear with the girl's body and one drove it away by shooting it with a small-caliber pistol. The bear was later tracked and killed by authorities.

Both of the bears involved in these fatal Tennessee attacks were healthy and were apparently motivated only by predatory instinct. Similarily, in Utah, an 11-year-old boy was dragged out of his tent and killed by a black bear while camping with his family in Uinta National Forest in 2007. A 31-year-old woman named Robin Kochorek was killed and partially eaten in 2007 by a black bear while mountain biking at Panorama Mountain Resort in British Columbia, and in 2008, 70-year-old Cecile Lavoie was killed and dragged into the woods by a black bear while fishing near her cabin in Quebec.

walk a hundred yards or so back down the path that brought you here before you hear something moving in the dense spruce forest off to your right. Your first thought is that it could be a moose, as it sounds big, but then you see something black, moving slowly. You stop and strain to see what it is through the thick growth, but whatever it is has also stopped moving. A bit

What Should You Do if Confronted or Attacked by a Bear?

Every bear attack is different. Bears are generally intelligent creatures that adapt well and come up with surprisingly creative solutions to problems, like how to steal food from campers. It's true that many people spend years hiking and camping in bear country without an encounter, and on most long wilderness trips you are unlikely to even catch a glimpse of one in the wild. Most of the bears you do see will run away from you, and the few that do not may regard you with curiosity or indifference before continuing to go about their business. But one thing is certain: All bears are dangerous, no matter how cute and furry they may appear.

The nature of the confrontation will have a lot to do with how you should react and what you can expect might happen. If you surprise a bear by suddenly getting too close to it or its food supply, or if you happen to get too close to a sow bear with cubs, the bear will be defensive, and may attack to eliminate what it perceives as a threat. In this situation, you *must not* come across as aggressive or challenging. You must show that you are submissive if you want to survive. Be especially careful to avoid a bear that has made a kill or taken an animal carcass killed by hunters. Bears are omnivorous and just as likely to feed on berries as meat, but when they have a fresh kill, they will aggressively defend it.

nervous, you resume walking but at a slower pace, still look-ing in the direction of the sound. Movement catches your eye and you stop again. This time, whatever it is keeps walking, and it's coming closer to you. You squat down to see under the low-hanging branches, and then it comes into view among the shadows. It's a large bear!

A different type of confrontation occurs when bears associate humans with food, not in a predatory way, but be-cause they have learned that campers and hikers carry lots of goodies. Bears looking to steal food may come into a camp at night, or even threaten hikers on a trail in broad daylight. Some will break into cars or houses to get at an easy source of food. In this kind of encounter, you may have to aggres-sively drive the bear away, as it can hurt you inadvertently in its attempt to get your food, especially if it comes through the walls of your tent in the night. Many bear attacks occur this way, and if you find yourself in this situation, do all you can to try to frighten the bear or fight back.

The rarest type of bear confrontation is the predatory attack, in which the bear hunts or stalks you, intending to make a meal out of you. Most bears don't think of humans as food, but taking an adult human is easily within their capabilities. This kind of attack is more common with black bears than with the larger grizzly or Alaskan brown bear, although there are occasionally incidents like this with all species of bears. In this kind of predatory confrontation, the bear will persistently follow you and may attack before you even know it is stalking you. The charge will not be a bluff and it may not assume a threatening posture beforehand. In this situation, fight back with anything and everything you have. You must convince the bear that you are no easy prey.

Your grip on the stick in your hand tightens as you peer through the branches trying to get a better look at the bear. It's still a hundred feet or more away. You decide that maybe it's just curious and it won't get any closer, so maybe you'd better keep moving away. You take a few steps along the trail and stop to look again. The bear has matched your pace. It is walking slowly and quietly, staying among the spruce trees but keeping up with you, parallel to the trail. When you stop moving, it stops too, staring at you intently. Then it starts coming toward you even though you are no longer moving. You don't want to let it out of your sight, so you back slowly away, trying not to make any

Stand Your Ground

One thing all bear experts agree on is that you should not run when confronted by a bear. It's a race you won't win, no matter how fast and fit you are. Bears may appear awkward and slow because of their great size and weight and their clumsy-looking movement patterns, but when they want to, even big grizzlies can run up to 30 miles per hour. One study showed that in 83 percent of cases where a person chose to run from a bear, the bear gave chase, often attacking and mauling the runner. Running is a message to the bear that you are weak and might even be good for lunch.

Your first line of defense in any bear confrontation is standing your ground. This shows strength, which the bear may respect. You are telling it that you may be smaller, but you are unafraid, and attacking you could cause it pain as well. Standing your ground doesn't mean you should challenge the bear, unless all else fails. Avoid staring directly into its eyes, as this may be interpreted as a confrontation. If it doesn't lose interest and leave at this point, try speaking to it in a low voice while backing away slowly. This shows

sudden movements. You can see it clearly now, as it emerges from the thicket. It's a huge black bear, obviously fully grown and probably a male.

About now you wish that you had not walked this far from camp alone. You know it wouldn't do any good to shout for your friend; even if he is off the lake and back in camp, it's still too far away for your voice to carry. You try backing down the trail some more. The bear stays where it is. This is encouraging and you take more backward steps. When the bear does not follow, you start to think that maybe it has satisfied its curiosity and doesn't want anything else to do with you. You turn to walk at

that you do not wish to fight without sending the message that you are afraid, and it gives the animal a way out without relinquishing its dominance. But sometimes no matter what you do, the bear may still want to challenge you by growling and popping its teeth and possibly even making bluff charges at you that stop short or deliberately miss. It will be hard to resist running at this point, but you must.

If the charge is not a bluff and the bear makes contact, your first action should be to protect your face and neck while trying to curl up into a fetal position as you are knocked down. The bear may not even bite you if you are still and it thinks you are no longer a threat. Considering the power they have to do horrendous damage, many victims of bear attacks come out with only superficial wounds and scratches. If the bear does begin biting you and continues despite your submissive posture, you must fight back with everything you have to try and drive it away. Focus on hitting its head, eyes, or nostrils with anything at hand and try to protect your head, neck, and other vulnerable areas from a fatal bite.

a normal pace, looking over your shoulder every few steps. After covering a hundred yards or more, you think you are in the clear when you look again and see the bear following you down the trail!

When you turn to face it, it keeps coming, moving forward with a confident, determined pace. It stops again 30 feet away from you. You try talking to it, telling it to go away in a soothing voice as you grip the heavy hiking stick with both hands. It takes a few steps forward, and you raise the stick in a defensive position as you step back by the same distance. Now you are *really* wishing it was a high-powered rifle instead of a piece of wood!

You are shouting, yelling at the bear and telling it to get out of here. It just looks at you impassively. As big as it is, you know that it's accustomed to doing whatever it wants, and there's

REAL LIFE | *Attacked by a Bear in Her Own Home*

Most bear attacks happen out in the wilderness where bears are in their natural environment and far outnumber humans. But as new developments encroach into areas surrounded by forests or other wildlands, news reports of dangerous wildlife such as mountain lions and bears roaming into suburban neighborhoods seem to be more common all the time. Usually, such prowling bears don't cause any trouble, other than maybe tearing up garbage cans to get at food scraps.

In areas with large bear populations like the 20,000 black bears that roam the state of Minnesota, frequent encounters with humans are bound to occur. But despite this, 37-year-old Kim Heil-Smith was not expecting to be

nothing in these woods it needs to fear. You fight the urge to turn and bolt down the trail to your camp. You know from seeing many nature documentaries on television that trying to run from a bear is a bad idea, and that it will only incite a pursuit that no human can hope to outpace. But it's hard to stand your ground in the face of such a fearsome threat. You yell louder and take another step back, holding the stick like a five-foot-long baseball bat, ready to whack the animal in the head as hard as you can if it keeps coming. But with another step back, you stumble over a rock. That's when the bear charges—launching into a blur of motion you'd have no hope of reacting to in time even if you had not lost your balance—and it's on you so fast the next thing you feel is its encircling paws grabbing you as its crushing weight takes you to the ground on your back.

attacked by a bear in her home near Grand Marais when she went out into her garage one night in 2003 to get something out of the car. She was talking on a cordless phone when she opened the door to the garage and found it occupied by a female bear and her cub, probably looking for food in the garbage. The adult bear was between Kim and her car and had nowhere to go. It grabbed her and took her down despite her attempts to shut the door on it. In her account of the incident she claimed she was scared at first, but then got mad about the bear being in her house and struck and grabbed its nose and yelled at it to leave, which it did, but not before doing significant damage. Her wounds were not life-threatening, but the scratches and punctures left her kitchen floor covered in blood and required many stitches when the paramedics got her to the hospital.

One Minute into the Attack

The bear continues to focus on mauling your left shoulder. You are aware of the pain, but the terror of what's happening to you keeps you from focusing on how badly it hurts. The only thing

The Differences among Bear Species

If you should ever have a dangerous encounter with a bear, it may just save your life to know what kind of bear you're dealing with and how it's likely to behave.

Black Bear Although many people regard the black bear as much less dangerous than the brown or grizzly bear, black bears can and do kill people. Although they are the smallest of the North American bears, a full-grown male can weigh 550 pounds. Attacks seem to be more often motivated by hunger  and the association of humans with food rather than territorial or reactionary. If you are attacked by one, it is essential to fight back rather than play dead, because if it starts biting you and you are not moving, it may begin eating. In identifying them, you should also be aware that not all black bears are black, and brown or cinnamon-colored varieties are common in the Rockies and other areas of the West.

Grizzly and Brown Bear The grizzly bear is simply a variety of the widespread species of bears collectively called brown bears, which range throughout northwestern North America including Alaska and much of western Canada, as well as most of Siberia and parts of Northern Europe. These huge bears are often completely indifferent to man. They are the world's largest land carnivores, and whether they attack or run away depends mostly on what kind of mood they're in. The best policy around brown bears is to keep your distance

that matters now is to get this animal to stop and to get it off of you. You bring one knee up into its underbelly with as much force as you can muster. It seems to have no effect, but you keep at it, each time trying to strike harder. At the same time,

and avoid surprising one. Females are notorious for aggressively defending their cubs against any perceived threat.

Since this type of attack is reactionary rather than predatory, playing dead often works well with grizzlies, which is a good thing, since fighting back would be even more hopeless. A big male grizzly can weigh more than a thousand pounds. The biggest Alaskan brown bears weigh as much as 1700 pounds and reach a length of nine feet. Because of their great size and weight, any attack is dangerous, even if the bear doesn't really want to hurt you. Their weight alone can kill you, never mind the three-inch-long claws and crushing teeth.

Polar Bear The polar bear is the most dangerous of all bears, because it makes no distinction between humans and its regular prey of seals. A polar bear is a supreme predator perfectly adapted to its Arctic environment and extremely

difficult to escape from or stop if it wants to eat you. Until the introduction of firearms, the native people of the North lived in constant fear of polar bears, which have long been known to stalk and hunt humans. Polar bears can weigh over 1000 pounds and reach nine feet in length, standing five feet at the shoulder when on all fours.

Fortunately, their habitat is limited to the far north beyond the areas that most people frequent recreation. If you are an Arctic traveler or adventurer, however, you should be armed with a rifle capable of stopping a determined polar bear. A polar bear will outpace a human on ice or in the water.

you reach with your right hand to the bear's face, feeling until your fingers find its left eye. You push against its face as hard as you can with your thumb digging into the eyeball, which it the only vulnerable spot where you can have any effect. You dig in harder as you continue to pummel at its belly with your knee.

Should You Carry Bear Spray or a Firearm?

Before modern high-powered firearms, people who coexisted with big bears usually left them alone and maintained a healthy fear of them. Today, few people who pack a firearm in bear country would ever want to have to use it to destroy a bear in its own habitat. Still, having a weapon capable of stopping anything that walks is a comforting feeling when you come upon huge bear tracks in the mud.

If you carry a firearm for bear defense, make sure it is adequately powerful and that you can use it with skill. The worst thing you can do is shoot a bear with an anemic caliber that will only serve to enrage it. A 12-gauge shotgun loaded with slugs is considered by many to be one of the best weapons for bear defense. Hard-hitting rifles like the .45-70, the .450 Marlin, and the .454 Casull—all available in short, lightweight lever-action carbines—are more accurate than shotguns and can take down the largest bears. Some people carry large-caliber handguns instead, but you have to be even more expert at shooting to get the shot placement you need with a handgun. No handgun matches the power of a big-bore rifle and none will give you as much security. If you choose to carry a handgun, make it at least a .44 Magnum. Rifle and handgun bullets should be chosen for weight and penetration rather than expansion.

If you do find yourself in a bear confrontation and you are armed, make certain that it is really going to charge

The bear releases its grip on your shoulder and shakes its head to get your thumb out of its eye.

Seeing an opportunity, you push yourself away from it with your foot, sliding on your back until you are out from under its body. Growling in rage, the bear realizes you are trying to escape

before you shoot. If you can't prove it was self-defense, you can be subject to heavy fines for killing a bear protected by wildlife laws. More importantly, a botched shot that only wounds the animal will almost certainly provoke a charge, or cause it to run off where it might later become a killer because of its wound. If you do have to shoot once it has decided to attack, remain calm and make the shot count, because you may have time for only one before it is on you. Not everyone can stay this cool under pressure, and this is why many bear experts say you are better off carrying pepper spray.

Pepper spray formulated for bear defense has proven to be highly effective at stopping bear attacks, with up to a 94 percent success rate. The success rate for firearm defense against bears, by contrast, is only 65 percent, likely due to the greater difficulty of bringing a firearm into action quickly and accurately while under stress. Bear spray comes in a big can and when released makes a sudden, loud hissing sound, creating a billowing cloud of burning orange capsaicin mist that is effective out to 30 feet or so. Even the largest cans are lightweight and compact compared to firearms. Most come with holsters that can be clipped on a belt or pack strap, and these should be used to keep the spray readily accessible.

Having a weapon of deterrence will give you the confidence you need to stand your ground when faced with a bear.

and bites down hard on your left knee. Then it begins backing up on all fours, dragging you helplessly into the woods beside the trail. You claw at the ground with your one good hand, grabbing for anything to hold onto, but find nothing until your fingers slide across a baseball-sized lump of granite rock.

Two Minutes into the Attack

You scream at the top of your lungs as you feel the jaws of the bear crush the bones and tear the ligaments in your knee. As it drags you on your back, its strength makes you feel like you are being pulled into the trailside brambles and leaves by

A Scary Encounter in the Night

The prospect of getting attacked, possibly killed, and even eaten by a large carnivore inspires a primal fear that is unmatched by just about anything else that can happen when venturing into a wild place. This is a fear that keeps many people from going out into the woods, especially overnight. When darkness falls and every crackling leaf or breaking twig could be an approaching bear, it's hard to relax and even harder to get any sleep.

Those of us who have spent a lot of time alone in the mountains or forests where bears are more numerous than humans have certainly had moments of apprehension caused by encounters with these unpredictable animals. Though I've never been attacked, I had the fright of my life one pitch-black night while camping alone beside a stream in a remote Appalachian Mountain wilderness area. Used to spending a lot of time alone, I didn't give much thought to bears when I set up my tent, other than to hang my food bag out of their reach. But around 4:00 in the morning, I was awakened from pleasant dreams by deep growling just

a truck. You can't believe how determined this attack is, and if you had any doubts at first, you know for sure that this bear sees you as prey and will not stop short of killing you unless you can defend yourself. You only hope is the chunk of rock in your hand. When the bear pauses for a moment in its backward shuffle, you pull yourself into a sitting position so you can reach far enough to use the rock as a bludgeon to smash into the side of its head with all the force you can muster. It responds by shaking its head with your knee still clenched in its teeth, sending shockwaves of pain up your leg, but you draw back and strike again. After three blows with enough force to hurt your hand

inches from my head on the other side of the thin nylon of the tent door. I could feel the hot breath of the bear on my face, but it was so dark I literally could not see my hand in front of my eyes. The bear did not come through the tent to get me, but instead trashed my campsite, growling and breaking small saplings as it stomped around outside while I huddled in the middle of the tent trying not to make a sound. I was unarmed at the time and a full day's hike from even a dirt road. When the sounds stopped, I didn't know where the bear was, but all I could do was wait until daylight when I could see well enough to leave the area. I think it was upset by my intrusion iton its territory, but I don't know for sure. That particular wilderness area is one of the places where wildlife officials relocate problem bears from the nearby Smoky Mountains National Park. Despite this scary encounter, I have spent countless nights sleeping outdoors alone in both black bear and grizzly country without incident, and would never let the threat of bears keep me from exploring an interesting place.

where you are gripping the rock, the bear lets go and steps back away from you. It shakes its head and you see blood that is not yours dripping from the area behind its eye. The sharp-edged rock concentrated the force of your strikes and did some damage. Your own blood is soaking the evergreen needles of the forest floor, but you are afraid to put down the rock to use your good hand to try and stop the flow. The bear is still only a few feet away, and appears indecisive about what it will do next.

Four Minutes into the Attack

It feels as if both your heart and time itself have stopped as the bear shakes off the effect of your blows to its head and circles around to try and get behind you. You slide around on the ground, trying to keep your feet between it and your upper body, while clenching your rock—the only weapon you have— with a white-knuckle grip. It glares at you while growling menacingly, and you are certain that another attack is imminent. You yell at it to go away, cursing it and screaming and threatening to crush its skull if it gets any closer, though you know the chances of that are slim.

Suddenly another sound rings through the forest—a sound you can't believe you are hearing that breaks the bear's intent gaze and causes it to take a step back and cock its head to listen. It's the sound of your name being called. Your friend is yelling your name and you scream back at the top of your lungs that you need help. The bear backs away a few more steps as your friend comes running down the trail and bursts upon the scene. Taking in what is happening in a glance, he yells at the bear and throws several rocks that hit it as he gets closer to your side. With two of you to deal with, the bear decides it has had enough of the pummeling with rocks and turns to disappear back into the forest.

TOP TEN TIPS FOR SURVIVING A BEAR ATTACK

1. **Know your bears.** Know how to identify the different species of bears, as the behavioral patterns are different and they react differently to particular situations. Know their habitat preferences and the best way to avoid confrontations with the types of bears you will most likely encounter in any given location. The best course of action for you to take when threatened or attacked also depends on the species of bear.

2. **Make a lot of noise.** You can avoid most surprise encounters with bears by simply making a lot of noise when traveling in bear country. Talk, sing, whistle, or attach a bear bell to your belt or pack to alert any bears in the area that you are coming. They will usually clear out before you even see them. Many attacks occur because a person startles a bear from close range.

3. **Keep a clean camp.** Don't lure bears to your campsite by leaving food out or in your tent. When camping in bear country, do your cooking well away from your sleeping site, and wash all dishes carefully, and dispose of food scraps far away. If you are hunting or fishing, don't field dress game or clean fish near your camp. Before going to bed, hang all food far from the reach of climbing bears by suspending a line between two trees, or use bear-proof containers.

4. **Keep your distance, but don't run.** If you see a bear in the wild, don't approach any closer for a better look or a photograph, especially if you see young cubs. Keep your distance and slowly back away. Don't even try to outrun a determined bear, as that may incite the predatory instinct in the bear and cause an attack. Black bears can climb trees easily, and grizzlies can, too, if they really want to. A big grizzly can also reach 10 feet or more up a tree with its hind feet on the ground.

5. **Know the warning signs.** A bear that sees you may be frightened and run away, or may appear indifferent and then attack without warning. You can get a clue to its mood by signs of agitation, such as swaying its head, huffing, clacking teeth, or laying its ears back. A bear may stand on its hind legs to get a better view, but this is

not always a sign of aggression. The rare predatory bear may stalk or follow you without a sound or any indication of aggression.

6. **Don't appear threatening.** Assume a non-threatening posture. Do not make direct eye contact. Instead, turn sideways and use your peripheral vision to keep an eye on the bear. If slowly backing away agitates the bear, stop moving. Try talking to it in a calm voice.

7. **Use bear deterrent spray.** Even if you are armed with a firearm, always carry a powerful pepper spray rated for bear defense in a place where you can get to it immediately. You may be knocked down by a bear before you have a chance to use another weapon. Bear deterrent spray is proven as an effective means of preventing most attacks and is legal to carry in many areas where firearms are not, as well as easier to use under the stress of a charge.

8. **Carry an adequate firearm.** If you are spending a lot of time in prime habitat for grizzly or brown bears, such as the Alaska bush, carry a firearm with the power to stop a charging bear. A large-caliber rifle such as the Marlin Guide Gun in .45-70 or a 12-gauge shotgun loaded with slugs is better than any handgun for this purpose. But remember that no firearm will do you any good unless it is loaded and you can bring it into action quickly.

9. **Know when not to fight back.** If the bear attacks because you startled it or intruded into its territory, or because it is a female with cubs nearby, it may simply want to eliminate what it perceives as a threat. When it makes contact, protect your chest and abdomen by falling to the ground on your stomach or assuming a fetal position while covering the back of your neck with your hands. Don't move until the bear leaves you alone. It may be content to knock you down or bite once or twice.

10. **Know when to fight back.** If a bear attacks after stalking you or attacks in the night, it may be a predatory attack where you are seen as food. In this type of attack, you must not play dead, but try to escape or fight back with anything at hand. Use rocks, branches, or anything you can get while shouting and trying to intimidate the bear to let it know you are not easy prey.

CHAPTER TWELVE
BRACING FOR IMPACT

Your grip on the seat back in front of you strains every muscle and tendon from your fingers to your shoulders as you stare out from your window seat at the ground getting closer and closer. Endless subdivision tracts spread out below you and you're now close enough to see what kinds of cars are parked in the driveways and how the backyards are landscaped around the swimming pools. This is a sight you've seen countless times on every return flight to L.A. International, but this time it is not a routine landing. You are minutes away from experiencing your first plane crash and maybe from the end of your life.

You squeeze the seat harder as the cold sweat runs down your forehead and you wonder what it's going to feel like to die. Although the pilot has tried to reassure everyone on board that it will be a "hard landing" or, at worst, "a controlled crash" and that everyone will come through fine, you have little confidence that this will end well. A Boeing 727 is not designed to land on its belly without the landing gear deployed. You are almost certain that if it doesn't break up on impact, it will catch on fire and burn or explode from the friction of sliding across the tarmac at over 140 miles per hour. How could you have ended up in such a helpless situation with no control of your own destiny?

Just Another Routine Business Flight

You travel a lot with your job and flying is routine for you. It's never really bothered you except that you don't like being herded on and off crowded planes like so many cattle and you don't like the frequent delays that are seemingly more common every year. Of course, you've given some thought to the possibility

What Are the Odds?

Just how dangerous is air travel? What are the odds you'll ever end up in a plane crash to begin with, and if you do, how likely is it that you'll survive? We've all heard that statistically, it's safer to fly than to drive, but never mind statistics—when you're behind the wheel of your own vehicle, you usually feel in control of the situation. Step aboard a 200,000-pound jet airliner cruising at 600 miles per hour some 30 to 40,000 feet above the earth, and you're placing a lot of faith in technology, the competence of the pilot and the maintenance crews, and many other variables beyond your control. A lot can go wrong when those kinds of speeds and forces are involved, but accidents are surprisingly few and far between considering the number of flights taking place around the world every day.

Your safety in the air is also dependant upon where you are flying. The statistics show that air travel in the U.S. is quite significantly safer than anywhere else in the world. According to an MIT professor who is a leading expert on aviation safety, your chances of dying on your next U.S. flight are only 1 in 35 million. Those odds go up to 1 in 10 million for international flights in the industrialized "first" world, Europe for example. But if you fly in developing or "third-world" countries, such as most of Africa, your odds of death soar to one in two million. It's also a fact that some airlines

of a plane crash. Who has ever flown on a big jet without mar-
veling at the speed and power, and thinking about how much
could potentially go wrong on an aircraft that is so dependent
upon those powerful engines?

You've been through a couple of rough landings in bad
weather when you wondered whether or not the pilot was still

are safer than others. Because of their safety record, more
than 160 airlines are on a black list in the European Union,
meaning they are not allowed to fly into or out of EU countries. These include carriers registered in such places as
Sudan, Angola, and Rwanda.

So if your odds of being on a plane that crashes are
reassuringly low, what about your odds of survival if you do
happen to be on one of the very few commercial airliners that
goes down? You might think that a plane crash means you
are doomed to certain death, but that's far from the truth.
You actually have a good chance of surviving, as statistics
show that 95.7 percent of passengers make it out of aviation accidents alive. Most of these accidents are considered
"survivable crashes." Occasionally, there are also extraordinary stories of people living through crashes that would
seem certain to kill everyone on board. An example of this
was mentioned in Chapter Two, in the description of how
Juliane Koepcke lived through a midair explosion that left her
literally free-falling thousands of feet into the jungle canopy,
still strapped to her seat. Surviving this kind of crash seemingly has no logical explanation and leans more toward the
miraculous. But Koepcke was not the only one. It seems that
children are more likely to survive such a fall, and in a couple
of recent crashes the lone survivor has been a single child.

in control and if the jet was going to stop before running out of runway, but none of these caused more than a few seconds of anxiety. And like everyone else who flies, you've watched the news footage of burning wrecks and seen the reports of airline disasters in which every person on board died. You occasionally think about past terrorist attacks and seizures of airliners in flight, both the successful ones and the ones that were thwarted

REAL LIFE | *A Single Survivor in a Crash That Kills Everyone Else*

It's hard to imagine how and why just one person can survive a plane crash that kills everyone else on board, but this has happened at least 15 times in the last 40 years according to data collected by one researcher. In the case of Juliane Koepcke (page 38), the turboprop aircraft she was traveling on was destroyed by a lightning strike. Her mother was among the 91 other passengers on board, all of whom were killed.

Much more recently, in June of 2009, a 13-year-old girl named Bahia Bakari survived a Yemini Air Airbus crash into the Indian Ocean in which all of the 152 other passengers perished. She somehow lived through the impact and managed to cling to debris in stormy seas full of oil, floating luggage, debris, and the dead bodies of her fellow passengers. She hung on alone in shark-infested waters for several hours before being picked up by rescuers. She was suffering from hypothermia, but her only injuries resulting from the crash were a broken collarbone and cuts on her face. She later said she was somehow thrown out of the doomed Airbus 310 and found herself in the water beside it. Her father was truly amazed at her survival, saying she was not a good swimmer and was very shy and nonassertive. He

by the crew or passengers, and you wonder how well you would react in a similar situation.

But none of these thoughts stays with you long, and usually you spend your in-flight time reading a new novel or getting some work done on your laptop. Today's flight is no different, but the clock in the bottom corner of your computer screen tells you that you should be on the final approach into Los An-

would have never thought her capable of surviving such a crash, and simply accepted that it "must be God's will."

Another Airbus, Afriqiyah Airways Flight 771, crashed upon landing on May 12, 2010, at Tripoli Airport in Libya, killing all of its 11 crew members and 93 of the 94 passengers on board. The single survivor in this case was a nine-year old Dutch boy named Ruben van Assouw, who suffered broken legs but no life-threatening injuries. Ruben lost his mother, father, and older brother in the crash. Like the other two survivors mentioned above, Ruben was somehow flung clear of the aircraft upon impact. The fuselage of the Airbus virtually disintegrated during the crash, probably killing everyone else on board instantly.

Such escapes are often termed "miraculous," which is probably an apt description. There's just not much you can do to increase your chances of being thrown clear in such a crash. The forces involved in such an impact are nearly indescribable. Wearing your seat belt is considered the best thing you can do if there is any chance of a crash or hard landing. Juliane Koepcke was wearing hers, and during her free fall she remained strapped to a row of seats the whole way down, so no one can say that it would be safer not to wear one.

geles by now. Instead, the airplane is circling the city. You close the laptop and look out the window, wondering what the delay is this time: inclement weather, ground control traffic congestion, airline crew shifts? It seems that landing delays like this are happening a lot at the busiest airports—but it's just another aggravation that goes along with your job.

REAL LIFE | *Real Cases of Landing Gear Failure on Commercial Airlines*

Jet airliners can slow down quite a bit from their normal cruising speed when approaching the runway for a landing, but they still have to maintain enough speed to prevent stalling and to maintain sufficient airflow over the control surfaces. This typically means at least 110 knots (126.5 miles per hour) of airspeed (significantly more for some designs) when touchdown occurs. Even at this greatly reduced speed, stresses on the landing gear are tremendous, and in the event of a landing-gear failure, the aircraft can slide a long way before friction brings it to a stop. During this slide, it can catch on fire from the friction, or flip or cartwheel on the runway and break up. Just because the crash occurs on the ground does not mean that it is any less deadly, and many such crash landings have killed in everyone on board. Until the aircraft comes to a complete stop, the crash isn't over, and until you get out and get away from it, you are not safe.

In 2010, two commercial airliner landings made the news because of the skill of their crews, who in both cases brought their aircraft down safely with only part of the landing gear deployed. In September 2010, Delta Airlines Flight 4951 was diverted to JFK Airport after the crew discovered that the right wheel was jammed in the

3:25 PM

There hasn't been an announcement from the cockpit yet concerning the delay, so you ask a passing flight attendant how much longer it's going to be before landing. You had plans to meet a friend for dinner, and if this goes on much longer,

up position. The pilot warned the 63 passengers and crew to "brace for landing" before he brought the CRJ900 jet to a skidding stop on the runway in a shower of sparks. No one was injured but everyone on board certainly had some nervous moments.

Earlier in 2010, United Airlines Flight 634 experienced a similar problem on its approach to Newark Liberty International Airport. The plane was approaching the runway when it pulled up again and began circling the airport. When the pilot announced an issue with part of the landing gear and told them to prepare for a crash landing, 48 terrified passengers crouched in their seats to await their fate. But despite missing part of the gear, the pilot skillfully brought the jet to a stop after the belly of the fuselage scraped down the runway. Everyone on board made it off OK.

A landing gear failure of a Boeing 737 that occurred in Yogyakarta, Indonesia, in 2007 did not turn out so well. In this case, the front gear failed catastrophically when the wheels snapped off upon touchdown, sending the airliner careening off the runway. It burst into flames when the fuel tanks in the right wing ruptured. Once the wreckage came to a stop in a rice paddy, 117 battered and bloody survivors escaped, but 21 people were killed. Those who died were trapped inside the wreck when it caught fire.

you're going to be late. The flight attendant doesn't know, but says there should be an update from the pilot soon. You put the computer back in its bag and look at your watch again, wishing you didn't work for a company that makes you travel on low-budget airlines.

3:40 PM

After 15 more frustrating minutes of not knowing what's going on and assuming it's just the usual traffic control problem, with many other airliners likely in a holding pattern waiting to land as well, a chilling announcement comes from the cockpit. The pilot says that he wants to inform everyone that there is a problem with the aircraft's landing gear, and that they are trying to come up with a solution but it's not looking good. Immediately after he says this, there is a murmur of worried conversation throughout the passenger cabin that is interrupted when the pilot continues speaking. He goes on to say that there options for getting the plane back on the ground but that it may require a "hard" landing. He assures everyone on board that they are doing everything they can to resolve the problem, and that he will provide updates as they become available.

Hearing this, you look outside nervously from your window seat at the sprawling city below. The plane is a few thousand feet above the ground at this point, and you wonder how long it can fly before they have to bring it down because of the fuel supply. The flight originated in New York, so you know it must be

getting on the low side. You glance around you and take note of where the closest exit door is for the first time since you boarded the flight. You fly so much that you have long ignored the safety briefings given by the flight attendants on every flight as it taxis out to the tarmac for take-off. Now you see that you are not really so close to an exit. Counting the rows, it is seven rows forward to the nearest one. You are boxed into your window seat on the full flight by a young couple returning from a trip to visit family. They are occupying the aisle and middle seats of your row, but it's a relief that they are in good shape and will be able to move quickly. You

discuss the situation with them and the three of you agree to work together.

The other passengers around you are reacting in different ways. Most are talking excitedly and looking nervous. Others are in worse shape—trembling with fear, sobbing, or hugging their loved ones as they try to reassure each other. One man near the front of the cabin is getting belligerent and arguing with a flight attendant, demanding to be allowed to go forward to the cockpit to talk to the pilot.

You don't really know what to do at this point, other than to pass your computer case over to the young man in the aisle seat and ask him to put it in the overhead bin, out of your way. The flight attendants are telling everyone to do the same, and are hurriedly scanning the areas around the passenger seats for loose baggage as they urge everyone to quickly stow their things and get seated and strapped into their seat belts.

3:45 PM

The flight attendants are trying to reassure everyone in the passenger cabin that the aircraft is still under control and that the pilot is very experienced and will be able to get the plane on the ground safely. They go through the location of the emergency exits and the evacuation procedures that will be used to get everyone off the plane quickly once it comes to complete stop. They are not showing any fear themselves as they urge everyone to remain calm and resist the urge to panic, which will only

How Can You Increase Your Chances in Advance of a Crash?

There has long been a lot of discussion about which area of seating is the safest place on an airliner. It appears that you have about a 40 percent better chance of living through a crash if you're near the tail of the aircraft rather than the front. All of this depends upon the exact nature of the crash, as the impact area is different in each situation. One thing that is certain is that the closer you are sitting to an exit, whether front, middle, or back, the better your odds of living through a survivable crash. In many crashes, a large number of people survive the initial impact only to succumb to smoke inhalation or flames because they are unable to escape fast enough. Be aware of passengers between you and the nearest exit, especially those with small children, those with handicaps, or the elderly. You may have to assist those who are not as strong or as fast as you before you can get out yourself.

There are a few other things you can do to increase your odds of getting through a survivable plane crash. For one, wear clothing that allows freedom of movement and at the same time gives you some protection. Don't fly in high heels or sandals, for instance, and avoid synthetics like nylon that can melt in the heat of a fire. Avoid dangerous items like pens and pencils in your clothing that could increase your injuries in a crash. If a crash is imminent, remove eyeglasses, dentures, or other items that could come loose. Empty your bladder if at all possible to decrease the chance of serious internal injury in the impact. Prepare a cloth to function as a

make things worse. The man who was arguing with them earlier is now back in his seat. Some passengers are still crying, but at the moment there are no outbursts. Others are praying quietly or holding hands with their loved ones. You focus on your

smoke filter to hold over your mouth by wetting it in advance. If there is time to think about what you will do once you're outside the plane, get the appropriate clothing for the environment from your carry-on, and also take any medications you will need, but leave the luggage on the plane.

When bracing for the impact, cover your head with a pillow if possible. Make sure your seat belt is secure and in the correct position over your hips. Brace yourself by crossing your arms, palms forward, on the seat back in front of you with your head against your crossed wrists, and slide your feet forward until they touch the seat legs in front of you, so they won't snap forward on impact. Or cross your arms over your calves and grab your ankles.

If you live through the impact, get out as fast as you can. Many will just sit there, and even the flight attendants may fail to give directions in the shock of the aftermath. Don't wait until the plane fills with smoke or flames. Undo your seat belt, get out of your seat, and leave your hands free to use them to climb over bodies or luggage. Climb over the seat backs if you must. Don't push passengers in front of you, as it won't be any faster, and you may get punched or taken down only to be trampled in the rush when others behind you panic and run for the exits.

Jump feet-first into the escape chute at the exit if it is available. Don't waste time trying to sit down and slide. Once you're on the ground, get as far away from the aircraft as you can as quickly as possible.

view out the window, leaving your seatmates alone with each other. You can overhear their conversation, and since they seem relatively composed given the circumstances, you don't want to bother them by talking about the situation.

The pilot's voice comes back over the intercom system to announce that the reason the aircraft is still circling the airport at the same altitude is that he wants to burn off most of the remaining fuel on board, reserving just enough for the landing. He explains that the fuel level is already low from the transcontinental flight, but that every bit of excess weight that can be shed will reduce the landing distance needed and allow him to bring the aircraft to a stop faster. The extra time spent circling will also allow more time for planning and for the airport's fire department to cover a large area on and around the runway with a layer of

A Plane Crash Can Put You in Any Situation

Despite the fact that flying has become so routine for many of us that we hardly give it any thought, when an aircraft of any type goes down, it still makes the news, and often causes us to contemplate what it would be like to live through or die in a plane crash.

Travelers board airplanes fully expecting to arrive safely at their destinations, but when things go wrong, a plane going down in a harsh environment can cast almost anyone into the most dire circumstances described in other chapters in this book. Those who make it through the initial impact alive may then find themselves in a situation like Juliane Koepcke (alone in trackless jungle, Chapter Two), Lauren Elder (high on a snow-covered mountain, Chapter Seven), or like Steve Callahan (adrift in the open ocean on a life raft, Chapter Nine). Like the survivors of Uruguayan

fire-retardant foam. His voice is calm and reassuring, and he says that he and the copilot have been trained for such scenarios.

4:05 PM

It's been 20 excruciatingly long minutes since there's been an announcement from the cockpit. Something is changing now, though, as you feel the aircraft dropping in altitude and hear a change in the sound of the engines. Looking out the window, you see an endless landscape of suburbs and strip malls interconnected by streets jammed with traffic. The drivers are oblivious to the drama that is taking place overhead in what to them is just another passing jet. You would give anything to be sitting in a city traffic jam about now. Instead, you feel your stomach tighten into knots as the details below come into clearer focus

Air Force Flight 571, which crashed into the Andes in 1972, passengers who live through plane crashes can end up in some of the most remote locations on earth, simply because many commercial flight paths traverse these areas.

But regardless of where it happens, no one who flies on commercial aircraft wants to experience a plane crash, even a controlled one on an airport runway. The closest I've come to being in a crash was a botched landing in a Cessna 182 at an airport in Honduras. The pilot bounced the aircraft too hard onto the tarmac, somehow causing the tail to lift suddenly and the prop to come within inches of hitting the ground and causing the plane to flip. We bounced and swerved down the runway mostly out of control until at last it came to rest. Even such a relatively minor crash could result in injuries similar to a bad car accident, or the plane could have caught on fire or exploded before we could get out.

with every bit of elevation loss. It looks to you like you must be below 1000 feet by now.

4:06 PM

Sure enough, this is the final descent, as confirmed by the pilot—who still sounds calm and confidently says that he will bring the plane safely to a stop. He says that this is the final announcement from the cockpit, as he will be busy in the next few minutes, and that everyone should follow the flight attendants' instructions and "brace yourselves for a hard landing."

You wonder if it will truly be *your* final descent, and you know from so many landings how fast approach and touchdown happens from this point forward. If this *is* really it and this plane breaks up or explodes upon coming to earth, then the length of your remaining life can be measured in just minutes. It's hard to believe that you could be so out of control of your destiny. At least if you were in an imminent car crash you could swerve or hit the brakes or do *something*. But here you are just along for the ride with no active measure you can take other than to brace yourself and hold on tight.

The flight attendants are all in their seats and strapped into their seat belts, but still looking around to see that everyone is in the correct bracing position, which they had demonstrated while the aircraft was still circling. You wish the young couple next to you luck, and they do the same for you as you all assume the position. It makes about as much sense to you as anything else you could do. With your arms crossed and your hands palm out, clenching the seatback in front of you, the X formed where your forearms cross with your elbows bent creates a cradle to press your forehead against. The idea is to keep your head from suddenly snapping forward upon impact, and also to keep it down and out of the path of objects that may become flying projectiles as they dislodge. Your feet are likewise planted against the rails under the seat in front of you. You figure that those who study such things have devised the safest position possible, but it still doesn't give you a lot of comfort facing the prospect of a 140-mile-per-hour crash. That's still much faster than any but the most extreme car crashes, and in your car you are surrounded by airbags in the dash and the doors.

4:07 PM

You feel the aircraft drop sharply in altitude and raise your head to steal a glance out the window. It must be less the 500 feet above the ground now. There's a busy highway and then the flight path crosses over a fence into a no-man's land of green turf and asphalt. You're over airport property, and the moment of truth is imminent. You can't tear your eyes away from the window, even though the head flight attendant is rhythmically shouting over and over, "Heads down! Heads down! Heads down!" She will keep this up until the plane comes to a stop, not so much as a reminder perhaps, but really just a distraction to keep the passengers focused on their task of holding on so that they don't panic. Despite her mantralike chanting, one or two people are wailing loudly in the background.

You remain glued to the window until you see the end of the runway upon which the pilot will attempt to land. There is a sudden deceleration and drop and the last thing you see out the window before moving your head into the brace position is fire trucks and ambulances paralleling the runway with lights flashing. The tarmac and the ground beyond are covered with foam. You press your head into your arms and begin counting to yourself to ease the suspense. At first, the landing seems like any other as the one good wheel kisses the tarmac. But then there is a swerving motion and the entire fuselage begins to oscillate side to side and up and down as the pilot struggles to maintain directional control using the rudder. You hold your breath as you feel the speed slowing. The airplane is on the ground but probably still traveling at over 100 miles per hour.

The crash happens when the airspeed decreases too much for the rudder to be effective. The right wing dips and hits the tarmac and the aircraft slides around as the tail end attempts to swap places with the nose. Sliding sideways on one wingtip and the landing gear opposite, the aircraft begins leaving pieces in its wake. You feel yourself pressed against the side of the cabin and the window, and the weight of the young woman and man jammed against you from the other side. But when at last the out-of-control ride ends and the skidding plane comes to rest, the three of you are uninjured.

4:09 PM

Cheers and hand clapping erupt from relieved passengers in the cabin, but the flight attendants spring into action, ordering everyone to remain calm, but saying that they must begin evacuat-

ing the plane immediately. Sirens pierce the air outside the fuselage, and you feel a moment of panic as you wonder how long it will be before the wreck catches fire or explodes. You don't have to wonder long—smoke begins to fill the cabin even as the exit doors are shoved open. Holding the tail of your shirt across your mouth and nose, you anxiously await your turn to move into the aisle behind your seatmates as those between you and the nearest door make their way to the evacuation chute. One woman balks at jumping and momentarily blocks the exit, prompting a flight attendant and a burly passenger to bodily lift her onto the chute and send her on her way. You get your turn at last and you hit the ground running, intent on getting as far away from the doomed 727 as possible.

TOP TEN TIPS FOR SURVIVING A PLANE CRASH

1. **Wear sensible clothing.** Wear casual clothing that allows freedom of movement. Natural fabrics such as cotton, wool, denim, or leather are better than synthetics, which may melt when heated and increase the severity of burns. Long sleeves and long pants are recommended. Avoid high heels or sandals, and wear shoes or boots with laces if possible.

2. **Pay attention to the safety briefing.** Seasoned travelers tend to tune out the flight attendants' safety briefing, but waiting a few minutes to start your book or nap can make a big difference if there's trouble later on. Every aircraft is different, and the best way you can prepare for an emergency is to think about what action you would take. Review the safety card in the seat pocket and know where the exits are, as well as additional emergency equipment.

3. **Count the rows.** Count the rows between your seat and the nearest exit so that if you have to try to get out in total darkness or in a cabin filled with smoke, you can find the exit by feeling the seat backs as you move toward the exit.

4. **Be aware of those around you.** Your fellow passengers can be either a help or a hindrance when it comes to reaching an exit in an emergency. Know in advance if they are handicapped, elderly, or in any other way likely to have difficulty reacting and moving out. Don't ignore strange behavior, as it may be an indication of danger that could develop into an attempt at sabotage or a terror attack.

5. **Fasten your seat belt.** The seat belt is one of the most important safety features on an aircraft. Fasten it snugly and keep it on. It can save you from injury in turbulence as well as in a crash.

6. **Brace for a hard landing.** Don't sit back or upright. The proper position is to cross your hands on the seat in front of you and put your head against your hands. Stay in this position for as long as it takes until the aircraft is on the ground and stopped.

7. **Evacuate the aircraft.** Once the aircraft comes to a rest, move toward the exit as quickly as possible. Forget about your carry-on bags; fire and smoke may quickly fill the cabin, trapping you inside if

you don't act immediately. If there is smoke, stay as low as possible and keep a wet paper towel, handkerchief, or extra clothing over your mouth to help filter it.

8. **Use the evacuation slide correctly.** If the crew is able to activate the evacuation slide, jump feet first into the center of the slide; don't waste time and hold others up by trying to sit down first. Keep your arms across your chest, elbows in, and keep your feet and legs together.

9. **Move away from the aircraft.** Once you're out of the aircraft, move away from it as quickly as possible and don't go back. As you move away, be watchful for fast-moving emergency vehicles and other hazards as the air may be filled with smoke, reducing visibility.

10. **Know what to do in the event of water evacuation.** If flying over water, know where the passenger flotation devices are and how to use them. Once outside the plane, try to get clear of fuel-covered water, as it may ignite, but remain in the vicinity of the plane if it doesn't sink to increase your chances of being found by rescuers. Try to help others and stay with a group if possible.

CHAPTER THIRTEEN
URBAN BREAKDOWN

You slowly slide backward in the foul-smelling mud as you work your way down the embankment into the drainage ditch behind your house. You are afraid of making the slightest sound as the mob enters your backyard and storms onto the deck, breaking the sliding glass patio doors with a thrown chair before the leader fires three rounds from a pump shotgun into the house at nothing in particular. A half-dozen of them push their way into the house behind him and within seconds you hear more crashes of broken glass, slamming cabinet doors, and the sound of tables and other furniture being overturned and smashed. Five of the looters remain outside on the deck, looking around the yard with nervous fingers on the triggers of the various rifles and handguns they are carrying.

Your heart seems to stop for a second as the one who is carrying an AK-47 looks intently in your direction, making you wonder if he can see your eyes staring back at him amid the thick bushes and weeds that conceal the ditch from what was once your tranquil suburban backyard garden. But his attention turns back to the house as excited yelling comes from within and you realize they probably found your well-stocked liquor cabinet. They will also be overjoyed with the amount of food you left behind, but you couldn't take any more of it with you than you have in your backpack and you realize with a chill that you got out just in time and were lucky to escape with your life. What could happen that would result in widespread raiding and violence in your quiet suburban neighborhood in one of the larger cities in the southern U.S.?

It Begins with a Far-Reaching Failure of the Power Grid

Everyday order in modern life is dependent on a complex industrial and technological grid that keeps cities and towns run-

REAL LIFE | *The Los Angeles Riots of 1992*

When large numbers of people in an urban environment who may feel they are not in control of their destiny do not get what they want, anything can happen. And the most unexpected circumstances can trigger it. Take for example the case of the Rodney King beating by Los Angeles police officers. After four officers were acquitted on charges they used excessive force to subdue King when arresting him after a high-speed car chase, a six-day period of nearly citywide civil unrest and rioting occurred in Los Angeles. Because the beating incident was captured on videotape and was the subject of extensive media coverage, many residents were not expecting the verdict that was delivered in the case. When the officers were not convicted of any wrongdoing, the riots began that very evening. The violence grew more intense over the following days, leading to looting, arson, assault, and murder. Some 2000 people were injured and 53 were killed as a result of the rioting, and 1100 buildings were destroyed by over 3600 fires set amid the chaos.

A large area of stores owned by Korean immigrants was targeted by the rioters, who were mainly African-American and Hispanic residents of the city. Underlying

ning so smoothly that this array of interconnected systems has faded almost to invisibility in the background, working unseen beneath the surface like the interlocking gears inside the case of an engine. Few people stop to consider how complicated all this is when they walk into a room and flip on a light. Instead, they take it for granted that the switch will always turn on the power they require to run their lives, just as they have been conditioned to expect that it will.

tensions between these ethnic groups that started before the Rodney King beating were responsible for this aspect of the unrest. Many of the Korean shopkeepers were well-armed with semi-automatic rifles and took up positions on the rooftops of the buildings to defend their stores from the mob. The resultant gun battles were televised all over the world, and viewers watched in amazement as large parts of a major U.S. city became a burning battleground. By the second day, California Highway Patrol officers were being airlifted into the city to reinforce the local police response, and 2000 California National Guard soldiers were called up. That number was doubled to 4000 by the third day, when the situation was beginning to be brought under control.

If this sort of eruption of violence can occur over what seems to be a small and isolated event, it's not hard to imagine how fast things could go downhill in a crisis of larger proportions affecting a much greater number of people. Such situations are widely referred to as SHTF (Shit Hits the Fan) scenarios and imply events of extreme disorder where most anything can happen and you had better be prepared to take care of your own security and escape from the scene.

Day One: Evening

Like most people, you've been annoyed before by a temporary power outage. In your particular city in the Southeast, this is usually caused by a severe summer thunderstorm in which

What Could Possibly Happen That Would Require Bugging Out?

If you don't think of yourself as a "survivalist" or a "prepper," you may wonder what in the world all these people are so worried about that makes them want to stock up on food, build a retreat, or prepare a bug-out bag. Many people don't want to be associated with survivalism because of the negative connotations it can have. Some survivalist bloggers and authors seem to look for the worst in everything and come up with outlandish theories about government conspiracies, convincing themselves and their readers that most everything that happens is a sinister plot to rob them of their freedom or destroy them to clear the way for some new world order. Many are doing this to sell books or products; others seem to simply enjoy stirring up anxiety and fear, along with hatred of government authority. Many ordinary people who might otherwise be interested in survival or preparedness skills may not want to be associated with such labeling and possibly perceived as anti-government or a member of some extreme militia movement.

The truth is that there are enough real possibilities for the destruction of all or part of modern civilization without bogus conspiracy theories. Natural disasters on a normal scale can be bad enough, but there is always the potential for even worse earthquakes, hurricanes, or other storms than have been seen before. Events happening beyond our planet can have a devastating effect—evidence has shown

lighting strikes a transformer or the occasional tornado that rips through a limited area, taking down power line poles. Such outages usually only last a few hours, or at most a couple of days, as was the case with one tornado.

that catastrophic asteroid strikes have occurred before the time of human history, and many scientists speculate that solar flares of sufficient intensity could take out our power grid. Aside from such natural events, we have advanced to the point of having the weaponry sufficient to destroy our own planet in the worst-case scenario of global nuclear war, and on a smaller scale, terrorist attacks have shown that no country is safe from those bent on surprise attacks that can cripple a city and kill thousands. No one knows when the next such attack could occur and whether it will be even larger in scale than the attacks of September 11, 2001.

As in the case of the Los Angeles riots of 1992 (page 262), mobs of people can be set off by a variety of events and can take to the streets and turn order into anarchy in hours. Again, large cities are among the most dangerous places to be in such events because of the sheer number of people and the uncertainty of what they might do. And cities are the most likely places for such rioting to occur. Some fear that with or without a government conspiracy, the collapse of the financial system is imminent and that if people lose access to their bank accounts a total SHTF scenario will occur. This is plausible, as without money or credit, life in modern society would grind to a halt for most people. Small-scale examples of this have already occurred, the 2010 riots in Greece being among the most notable (page 266).

So when the power goes out without warning one evening after you return home from work, you are surprised, because the weather is good, and you can only assume there is some technical problem and the power company has temporarily killed the line your house is on. You expect it to be back soon, but you are aggravated about missing your usual dose of the evening news on television because of it. It's also an inconvenience because you can't use the microwave to heat your leftovers from last night for this evening's dinner. You consider getting in your car and driving somewhere to a restaurant, but it's been a long day already. There are the makings of a sandwich in the fridge, and you figure it will stay cold enough as long as the lights are back on by morning. Feeling your way to your bedroom closet, you find the AA-powered headlamp that you bought for weekend camping trips. There are spare batteries as

REAL LIFE | *Greece Rocked by Rioters Protesting Government Spending Cuts*

In March 2010, tens of thousands of Greek protesters took to the streets wearing the masks and hoods of anarchy, attacking police with Molotov cocktails and smashing storefronts and cars with sledgehammers. The unrest brought the country to a standstill, shutting down public transportation, grounding all flights, and closing schools and public services.

The violence was brought about by a number of proposed measures the government enacted to avoid a nationwide bailout. This included public-sector salary cuts, hiring freezes, consumer tax hikes, and even pension freezes. Ordinary Greek citizens and workers were enraged that they were being called on to pay for the past mismanagement that led to their nation's financial crisis.

well among your other gear, and you find some comfort in the fact that you have a camp stove and fuel that you could cook with or at least make coffee with in the morning if the power should stay out that long.

Day Two: Early Morning

You find it hard to believe when you wake up in the morning and the power is still off. Barring a major storm, which didn't happen, you can't see any reason it should stay off this long. You're glad to have the camp stove as you set it up to brew your morning dose of caffeine. You need it more than ever, as you didn't get much sleep with the air conditioner not working. After getting the first cup of coffee and pouring some still-cool milk from the refrigerator over a bowl of dry cereal, you wonder

Many people see parallels with the economic recession, job losses, and housing foreclosures taking place in the U.S. during the same timeframe. They fear that if things were to get much worse or not improve soon enough, people might begin taking to the streets to vent their frustrations. Once again, this is a reason why if you reside in a large city, you should stay on top of the news and current events in order to be aware of what's going on and be prepared to act quickly if necessary. The particular SHTF situation that happens in your city may be localized to that one area, and by simply leaving early, you could avoid it entirely.

how you're going to get anything done at the office today. Surely the power can't stay off much longer.

You wait until it's about your usual time to go to work and then pick up your cell phone to call a coworker who lives in an-

Bugging Out vs. Bugging In

When I wrote *Bug Out: The Complete Plan for Escaping a Catastrophic Disaster Before It's Too Late,* I already knew there was lot of resistance to the idea of bugging out among those in the survivalist/prepper community. But modern and civilized individuals without specialized knowledge of survival have prevailed when cast away alone in some of the harshest environments on the planet.

But as I immersed myself in the survivalist culture, it became apparent that people are easily led to believe that the only way they can survive a catastrophic event is to spend thousands of dollars on so-called preps that would allow them to "bug-in" at home or in a survival retreat. It also became clear that much of this thinking was fueled by the writings of those in a position to profit from the sales of these preps. Naturally, the concept of bugging out would be discouraged because it relies more on individual skill and the development of specialized knowledge than big spending, as well as people's natural aversion to discomfort that has become so commonplace in the modern age. But sometimes, if you want to live, you have to go.

Sometimes natural disasters like hurricanes can turn into a combination of a storm and a SHTF event, as was seen in parts of New Orleans after Hurricane Katrina. Before Katrina, New Orleans was a good example of a city in which many residents literally never left for any reason.

other part of the city and see if she knows what's going on. The battery is almost dead since you couldn't plug in your charger and you plan to charge it in your car on the way in. But when you try to dial out, you find that the battery is the least of your

But when the flood waters came, the reality they faced was that they were trapped in an unsustainable environment. Without power, without access to food or water, and without police protection, law and order quickly broke down and anarchy ruled in the days that followed. The world watched as this scenario unfolded, with refugees crowded into the Superdome while authorities fumbled around with a response that was slow and inadequate due to lack of prior planning and poor staging of supplies. This created desperation among the survivors, many of whom were simply looking for basic necessities. But another element of society saw this as an opportunity, and the result was widespread looting, pillaging, arson, and even murder. Local law enforcement was helpless to contain it.

The nightmare in New Orleans after Katrina was relatively short in duration but illustrates how bad things can get in a hurry when the lights go out in a big city. Even with the rest of the country functioning normally, the city was essentially a no-man's land cut off from the world during this time.

The lesson learned from the Katrina aftermath is that staying in a large city after a breakdown is unsafe. No matter how well-prepared you may be to bug in, you put yourself at a distinct disadvantage by remaining in a place that may be swarming with gangs of rampaging looters. In a big city, there are simply too many people and too few resources for the unprepared, many of whom will quickly resort to anything when everything is taken away from them.

problems. There is no signal at all. The only other time you've experienced this with this particular phone was when you went on a backpacking trip far out in the mountains a few months ago. There's never been a dead signal area anywhere else. You put the phone down and finish your breakfast so you can get dressed and go see what's going on.

Day Two: Midmorning

You pull out of your neighborhood to head to the office, and notice that your gas gauge is below a quarter of a tank. You meant to fill up again the afternoon before but were too tired from your long day. Intending to stop at the first convenience store on the way to your office, you find long lines of cars backed up several blocks at the gas pumps. You pull in and get out to ask another driver what's going on. He looks at you in surprise and asks if you have been listening to the radio. You say that you haven't and wonder why you didn't think of the radio in your car, but you always listen to music on CDs instead. The man tells you that none of the local FM stations in the region are on the air, but reports are coming in on AM stations broadcasting from the other side of the continent that there's been a massive power and communications outage across most of the eastern half of the country. No one knows what caused it, but there are speculations of everything from a terrorist attack to intense solar flares or even alien interference. As he goes on, you begin to immediately see the implications of such an event. It doesn't matter what caused it, this is something that's not going to get fixed in a hurry and people will start going crazy because of it.

One thing is for sure, there's no point in sitting in line at a gas station that is unable to pump fuel from underground storage tanks without electricity. Even if you could get gas here, it wouldn't do you much good if the grid is down over such a big area. Driving out would just leave you stranded on the road somewhere when you inevitably run out again. But you know that most people will sit in this line, wasting time hoping when all that is going to do is lead to frustration. The man tells you there have already been fistfights in the gas line, and carjackings have started on the roadways as some people have figured out that cars not in line at the pumps may have plenty of gas in the tank.

You wish the man good luck and do a U-turn out of the line to head straight back to your house, thankful that it's early in the month and you usually do your main grocery shopping once a month so you don't have to run out to the store every couple of days during the work week. You can only imagine what it's going to be like around the shopping centers in the area. You've seen it before when you lived on the coast and went through the aftermath of a hurricane. The looters will come out in force, taking anything and everything they can wheel away in shopping carts stacked to overflowing. There's bound to be violence, and probably on a scale that will make similar events pale by comparison.

Day Three: Midafternoon

So far your neighborhood has remained quiet since you came home yesterday morning and began going through your gear and making preparations. Since you can't get out by car, there's not much advantage in leaving yet, as you are in a residential area far enough away from main streets and shopping centers that the looters will have no reason to come here first. But you're under no illusion that it will be safe to stay in your home long-term. Your neighbors, whom you don't really know all that well, have apparently already left. They probably had just enough gas to get out of the city and get stuck in what surely must be massive traffic jams on the interstate leading north.

Part of your decision to stay this long is based on the amount of food you have in the house. You can't take it with you traveling on foot, so you might as well take advantage of it and eat well while you can. You start with the perishables in the refrigerator and freezer, all the while keeping your gear close at hand in the backpack you have prepared as a bug-out bag.

You've never considered yourself a survivalist, but you have long had an interest in wilderness survival skills, perhaps stemming from all the tales of Indians and mountain men you read as a kid. You know your way around in the woods, as your childhood was spent in a small country town where you enjoyed hunting and fishing when you weren't in school. As an

Bugging Out Does Not Always Imply a Long Stay in the Woods

Having a well-thought-out bug-out plan prepares you for the *worst-case* scenario. That doesn't mean an all-out SHTF total-breakdown scenario is bound to happen, and the plan or parts of the plan can serve you well in a lesser event. It's true that you may need to get out of the danger zone of a terror attack, retreat from an approaching hurricane, or leave a city that has broken out in riots. But the bug-out bag can also serve as a *get-home* bag in certain situations when you are traveling and some event happens that would make it difficult to reach your family and get them to safety if not for the gear you are carrying.

With this in mind, the well-stocked bug-out bag will have everything you need to meet the essentials of survival: shelter and the means to make fire; food and water for

adult, it's been years since you did any hunting, but you have taken up recreational backpacking and have invested in some lightweight camping gear. Now you realize that this equipment and your skills acquired from many days and nights spent outdoors are among your most valuable assets. You don't know how far you'll have to go, but you do know that the time will soon come when you must leave.

You feel confident you can get out of the city safely, as there is a drainage ditch right behind your house that winds through more residential neighborhoods before emptying into a nearby river. You've viewed the river and the ditch on Google Earth, as you have done a canoe trip on the river and were curious about

the first three days; and the means to purify water you find and procure more food from the natural environment. It will also include essential survival tools such as a good knife and a weapon for self-defense that can double for hunting.

You may not need to hunker down in the nearest river-bottom swamp or national forest at all. Perhaps you simply need the gear to travel cross-country to reach your own retreat cabin, or the home of a friend or relative in an area unaffected by the event that forces you to leave. By having the gear and a plan of action, you have taken the necessary steps to look out for your own evacuation and security and you will *not* become a refugee, as so many who bash the bug-out option would have you believe. Refugees are the unprepared who are waiting to be rescued or moved to a safe area, leaving their fate in the hands of the authorities and others. If your bug-out bag includes everything you need to survive an extended stay in an uninhabited area, and you have the skills and knowledge to do so, then anything less will be that much easier.

where your house was in relation to it. As with most modern cities, the river was the original reason people settled here over two centuries ago, but now its winding course lies forgotten in bottomland swamps and overgrown woods. Modern commerce has long since been conducted on roads, and insurance companies have discouraged construction and development in the river's flood plain. When the time comes, you will follow the ditch to the river, and then somehow make your way downstream to even more remote swamps far beyond the

Don't Take Peace and Security for Granted

In the complex web of society we've created, we take it for granted that all the intricate parts that keep the system moving smoothly will continue to function and that our lives will remain orderly, peaceful, and secure, even if we do sometimes get frustrated by technology, traffic jams, and minor glitches. But what happens if something throws a monkey wrench into the system and order turns to disorder, peace turns to violence, and there is no security except what you provide for yourself?

I wrote *Bug Out: The Complete Plan for Escaping a Catastrophic Disaster Before It's Too Late* to present an option to those who might get caught in such a scenario. Keeping tabs on current events around the world and looking back on relatively recent incidents that have already happened, it's not hard to imagine how such a breakdown of law and order could occur. Most residents of highly developed and technologically dependent nations such as the United States

city limits. Perhaps, eventually, your plan may include an attempt to travel all the way to the salt marshes of the coast.

Day Four: Sometime after Midnight

You've been sleeping in short shifts of no more than an hour between getting up to look around and listen. The darkness that enshrouds the city each night is still hard to get used to. It's amazing think how much the landscape has changed without electricity. Tonight your most recent nap was shattered by the sound of gunfire. You realize it can't be very far away. Some of the houses in your subdivision are still occupied. You've seen some activity on the street during the daytime, but you've kept

are so reliant on the power grid that they would not know how to function if it went down on a large scale and stayed down for an extended period of time. While scenarios that could cause such a breakdown may seem like science fiction, some of them are within the realm of plausibility. One thing is certain: Most people will not be prepared or equipped to survive the aftermath of such an event, even if they know there is a possibility of it happening.

Having a bug-out plan doesn't imply that you are paranoid and living in fear. Many people already enjoy the challenge of testing their wilderness survival and woodcraft skills without a specific reason. Preparing for a theoretical bug-out scenario and doing test runs with your gear can add a dimension of excitement to outdoor activities that might otherwise become dull and routine. And by planning and preparing for the worst case, you will always be better prepared for minor glitches and emergencies that will seem small by comparison.

a low profile yourself, not wanting anyone to know you're still home. The nearby gunfire sends a chill up your spine. The last thing you want is an armed confrontation with rampaging outlaws. You are not in an advantaged position to defend yourself, as your only firearm is the bolt-action, scoped .22 rifle that you hunted small game with as a teenager and have carried around through your various moves all your life. If you have to, you could certainly take out one or two aggressors with it before they know you are there, but the sounds you are hearing now are the reports of high-powered rifles and shotguns, many of them firing in rapid semi-auto mode, a dozen or more rounds at a time. People are killing each other out there somewhere in the night, and you decide that it's getting too close for comfort.

Day Four: Morning

You've been ready to move out since daylight and have already concealed your backpack in the thick vegetation growing on the banks of the ditch behind the house. You're back inside to look out the front windows to see which house it is that is burning just a couple of blocks away. What you see confirms that gangs are now invading the neighborhood and setting fire to every house after ransacking it. Sporadic gunshots ring out, making you wonder how many people stayed behind only to get shot in their homes. You slip out the back door and make your way into concealment as a group of thugs finally reaches your own home.

They split up, and half of them come around the house into the backyard, almost catching you before you slide out of sight into the mud and weeds. You don't dare move until they are gone, and it is a least an hour before they leave as they pack your food and liquor in pillowcases and haul it out the front door before torching the house.

Day Four: Late Afternoon

You spend the better part of the day picking your way stealthily down the drainage ditch, which is running with three or four inches of water that smells of sewer and is choked with briars and other vegetation. You detour around a cottonmouth snake sunning itself in a bush, and when you come to road crossings, you stop to look and listen carefully before proceeding under the bridges that span the stream. All through the day you smell the smoke of burning buildings and hear gunshots and screams. But the ditch is like a secret corridor that winds forgotten in overgrown thickets behind the six-foot-high privacy fences that partition the backyards of the neighborhoods it traverses.

Eventually, you succeed in covering the seven or eight miles to the river, and in the last mile the ditch broadens to a small tributary stream, flowing through a mature stand of hardwood forest. Deer tracks are everywhere in the mud, but not one human footprint can be seen among them. As darkness approaches, you reach the stream's confluence with the river and are relieved to find the banks quiet and deserted. An owl hoots nearby, answered by one of its kin somewhere far away on the opposite bank. You find a place to bivouac for the night in a dense grove of willows on a riverside sandbar. This river will become your home for the time being, providing a sanctuary removed from the insanity of violence you left behind, as well a source of food, water, and most importantly *hope* that something may be better downstream.

TOP TEN TIPS FOR BUGGING OUT
IN AN URBAN BREAKDOWN

1. **Understand the risks.** Stay tuned in to current events, weather, and science so you will be aware of any potential threats to normal life in your area. Be aware of specific natural disasters, terror threats, or political situations that can pose a risk where you live or work. The more urban the environment, the more likely you will have to bug out if something serious happens, as areas with large populations will be full of desperate people.

2. **Prepare a bug-out bag.** Once you accept the possibility that you may have to bug out someday, prepare your bug-out bag in advance. Gather the necessary gear and supplies, and learn to use any items that you may not be familiar with. Make sure all the stuff you need fits in the bag and that you can carry it on your back while traveling on foot if you have to.

3. **Have a pre-planned bug-out location.** Being prepared to leave will do you little good if you don't know where to go. Scout the potential bug-out locations in your region by studying maps, researching both online and in books, and doing on-the-ground reconnaissance. Evaluate a bug-out location based on remoteness and inaccessibility to the masses; natural hazards such as wildlife and climate; available resources such as water, plant foods, and game; and reasonable proximity to your starting point.

4. **Know the best escape routes.** Know in advance the route you will take to your bug-out location using your chosen transportation option, and have one or more contingency plans. Choose routes that are not likely to be the scene of mass evacuations and traffic jams, and practice traveling them so you will know the way no matter what the circumstance. Consider unconventional routes that will allow you to avoid as many people as possible.

5. **Keep your vehicle ready.** If a motor vehicle is part of your bug-out plan, make sure it is well-maintained and that the fuel tank is kept topped off as much as possible. Equip your vehicle with the necessary equipment to deal with different weather conditions; any spare parts

that commonly need replacing and the tools to install them; towing gear and a winch; and bolt cutters to open padlocked gates.

6. **Consider alternate transportation.** In many areas, motor vehicles may not be the best option. A bicycle can get you out of a gridlocked city faster than sitting in a traffic jam with thousands of stalled cars. If there is navigable water such as a stream, river, lakeshore, or coast, a boat may be the best option, as there will be far fewer people trying to bug out by boat, and it will get you to areas those without boats cannot reach.

7. **Be prepared to walk.** Always be prepared to bug out on foot if all else fails. In some cases, walking may be the best option even if you have other choices. Unconventional routes you can take on foot include railroads, storm drains, and many other cross-country options. With careful planning, you can find a way out while those confined to vehicles remain trapped.

8. **Be inconspicuous and blend in.** Remain as unobtrusive as possible by not dressing in a way that says you are a prepared survivalist or openly carrying a weapon such as an assault rifle. If you do, you may be detained by the police or other authorities, or have your weapon and other gear confiscated. You could also be targeted by others who see that you are prepared and want your stuff.

9. **Avoid confrontations.** Although being armed is a good idea and suitable firearms for both hunting and self-defense should be part of your bug-out bag, you should seek to avoid confrontations at all costs. Chances are you will be outnumbered or outgunned anyway. Staying hidden, moving at night, and choosing routes away from mass evacuations are among the best tactics for avoiding confrontations.

10. **Resist the urge to go back too soon.** If all has gone well and you've reached your bug-out location safely, stay there and try to remain out of sight until you are sure that order has been restored and it is safe to return to the city. It may be lonely out in a wilderness of forest, desert, or mountains, but you will be safer there than among a lawless population without adequate resources.

BIBLIOGRAPHY/ RECOMMENDED READING

Adams, Carl. *The Essential Guide to Dual Sport Motorcycling: Everything You Need to Buy, Ride, and Enjoy the World's Most Versatile Motorcycles.* Center Conway, NH: Whitehorse Press, 2008.

Alloway, David. *Desert Survival Skills.* Austin, TX: University of Texas Press, 2000.

Anderson, Ellis. *Under Surge, Under Siege: The Odyssey of Bay St. Louis and Katrina.* Jackson, MS: University Press of Mississippi, 2010.

Artwohl, Alexis, and Loren W. Christensen. *Deadly Force Encounters: What Cops Need to Know to Mentally and Physically Prepare for and Survive a Gunfight.* Boulder, CO: Paladin Press, 1997.

Ayoob, Massad. *The Gun Digest Book of Concealed Carry.* Iola, WI: Gun Digest Books, 2008.

Becker, Greg. *The Seagoing Hitchiker's Handbook: Roaming the Earth on Other People's Yachts.* High Adventures Publishing, 1993.

Bennett, Alison Muir. *The Hitchhiker's Guide to the Oceans: Crewing Around the World,* 6th ed. London: Adlard Coles, 2008.

Brown, Tom. *Tom Brown's Guide to Wild Edible and Medicinal Plants.* New York: Berkley Books, 1985.

Brown, Tom. *Tom Brown's Field Guide to Living with the Earth.* New York: Berkley Books, 1986.

Brown, Tom. *Tom Brown's Field Guide to Wilderness Survival*. New York: Berkley Books, 1987.

Burns, Bob, and Mike Burns. *Wilderness Navigation: Finding Your Way Using Map, Compass, Altimeter and Gps*. Seattle: Mountaineers Books, 2004.

Callahan, Steve. *Adrift: Seventy-six Days Lost at Sea*. New York: Mariner Books, 2002.

Cannon, Lou. *Official Negligence: How Rodney King and the Riots Changed Los Angeles and the LAPD*, 2nd ed. New York: Basic Books, 1999.

Christensen, Loren W. *Surviving a School Shooting: A Plan of Action for Parents, Teachers, and Students*. Boulder, CO: Paladin Press, 2008.

Churchill, James. *Paddling the Boundary Waters and Voyageurs National Park*. Guilford, CT: Falcon, 2003.

Clarke, Thurston. *Searching for Paradise: A Grand Tour of the World's Unspoiled Islands*. New York: Ballantine Books, 2002.

Craighead, Frank C. *How to Survive on Land and Sea*. United States Naval Institute, 1984.

Curtis, Rick. *The Backpacker's Field Manual: A Comprehensive Guide to Mastering Backcountry Skills*. New York: Three Rivers Press, 1998.

Downey, Tom. *The Last Men Out: Life on the Edge at Rescue 2 Firehouse*. New York: Holt Paperbacks, 2005.

Drye, Willie. *Storm of the Century: The Labor Day Hurricane of 1935*. Washington, D.C.: National Geographic Society, 2003.

Fletcher, Colin. *The Complete Walker IV*. New York: Knopf, 2002.

Forstchen, William R., *One Second After*. New York: Forge Books, 2009.

Ghinsberg, Yossi. *Lost in the Jungle*. New York: Skyhorse Publishing, 2007.

Gibbons, Euell. *Euell Gibbons' Beachcomber's Handbook*. David McKay Co., 1967.

Gibbons, Euell. *Stalking the Wild Asparagus*. Chambersburg, PA: Alan C. Hood, 1962.

Gero, David. *Aviation Disasters: The World's Major Civil Airliner Crashes Since 1950,* 4th ed. Charleston, SC: The History Press, 2006.

Gonzales, Laurence. *Deep Survival: Who Lives, Who Dies, and Why.* New York: W.W. Norton, 2004.

Gray, Michael E., and Linda E. Gray. *Auto Upkeep: Basic Car Care, Maintenance, and Repair.* Ozark, MO: Rolling Hills Publishing, 2007.

Hansen, Eric. *Stranger in the Forest: On Foot Across Borneo.* New York: Vintage, 2000.

Herndon, Ernest. *Into the Hearts of Wild Men.* Sand Springs, OK: Grace and Truth Books, 1998.

Herrero, Stephen. *Bear Attacks: Their Causes and Avoidance.* Guilford, CT: Lyons Press, 2002.

Hinch, Stephen W. *Outdoor Navigation with GPS.* Birmingham, AL: Wilderness Press, 2007.

Hinz, Earl R., and Jim Howard. *Landfalls of Paradise: Cruising Guide to the Pacific Islands,* 5th ed. Honolulu: University of Hawaii Press, 2006.

Horne, Jed. *Breach of Faith: Hurricane Katrina and the Near Death of a Great American City.* New York: Random House Trade Paperbacks, 2008.

Johnson, Mark. *The Ultimate Desert Handbook: A Manual for Desert Hikers, Campers and Travelers.* Camden, ME: International Marine/Ragged Mountain Press, 2003.

Kaniut, Larry. *Danger Stalks the Land: Alaskan Tales of Death and Survival.* New York: St. Martin's Griffin, 1999.

King, Dean. *Skeletons on the Zahara: A True Story of Survival.* New York: Back Bay Books, 2005.

Knowles, Thomas Neil. *Category 5: The 1935 Labor Day Hurricane.* Gainsville, FL: University Press of Florida, 2009.

Krakauer, Jon. *Into the Wild,* New York: Anchor Books, 1996.

Kuhne, Cecil. *Near Death in the Desert.* New York: Vintage, 2009.

Leslie, Edward E. *Desperate Journeys, Abandoned Souls: True Stories of Castaways and Other Survivors*. New York: Mariner Books, 1998.

Little, Ida, and Michael Walsh. *Beachcruising and Coastal Camping*. Rockledge, FL: Wescott Cove, 1992.

Maclean, Norman. *Young Men and Fire*. Chicago: University of Chicago Press, 1993.

McCarthy, Cormac. *The Road*. New York: Vintage, 2006.

McMillon, Scott. *Mark of the Grizzly: True Stories of Recent Bear Attacks and the Hard Lessons Learned*. Guilford, CT: Falcon, 1998.

McNab, Chris. *Special Forces Survival Guide: Wilderness Survival Skills from the World's Most Elite Military Units*. Berkeley, CA: Ulysses Press, 2008.

McPherson, John and Geri McPherson. *Ultimate Guide to Wilderness Living: Surviving with Nothing but Your Bare Hands and What You Find in the Woods*. Berkeley, CA: Ulysses Press, 2008.

Megee, Ricky. *Left for Dead in the Outback: How I Survived 71 Days Lost in a Desert Hell*. Boston: Nicolas Brealey Publishing, 2009.

Moitessier, Bernard. *A Sea Vagabond's World*. Dobbs Ferry, NY: Sheridan House, 1998.

Nalepka, James. *Capsized: The True Story of Four Men Adrift for 119 Days*. New York: HarperCollins, 1992.

Neal, Tom. *An Island to Oneself*. Woodbridge, CT: Ox Bow Press, 1990.

Nestor, Tony. *Desert Survival Tips, Tricks, and Skills*. Flagstaff, AZ: Diamond Creek Press, 2003.

O'Hanlon, Redmond. *Into the Heart of Borneo*. New York: Vintage, 1987.

O'Hanlon, Redmond. *In Trouble Again: A Journey Between the Orinoco and the Amazon*. New York: Vintage, 1990.

Olsen, Larry Dean. *Outdoor Survival Skills*. Provo, UT: Brigham Young University Press, 1976.

Parrado, Nando. *Miracle in the Andes: 72 Days on the Mountain and My Long Trek Home*. New York: Three Rivers Press, 2007.

Peterson, Lee Allen. *Edible Wild Plants*. New York: Houghton Mifflin, 1977.

Philbrick, Nathaniel. *In the Heart of the Sea: The Tragedy of the Whaleship Essex*. New York: Penguin, 2001.

Ralston, Aron. *Between a Rock and a Hard Place*. New York: Atria, 2005.

Rawicz, Slavomir. *The Long Walk: The True Story of a Trek to Freedom*. Guilford, CT: Lyons Press, 2006.

Robertson, Dougal. *Survive the Savage Sea*. Dobbs Ferry, NY: Sheridan House, 1994.

Sherwood, Ben. *The Survivor's Club: The Secrets and Science that Could Save Your Life*. New York: Grand Central Publishing, 2010

Simmons, James C. *Castaway in Paradise*. Dobbs Ferry, NY: Sheridan House, 1998.

Thayer, Samuel. *The Forager's Harvest: A Guide to Identifying, Harvesting, and Preparing Edible Wild Plants*. Ogema, WI: Forager's Harvest Press, 2006.

Wicks, Robert. *Adventure Riding Techniques: The Essential Guide to All the Skills You Need for Off-Road Adventure Riding*. Sparkford, Somerset, England: Haynes Publishing, 2009.

Wiseman, John. *SAS Survival Handbook, Revised Edition: For Any Climate, in Any Situation*. New York: Harper Paperbacks, 2009.

Photo Credits

p. 14: © Jens Ottoson/Shutterstock.com

p. 19: © David Yu/Shutterstock.com

p. 25: © Denis Pepin/Shutterstock.com

p. 26: © Konstantin Yolshin/Shutterstock.com

p. 28: © siloto/Shutterstock.com

p. 41: © Kolaczan/Shutterstock.com

p. 44: © Heiko Kiera/Shutterstock.com

p. 52: © guentermanaus/Shutterstock.com

p. 59: © Samuel Acosta/Shutterstock.com

p. 67: © Ramon Berk/Shutterstock.com

p. 70: © Scott B. Williams

p. 74: © Vladislav Gurfinkel/Shutterstock.com

p. 82: © Chuck Wagner/Shutterstock.com

p. 83: © Ferenc Szelepcsenyi/Shutterstock.com

p. 89: © George P. Choma/Shutterstock.com

p. 101: © urosr/Shutterstock.com

p. 106: © Niki Crucillo/Shutterstock.com

p. 107: © picturepartners/Shutterstock.com

p. 113: © Olmar/Shutterstock.com

p. 123: © Kobus Tollig/Shutterstock.com

p. 136: © Scott B. Williams

p. 139: © Sally Scott/Shutterstock.com

p. 146: © Pixinstock/Shutterstock.com

p. 148: © Pincasso/Shutterstock.com

p. 150: © Péter Gudella/Shutterstock.com

p. 161: © Sergey Rusakov/Shutterstock.com

p. 177: © Paul B. Moore/Shutterstock.com

p. 178: © Naaman Abreu/Shutterstock.com

p. 183: © Ivan Cholakov Gostock-dot-net/Shutterstock.com

p. 185: © Leo/Shutterstock.com

p. 205: © Kolaczan/Shutterstock.com

p. 210: © SVLuma/Shutterstock.com

p. 212: © Christophe Michot/Shutterstock.com

p. 218: © Condor 36/Shutterstock.com

p. 225: © Whytock/Shutterstock.com

p. 234: © Karel Gallas/Shutterstock.com

p. 235: © Thomas Barrat/Shutterstock.com

p. 250: © Vibrant Image Studio/Shutterstock.com

p. 251: © Xavier MARCHANT/Shutterstock.com

p. 258: © Zastol`skiy Victor Leonidovich/Shutterstock.com

p. 267: © forest badger/Shutterstock.com

p. 273: © Sergieiev/Shutterstock.com

p. 274: © Scott B. Williams

ACKNOWLEDGMENTS

I must first thank my dear Michelle for keeping me on track and helping me stay focused on the goal during the completion of this and every writing project. Without her I would probably still be wandering somewhere in the wild, never taking the time to stop and put my experiences into writing.

This book is my attempt to develop an excellent idea given to me by Keith Riegert, acquisitions editor at Ulysses Press. I feel fortunate to be working with Keith and the rest of the staff there on projects such as this that have led in a direction I could not have foreseen.

For help with specific content in this book, I must thank fellow sailor and writer James Baldwin, known for his contributions to sailing magazines such as *Cruising World* and for circumnavigating two and half times on an engineless Pearson Triton 28 named *Atom*. James provided advice regarding the setting for Chapter Five, and one of his articles about a drunken sailor swept out to sea in a dinghy inspired much of Chapter Nine. I would also like to thank Elaine Lembo and Susan Fennessey, editors of *Cruising World*, for digging up the September 1987 issue of that publication in which Gary Mundell told his story of becoming a modern-day castaway on a Pacific atoll. I am indebted to Lieutenant Scott Finazzo of the Overland Park Fire Department for relating some of his experiences in burning buildings and offering advice on Chapter Ten. Chapter Twelve was greatly enhanced by the thousands of hours of flight experience of my lifelong friend CMSgt Mike Jones of the Mississippi Air National Guard, who offered his suggestions for a realistic scenario. I also want to thank the members of the ADVrider forums (www.advrider.com) who responded to my questions regarding off-road motorcycling in Nevada that helped me develop Chapter Eight, as well as my own riding partners, Frank, Jeff, and Travis, who read the first draft. Finally, the first-hand experience I had in the subject matter of Chapter Two would not have been possible if not for the jungle trips I experienced with my long-time canoeing partner and fellow author Ernest Herndon.

ABOUT THE AUTHOR

Scott B. Williams has been exploring wild places and seeking adventure on both land and sea for most of his life. At the age of 25, he sold his possessions and embarked on an open-ended solo sea kayaking journey from his home in southern Mississippi to the islands of the Caribbean. His book *On Island Time: Kayaking the Caribbean* is a narrative of that life-changing journey that led to many years and many thousands of miles of kayaking and canoeing adventures. His enthusiasm for travel by water led him to learn the craft of wooden boat building and later to construct more than a dozen custom-built vessels, including a 26-foot sailing catamaran. In addition to paddling small craft and offshore sailing, he enjoys backpacking, bicycling, dual-sport motorcycling, and photography. He maintains several blogs related to these pursuits and occasionally writes for magazines including *Sea Kayaker* and *SAIL*. His most popular blog, *Bug Out Survival* (www.bugoutsurvival.com), expands on his book *Bug Out: The Complete Plan for Escaping a Catastrophic Disaster Before It's Too Late*. More information about all of his books, articles, and blogs can be found on his main website, www.scottbwilliams.com.